Praise for *An Elegant Madness*

"Murray paints such a vivid and entertaining portrait of the period between 1800 and 1830 that it's obvious why Austen's world strongly echoes our own."
—*Detroit Free Press*

"Combines gossipy enthusiasm with uncompromising attention to research and detail . . . Murray's gusto is giddily infectious."
—*Salon*

"Breathy, bracing . . . For anyone feeling a bit put off by the wanton excess, schlocky materialism, and general bad behavior of our own era, this is a tonic narrative indeed."
—*Mirabella*

"Entertaining, amusing . . . Murray is at her best when talking about sex and money."
—*Newsday*

"Ms. Murray has clearly enjoyed collecting this mass of gaudy trivialities, and anyone with a taste for informal history will enjoy reading it. The period produced splendidly mischievous cartoonists, whose work adds to the pleasure of the text."
—*The Atlantic Monthly*

"Venetia Murray has captured that era in all its glory with her witty, very readable social history."
—*W* magazine

"Glittering and gossipy, an extravagant panorama of 'The Age of Scandal' . . . both frivolously entertaining and assiduously researched."
—*Kirkus Reviews*

Venetia Murray worked as a journalist, writing for many major periodicals and newspapers, and published three successful novels before deciding to concentrate on social history. Her previous works include *Echoes of the East End* and *Castle Howard: The Life and Times of a Stately Home*. She lives in Wiltshire, England.

AN ELEGANT MADNESS

High Society in Regency England

VENETIA MURRAY

PENGUIN BOOKS

PENGUIN BOOKS
Published by the Penguin Group
Penguin Putnam Inc., 375 Hudson Street,
New York, New York 10014, U.S.A.
Penguin Books Ltd, 27 Wrights Lane,
London W8 5TZ, England
Penguin Books Australia Ltd,
Ringwood, Victoria, Australia
Penguin Books Canada Ltd, 10 Alcorn Avenue,
Toronto, Ontario, Canada M4V 3B2
Penguin Books (N.Z.) Ltd, 182–190 Wairau Road,
Auckland 10, New Zealand

Penguin Books Ltd, Registered Offices:
Harmondsworth, Middlesex, England

First published in Great Britain by Penguin Books Ltd. 1998
First published in the United States of America by Viking Penguin,
a member of Penguin Putnam Inc. 1999
Published in Penguin Books U.S.A. 2000

10 9 8 7 6 5 4 3

THE LIBRARY OF CONGRESS HAS CATALOGED
THE AMERICAN HARDCOVER EDITION AS FOLLOWS:
Murray, Venetia.
An elegant madness: high society in Regency England / Venetia Murray.
p.   cm.
Includes bibliographical references and index.
ISBN 0-670-88328-X (hc.)
ISBN 0 14 02.8296 3 (pbk.)
1. England—Social life and customs—19th century.   2. Aristocracy (Social class)
England—History—19th century.   3. Elite (Social sciences)—England—History—
19th century.   4. Upper class—England—History—19th century.   5. Nobility—
England—History—19th century.   6. Gentry—England—History—19th century.
7. Regency—England.   I. Title.
DA533.M983   1999
306'.0942'09034—dc21   98–31589

Printed in the United States of America
Set in Bell MT

To Ann and Oliver
— with love

Contents

List of Illustrations

Textual Illustrations

The author and publishers are extremely grateful to Simon Heneage for permission to use caricatures from his collection. Nathan Kelly did all the photography.

Preface

The educated classes during the Regency revelled in the written word. They were prolific correspondents, writing to their friends and families almost daily; they kept diaries and journals, common-place books and albums, menus and account books. They voiced their opinions on current affairs, dissected the latest scandal and described the characters of their acquaintance in acid detail. And it was an age when people put a high premium on the ability to express themselves with charm and wit. All this original material illustrates the reality behind the façade of the Regency period, the credits and debits of daily life amongst the privileged elite. It includes some of the most delightful and entertaining material for a social history ever written and is the foundation upon which this book is based.

On the other hand, the very fact that there are so many letters, diaries, journals and memoirs means that it is impossible to make use of them all: a book of this kind, therefore, is bound to be governed by personal taste. I have covered as many sources as I could but the list is obviously far from complete: I hope those readers who fail to find mention of their particular favourites will forgive me, and may even be pleased to discover some of mine that they may not have known.

Spelling during the eighteenth and nineteenth centuries was a matter of individual taste rather than accepted custom; readers will therefore find that in some cases in the text and illustrations the spelling of proper names may vary.

I must also explain my arbitrary choice of dates. The true, political, Regency lasted for only nine years, from 1811 to 1820. The term, however, is generally accepted to cover a much longer period, the fifty-odd years which span the turn of the century, from the French Revolution to the eve of Reform. I have therefore decided to widen the range of the book, starting with the first Regency crisis of 1788 and ending with the death of George IV.

Finally, I should add that the scope of *An Elegant Madness: High Society in Regency England* is largely confined to that tiny, but influential section of the population which was known as the '*beau monde*', or 'the *ton*'. These were the men and women who created the image of the Regency, and upon whose reminiscences I have based my research. I must emphasize, however, that the manners and mores of this aristocratic minority, sophisticated but dissolute, elegant but immoral, were by no means representative of the country as a whole. Many of the upper, as well as the middle, classes were God-fearing, conventional citizens who led more or less exemplary lives. *An Elegant Madness* was never intended to be taken as a sociological survey: the aim of this book was to convey the mood of the Regency, to entertain my readers and, perhaps, to enlighten a few.

Acknowledgements

I would like first to thank Her Majesty the Queen for her gracious permission to use material from the Royal Archives at Windsor. I am most grateful to Lady de Bellaigue and the staff at Windsor for all their help and co-operation during the time I spent working in the Archives. In particular, my thanks are due to Miss Clarke for taking the time to read and correct the chapters which quote from original menus and accounts at Carlton House and the Brighton Pavilion.

The book has been given a glorious extra dimension by its illustrations, all of which were provided by Simon Heneage from his unique collection of Regency cartoons, rare prints and caricatures. The period between 1780 and 1830 was the 'golden age of caricature', of such brilliant commentators on the contemporary scene as Gillray, Rowlandson and George Cruikshank, all of whose work is featured here. These illustrations are the perfect complement to the text and I am enormously grateful to Simon, not only for allowing us to use them but for taking so much time and trouble over the selection. On a personal level, too, many thanks to Simon and Liz for many a jolly lunch.

Similarly, I cannot sufficiently express my thanks to Philip Ziegler, who has encouraged and supported me throughout the project, calmed my doubts and fears, and resolved many of my practical problems. He was also kind enough to read the manuscript in its original draft. I am most grateful too, to Leslie

Mitchell, of University College, Oxford, both for sparing the time to see me in Oxford on several occasions and for reading the final script. Many thanks, too, to Claire Lamont of Newcastle University who has also contributed ideas and leads on different aspects of the Regency which have been of great help to the book.

The Duke of Devonshire allowed me complete freedom of access to the Chatsworth Archives and I am indebted to him for permission to quote from various letters and account books: Mr Peter Day, the Keeper of the Collections, and his staff could not have been more helpful and I am most grateful for all their courtesy and assistance. I would also like to thank the Duke of Devonshire separately for having me to stay at Chatsworth while I was doing my research. Needless to say, it was a delightful way to work.

Eleo Gordon has been the ideal editor, a marvel of patience as well as a most helpful and constructive critic. I am really grateful for her moral support and continuing faith in the book. My thanks are due too to my agent Jane Judd, who helped me to formulate the idea in the first place.

I am indebted to Miss Caroline Paybody for lending me a copy of the catalogue of the Carlton House Exhibition, from the Royal Collection; to John Roles, Senior Keeper (Curation) of Brighton Borough Council for photocopies and transcripts of various material relevant to the period; and to Hannelore Lixenberg who proved a most courteous and well-informed guide to the Pavilion. As always, I could not have produced the book without the aid of the London Library; in the same context I would like to express particular thanks to the staff of Frome Library who have been exceptionally helpful and found me the most obscure books via the public lending system with the minimum of fuss or delay.

Among the many other people who have helped in one way or another over the years it has taken me to write this book, I would particularly like to mention the following: Alexander Murray, Polly Devlin, Andy Garnett, Mark Jones, Robert Powell-Jones, Anthony Hobson, Antony Rous, Margaret Oborne, Anne and Peter Thorold, Shirley Conran, Patrick Hutton, Rupert Birch and Sophy Kershaw. Clive and Paul of Altek deserve a special mention for saving my sanity over innumerable computer crises: and my friends and family for putting up with my obsession with the subject for so long.

Finally, I would like to add that although this book is dedicated to my sister and brother, I had four other people in mind as well while I was working on it – Magnus, Ivan, Flora and Hugo. Although the last two were not yet born when I began it, one day one of them might even read it.

1

AN IMPOLITE SOCIETY

The years of the Regency have come to be synonymous with an elegance and style which are unique in the history of English culture: but they tend to be seen through a romantic haze. The vision persists of an elitist society, a time of grace and honour when manners were all and money irrelevant. So much evidence remains of Regency taste, in architecture, decoration and furniture, that it would seem reasonable to attribute an equal elegance of mind to its creators. But any such assumption would be wrong. The reality of life was far more robust than the romantic image suggests, and so was the behaviour of the ruling classes. The Regency was an exciting, dramatic and immensely entertaining time to be alive, and it is true that there has seldom been a period when so much flair and imagination has been spent on the arts, or a society which put such a high premium on civilized living. But it is also true that Society managed to behave at times with amazing vulgarity. Gluttony and gambling were the fashionable vices; the contemporary attitude to money was often dishonest by modern standards and sexual morality, at least among a certain section of the *haut ton*, virtually non-existent. A successful mistress had a lot more fun than a wife – and a much better financial deal since she was free to control her own money. On the other hand, a wife could, and often did, behave just as badly as a courtesan, provided she was reasonably discreet. The Regency was a time of glorious paradox.

The romantic image of the Regency, furthermore, tends to concentrate on the artistic achievements of the period, and forgets that it was also a time of tremendous innovation in the world of science and technology. The same year, 1816, that Jane Austen dedicated *Emma* to the Prince Regent, William Hedley built a primitive train and called it the *Puffing Billy*; Charles Babbage began work on the first calculating machine and Sir Humphrey Davy joined forces with Michael Faraday; the first steam ships appeared on the waterways of Britain and the first gas lighting in the streets of London. By the closing years of the Regency the Duke of Devonshire had been notified of Princess Charlotte's death by means of the new telegraph service, Daguerre had produced a prototype camera, Sir William Herschel had published his catalogue of the stars and Thomas Telford had built more than a thousand miles of roads. During the eighteenth century a letter from London to Bath could take three days to arrive, but, by the 1820s, mail was delivered the morning after posting in towns more than 120 miles apart. In central London the postal service was so efficient, and there were such frequent deliveries, that an invitation issued in the morning could be acknowledged the same afternoon.

The tone of a society tends to be set by its titular head and there can be no better example of the double standards prevalent at the time than that of that Prince of Paradox, the Regent himself. In 1788, when the question of a Regency first arose, the Prince of Wales, as he then was, had already made himself notorious for his wild behaviour and appalling extravagance. Yet he was a man of enormous charm, intelligence and taste, with impeccable manners when it mattered. Canning, a man of great discernment himself, was 'charmed beyond measure' by 'the elegance of his address and the gentlemanliness of his manner'; and William Beckford, too, thought that the Prince was 'graciousness personified' and wrote that, 'brighter than sunshine', he 'cast a brilliant gleam wherever he moved'.[1] The Prince, after all, was known as 'The First Gentleman of Europe'. But the heir to the throne was also a dedicated hedonist, drunkard and lecher; and, unfortunately, by the time he was thirty, this was the image the public recognized.

The Prince's headquarters were at Carlton House, a mansion off Pall Mall, where he gathered around him a circle of friends, ranging from politicians to gamblers, scholars to courtesans, and society hostesses to suspect jockeys. And it was the exploits and behaviour of this 'Carlton House Set', as they came to be known, which dictated the mood of Regency society. This powerful little group included some of the most brilliant figures of their generation: Charles James Fox, who was both a political ally and a convivial drinking companion; Georgiana, the legendary Duchess of Devonshire, one of the great Whig hostesses, with whom the Prince may or may not – opinions differ – have had an affair; Richard Brinsley Sheridan, playwright, politician and serious drunkard; and 'Beau' Brummell, King of the Dandies, the man who ruled society for years and created a revolution in masculine fashion, but was ruined by gambling debts and ended his life in impoverished exile. But there were others among them, who, though they have been largely ignored by posterity, were equally responsible for the image of the group as a whole – and several of these were distinctly dubious characters, or, at best, confirmed eccentrics.

Sir John Lade, for example, who managed the Prince's racing stable for a time, affected to dress and speak like a groom: he married the notorious 'Letty', who started life as a servant in a brothel and was said to have been the mistress of 'sixteen-string Jack', a highwayman who ended his career on the gallows in 1774. Lady Lade was also reputed to have been the mistress of the Duke of York, and to have acted as procuress for the Prince himself. Colonel George Hanger, another somewhat tarnished star of the inner circle, was at least literate and intelligent; but he was a gambler and a rake, a typical 'Regency Buck'. Hanger married a beautiful gypsy girl who played the dulcimer to perfection: she was christened 'the lovely Aegypta of Norwood' by his fellow officers, but, in the end, ran off with a bandy-legged tinker. Hanger lost a fortune at cards and was imprisoned for debt in 1798, but survived to make another fortune in trade, as a coal merchant. The notorious Earl of Barrymore was known as 'Hell-gate', in recognition of his wild behaviour, while his brother, who limped, was 'Cripplegate', and their foul-mouthed sister 'Billings-gate'. The Prince's new bride, Princess Caroline, was justified when she complained a few weeks after the wedding that her husband's 'blackguard companions ... were constantly drunk and filthy, sleeping and snoring in boots on the sofas'.[2] The Regency was certainly not an age to be remembered for decorum.

As for sexual morality, the Prince's example again set the standards for society. His love affairs became the serial scandal of his generation: they began with his passion for 'Perdita', a lovely young actress, carried on through numerous mistresses, and included a clandestine, and illegal, 'marriage' to Mrs Fitz-herbert. His actual marriage, ten years later, to the unattractive, but nevertheless unfortunate, Princess Caroline was an unmit-igated disaster. Upon meeting his future wife for the first time, the Prince turned to his aide and said, 'Harris, I am not well. Pray get me a glass of brandy.' To be fair to the Prince, Caroline, whom he had never met before the marriage, was blowsy, petulant, noisy, vulgar and dirty. She was also silly: one of her ladies-in-waiting reported that Caroline hated her husband so much that she made wax effigies of him, stuck the figurines through and through with pins from her own dress, roasted them, chanted a few curses and actually believed that such methods would succeed in killing him. In spite of all this, she was much more popular with the public than her husband.

In later years the Prince confined his amorous attentions to a succession of society ladies, including several of his friends' wives, most of whom were old enough to be grandmothers. On the subject of the Prince's preference for older women, Peter Pindar (John Wolcot), the most popular satirist of the Regency, wrote the following:

> The foremost of the royal brood,
> who broke his shell and cried for food;
> Turn'd out a cock of manners rare,
> A fav'rite with the feather'd fair ...

> But though his love was sought by all,
> Game, dunghill, bantam, squab and tall,
> Among the whole, not one in ten
> Could please him like a tough old Hen.

By the time he became Regent, in 1811, the Prince's charm, intelligence and great aesthetic sense had fallen victim to public calumny. He was endlessly caricatured as a drunken buffoon and dismissed as a boor and a lecher by most of his contemporaries. When the Grand Duchess of Oldenburg met the Prince she found his behaviour so coarse that she was embarrassed: 'Handsome as he is,' she wrote to her brother the Tsar, 'he is a man visibly used up by dissipation and rather disgusting. His much boasted affability is the most licentious, I may even say obscene, strain I have ever listened to. You know that I am far from being puritanical or prudish; but I avow that with him . . . I do not know what to do with my eyes and ears – a brazen way of looking where eyes should not go.'[3] Leigh Hunt, editor of the *Examiner* at the time, was admittedly a Radical, but he was not alone in his judgement when he described the Regent, on his fiftieth birthday, as: 'A libertine over head and ears in debt and disgrace . . . a man who has just closed half a century without a single claim on the gratitude of his country or the respect.'[4] Yet this was the man who had been instrumental in founding the National Gallery, built the Brighton Pavilion, commissioned Nash to redesign the West End of London and create Regent's Park, revolutionized the art of interior decoration and became one of the greatest royal patrons of the arts this country has ever possessed.

The Prince Regent was by no means unique in his blatant approach to sex. All the royal brothers were dedicated lechers, with the possible exception of the Duke of Kent. The Duke of Clarence had ten illegitimate children by Mrs Jordan, the Duke of York's affair with Mary Anne Clarke caused a major scandal because it involved the sale of army commissions, and the Duke of Cumberland was rumoured to be guilty of incest.* But then a considerable proportion of high society, including its most enlightened, cultured and liberal members, were equally indifferent to the concept of fidelity. Round the corner from Carlton House, where the Prince held Court, the fifth Duke of Devonshire lived for years in a *ménage à trois* with his wife, the beautiful Georgiana, his mistress, Lady Elizabeth Foster – who was also his wife's best friend – and their assorted children. The Duke had three legitimate children by his wife and two by Lady Elizabeth, while the Duchess had a couple by Lord Grey. According to contemporary gossip the parentage of some, at least, of Lady Melbourne's six children was a matter of speculation: her second son, William, the future Lord Melbourne and Prime Minister, was thought by many to have been fathered by Lord Egremont. As for Lady Harley, later Countess of Oxford, she had so many lovers that her numerous children were known as 'the Harleian Miscellany'.

Most of these upper-class bastards were given the family surname, brought up in the same household as the legitimate heirs and introduced to society on equal terms, or at least acknowledged quite openly; but a few, the real mistakes, would be born abroad, reappear at a suitable age and suddenly acquire a benevolent 'godfather'. One particularly fortunate product of disputed parentage was a charming girl called Maria Fagniani, known as 'Mie-Mie'. She was the daughter of the Marchesa Fagniani, a famous beauty who was particularly free with her favours at the end of the eighteenth century. In effect, Mie-Mie had three fathers, all of them rich and all of them claiming paternity. The

* Although there is insufficient evidence to prove the point, it has frequently been suggested that incest was the spectre which haunted the eighteenth century and the Regency period in the same way that homosexuality scandalized the late Victorians. Byron's illicit relationship with his half-sister was one of the major scandals of the Regency and a contributory factor to his decision to leave England, but his case was by no means unique. T. H. White refers to incest as 'the *frisson* of the century' and cites Walpole on the subject: 'I am glad you are aware of Miss Pitt ... Her very first slip was with her eldest brother; and it is not her fault that she has not made still blacker trips' (*The Age of Scandal*, Jonathan Cape, 1950, p. 138).

first candidate was her mother's husband, the Marchese, and the others were Lord March, later Duke of Queensberry, and George Selwyn. The last two, both well-known rakes, had been lovers of the Marchesa at the same time, and each regarded Maria as his daughter and heiress. Selwyn left her £20,000, and cynically appointed the Duke as trustee. 'Old Q', as the Duke was usually called, went on to leave her another £100,000 and so Mie-Mie, in spite of her doubtful lineage, became one of the most eligible girls on the market. At twenty-one she married Lord Yarmouth, a man whose reputation was already as bad as that of her putative father's.

The mood and manners of any society are formed as much by events as example and England at the time was in a constant state of crisis: the period which began with the first Regency crisis in 1788 and ended with the death of George IV in 1830 stretched from the eve of the French Revolution, via the Napoleonic Wars, to the Congress of Vienna and the Age of Reform. The French Revolution caused a panic among the landed classes which affected the whole of Europe, but was particularly strong in England, thanks to the sudden influx of refugees. The thousands of French aristocrats who fled to England in the wake of the Terror added a new dimension to society: one estimate put the number as high as 40,000 by the end of the eighteenth century. Brighton, at the time, was the most accessible port to the French coast, and became the main reception centre for the fugitives. Some had only just managed to get out in time and arrived with nothing but the clothes they were wearing, and even these could be of the wrong sex. The Marquise de Beaulle escaped by dressing as a sailor and pretending to be part of the crew on a fishing boat, while her maid was smuggled on board in a trunk, in which she spent the whole crossing. The Comtesse de Noailles, who was twenty-one and pregnant, also dressed in boy's clothes and hid in the middle of a large coil of rope for fourteen hours on the same boat.[5] Mme de Noailles was taken in by Mrs Fitzherbert, an old friend, dressed as a woman again, and the next day went to a cricket match with her hostess and the Prince of Wales. The tales of such escapes were dramatic enough, but the stories of life in the Paris the émigrés had left behind were horrific. A particularly ghoulish example was the series of parties given by survivors of the Terror whose relatives had been executed: they were known as 'Victims' Balls' and the only criterion of admission was a certificate to prove that a member of the immediate family had been guillotined. The men, on entering the ballroom, had to salute, by a movement of the head, in the manner of a victim as he bent to be guillotined, while the women wore a thin red ribbon round their throats in another ghastly piece of mimicry.[6] This sort of story horrified the débutantes at Almack's and, incidentally, made their fathers even more wary of Reform. Prior to the French Revolution the country had begun to realize that the movement towards Reform was more than just an idealistic dream. The more enlightened politicians, including a few of the Tories, were prepared to accept that a change might be needed in the electoral system, and that the time had come for a softer approach to the working classes. The events of 1789 reversed any such liberal thinking and talk of Reform took on the taint of treason. The effects of the Revolution, coupled with the uneasy wind of democracy arriving from America, delayed the cause of Reform by more than forty years. In 1817 Lord Holland might write, 'That cursed business of Reform of Parliament is always in one's way. With one great man nothing is good unless that be the principal object, and with another nothing must be done if a word of Reform is even glanced at in requisition, petition or discussion.' But it was to be another fifteen years before the Bill became law.

The Revolution was followed in 1793 by the declaration of war with France, a war which was to last almost continuously for nearly twenty-two years. Admittedly the war was unpopular with a large proportion of the public, who saw no reason for England to become involved, but one of its most curious aspects was the reaction of society in general and the Whig aristocracy in particular. At the end of the eighteenth century the love affair of the English upper classes with France was at its peak and it

A FRENCH INVASION OR THE FASHIONABLE DRESS OF 1798
Caricature by G. L., published by Fores, 1798.
*All those with the slightest pretension to fashion remained dedicated Francophiles
even during the war.*

continued in spite of the war. The educated classes had always
spoken French as easily as English and saw no reason to change
their ways: people continued to break into French at parties,
sprinkle their letters with French phrases and hanker after Paris
as their spiritual home. It must, however, be added that such an
attitude was confined to a small section of society, the élite and
the liberals: the great majority of the public were violently
anti-French, as the cartoons of the period show. (Nevertheless it
is easy to imagine the public reaction if the upper classes in
Britain had spoken German to each other at parties in 1940 and
made it obvious that they could not wait to revisit Berlin.)

All those with the slightest pretension to fashion or taste
remained dedicated Francophiles, filling their houses with French
furniture, eating French food and drinking French wines. The
Regent himself carried on decorating his houses in the French
mode and adding to his collections of Sèvres porcelain, clocks

and other exquisite *objets d'art* from the Continent. It was more difficult to get hold of such things, of course, but some of the émigrés had managed to escape with valuables, and others were smuggled by agents. The import of luxury foods from the Continent, as well as wine and brandy, also seems to have carried on throughout the war. Regency society had no intention of allowing Napoleon to interfere with their gastronomic pleasures. Such was the belief in Paris as the arbiter of taste that even the fashions initiated by the enemy were copied in London. When the opera house was redecorated at the beginning of the nineteenth century the silver and blue associated with the Bourbons was replaced by scarlet and gold, the colours Napoleon favoured. They were also the colours adopted by the Prince Regent when he redecorated Carlton House yet again in 1815;[7] although, at least, by then peace had been declared. The love affair between French and English society was occasionally reciprocal: for example French ladies came to London to buy their riding habits in London and the Bond Street tailors were considered the best in Europe. English coachmakers, too, were greatly in demand and as soon as the war was over trade was resumed. In 1817 the French government put in an order for 900 mail coaches from a London firm, at a price of £150 each.

Most intelligent people realized that the Treaty of Amiens, in 1802, would never work and that the subsequent peace was only temporary, but they made the best of it while they could and high society streamed over to Paris *en masse*. The Whig grandees led the stampede, headed by Charles James Fox and his new wife, Mrs Armistead, Lady Holland, and the Duchess of Devonshire with her entourage. The Prince of Wales's sister-in-law, the Duchess of Cumberland, was another visitor, and Lady Conyngham (later the mistress of George IV), who was deemed by French society to be the most beautiful woman in Paris at the time. Another contemporary account even insists that the English ladies were much better dressed than the French. Gronow, for one, disagreed. Describing the English exodus to Paris, he wrote that 'Thousands of oddly dressed English flocked to Paris immediately after the war ... and our countrymen and women having been so long excluded from French Modes ... adopted fashions of their own, quite as remarkable, and eccentric as those of the Parisians, and much less graceful. British beauties were dressed in long straight pelisses of various colours; the body of the dress was never of the same colour as the skirt; and the bonnet was of beehive shape, and very small.'[8] And, again, no one seemed to feel the slightest embarrassment about the situation. All the English ladies wanted to be presented to Napoleon: Sheridan put Lady Elizabeth Foster in a fury by saying that she would fake a faint, or rather seven faints, if that was the only way she could attract his attention, while Lord Lansdowne and his wife had breakfast with Josephine and 'liked her very much'.[9] Lord Morpeth, later sixth Earl of Carlisle, was definitely in a minority when he refused to allow his wife to be presented to Josephine, but that was probably because he disapproved of Josephine herself, rather than from a residual sense of patriotic loyalty – her behaviour while Bonaparte was in Egypt had caused an international scandal. Everyone fraternized happily with their erstwhile opponents: General Menou, for example, had been defeated at Alexandria only a few months before, by Sir Ralph Abercrombie, but was asked to dine by all the English nobility in Paris; and another of Napoleon's commanders, General Andreossi, was appointed ambassador to the Court of St James almost immediately after the war.

Paris became the scene of a strangely unreal social season during that spring of 1802, when Europe was sandwiched between two furious bursts of warfare. (Hostilities were resumed fourteen months later and continued with even greater ferocity until 1815.) Madame Recamier was the great hostess of the day, and her parties were reported back to the unfortunate friends left behind in England. Frederick Foster wrote to Lady Melbourne that: 'We have been very gay lately. Last night we went to a Ball at M[adame] Recamier's, it was a very pretty one & lasted till 5 in the morning. Vestris danced & most excessively well.' He goes on to report various social encounters with some of the most infamous leaders of the late Revolution, showing no hesitation at meeting them. Admittedly Tallien, whom he met at a dinner party, had 'the appearance of *a Gentleman Murderer*, and talks of Guillotines & slaughter with the greatest coolness & composure', but he later qualifies this stricture by adding that Tallien's 'manners are very civil & his Conversation & look give me the idea of a Philosophe-Bourreau [intellectual executioner].'[10] This passion for the French lasted throughout the Regency and well into the nineteenth century. Although none of the English found anything strange in conducting their social life in the language of a country which they had been fighting for the last twenty-odd years, foreign visitors to London did. Richard Rush, the American ambassador, was clearly surprised to find that, not only were the guests served French food and French wines but, even though all 'The foreigners spoke English: nevertheless, the conversation was nearly all in French. This was not only the case when the English addressed the foreigners, but in speaking to each other.'[11] It was clear that nothing could shake the English infatuation with France and the war was regarded, by some, at least, as no more than a tiresome hiccup.

For others, however, the war was a violent reality. Too many scions of the English gentry were killed or maimed for society to be able to ignore it. The scarlet uniforms disappeared from the ballrooms and boys in their teens rushed off to seek action and glory in the Peninsular Campaign. Anxious parents searched *The Times*'s dispatches for news of their sons and letters from the front were passed round drawing-rooms all over the country. Lady Bessborough's son, Frederick Ponsonby, a young cavalry officer, described the Battle of Talavera in a letter to his mother: 'We had the pleasing amusement of charging five solid squares with a ditch in front. After losing 180 and 222 horses we found it was not so agreeable, and that Frenchmen don't always run away when they see British cavalry, so off we set, and my horse never went so fast in his life.'[12] He adds that if it had not been for the hampers sent out to the army by his mother he would have starved. Later he reports on the hazards of waltzing in uniform and says that he stuck his spurs into one lady's gown and brought half Madrid down with him. Both Ponsonby and his sister, Lady Caroline Lamb, were guests at the famous ball given by the Duchess of Richmond in Brussels on the eve of Waterloo. Lady Caroline wrote to her mother-in-law, Lady Melbourne, that that 'fatal ball has been much censured; there never was such a Ball – so fine & so sad – all the young men who appeared there shot dead a few hours after.'[13] She rather spoiled the effect of disinterested sympathy by adding that it was common gossip afterwards that it was Lady Frances Webster who made the Duke of Wellington late for the Battle of Waterloo.

Lady Caroline always exaggerated but the casualties at Waterloo were indeed horrific. The Allies lost 30,000 men, and almost all Wellington's aides-de-camp, most of them members of the English nobility, were either killed or wounded. Caroline's brother, Fred Ponsonby, was one of the casualties; he was badly wounded and lay on the ground of the battlefield for eighteen hours, yet survived. His extraordinary story has become famous, both as a testament to his own courage and to the way battles were fought during the Napoleonic Wars. It is so evocative, and, incidentally, so well written, that it deserves telling at length.

He begins by saying that most of the officers had been at the ball when they received their orders, and had only had time to dash back to their quarters, change and collect their gear before joining their men. Ponsonby and his regiment arrived on the scene at 6.00 in the morning and were sent first to Quatre Bras, where he found that the action was over and the ground covered with wounded from both armies, and the next day went on to Waterloo. Wellington, as usual, remained totally calm while the troops took up their positions. 'It was a most interesting time for the Duke,' Ponsonby wrote with glorious understatement and obvious awe.

[He] had every reason to expect that the whole of Bonaparte's army would immediately fall upon him, before he could collect his army on the position of Waterloo.

I was with him, the Duke, just in front of [the] line of cavalry, when we were all observing the preparations and movements of the immense mass of troops before us. He was occupied in reading the newspapers, looking through his glass when anything was observed, and then making observations and laughing at the fashionable news from London ... It is a very curious thing that very few of us expected a battle. Why, I cannot tell, but so it was. About 10 however the artillery began, and soon after we saw large bodies of the enemy in motion. The first attack was very formidable, it was repulsed, and my cousin General Ponsonby charged and had great success.

... my reg^t charged. It entered the mass and at the same time a body of French Lancers charged us on our flank. Nothing could equal the confusion of this mêlée, as we had succeeded in destroying and putting to flight the infantry. I was anxious to withdraw my reg^t, but almost at the same moment I was wounded in both arms, my horse sprung forward and carried me to the rising ground on the right of the French position, where I was knocked off my horse by a blow on the head.

I was stunned with the blow, and when I recovered, finding I was only wounded in my arms and seeing some of my reg^t at the foot of the hill, I attempted to get up, but a lancer who saw me immediately plunged his lance into my back and said: *Coquin tu n'es pas mort.* My mouth filled with blood and my breathing became very difficult as the lance had penetrated my lungs, but I did not lose my senses. The French tirailleurs ... took up their round again at the crest of the rising ground where I was; the first man who came along plundered me. An officer then came up and gave me some brandy; I begged him to have me removed, but this he could not do. He put a knapsack under my head and said I should be taken care of after the battle. He told me the Duke of Wellington was killed [he had not been, of course] and that several of our battalions in the night had surrendered. There was a constant fire kept up by those about me, a young tirailleur who fired over me talked the whole time, always observing that he had killed a man every shot he fired. Towards the evening the fire became much sharper, he told me our troops were moving on to attack and with his last shot he said: *Adieu mon ami nous allons retirer.* A squadron of Prussian cavalry passed over me. I was a good deal hurt by the horses – in general horses will avoid trampling upon men but the field was so covered, that they had no spare space for their feet.

Night now came on, I knew the battle was won. I had felt little anxiety about myself during the day as I considered my case desperate, but now the night air relieved my breathing, and I had a hope of seeing somebody I knew. I was plundered again by the Prussians. Soon after an English soldier examined me. I persuaded him to stay with me. I suffered but little pain from my wounds, but I had a most dreadful thirst, and there was no means of getting a drop of water. I thought the night would never end. At last morning came, the soldier saw a dragoon, he was fortunately of the 11th in the same brigade with me. He came and they tried to get me on his horse, but not being able to do so, he rode in to Head Quarters, and a waggon was sent for me. Young Vandeleur of my reg^t came with it, he brought a canteen of water. It is impossible to describe the gratification I felt in drinking it. I was of course very much exhausted, having lost a great deal of blood from five wounds. I had been on the ground 18 hours. I was taken to the inn in Waterloo, it had been the Duke's quarters. Hume dressed my wounds. I remained about a week in this village and was then carried into Brussels.[14]

   Ponsonby's family raced to Brussels to help nurse him and, after months of agony, he recovered.

Violence was endemic during the Regency, in civil life as much as on the battlefield. The ruffians of town and country, moreover, were restrained by no such code of honour as governed the conduct of the military. At the beginning of the nineteenth century muggers and cut-throats roamed the city streets virtually unchecked and a man took a serious risk if he walked alone at night, even in Mayfair. The Prince of Wales and his brother, the Duke of York, were attacked and robbed while walking near Berkeley Square; two young ladies returning from the opera in their own carriage were held up by a single footpad in St James's Square.[15] There was no centralized police force to cope with crime during the Regency: it was not until 1829 that the Metropolitan Police Act was passed, and even later before the rest of the country were required by law to maintain a regular constabulary. There were highwaymen on the open roads and heathland, 'wreckers' along the coast and bandits in the forests. Racecourses, country fairs, markets and prize fights were the natural habitat of pickpockets, con men and rogues of every calling. All these villains would cut a man's throat for a few shillings. The stories are legion – and explain why men carried swords and their servants pistols.

Violence, however, was not confined to the criminal classes. The cost of maintaining the war combined with the effects of the Industrial Revolution resulted in economic chaos. It was, as usual, the poorest section of society who suffered and they responded by some of the most vicious riots the country has ever known. The Luddite riots, in protest against the unemployment caused by the new machinery, began in 1811 (just as the Prince Regent was giving his inaugural, and appallingly extravagant, fête at Carlton House), and carried on intermittently for the next four years. They were followed by strikes and yet more riots all over the country. The incidence of civil disturbance throughout the Regency is not surprising in view of some of the economic facts. For a start, between 1789 and 1830, the population of Great Britain increased from eight and a half million in 1801 to almost twice that number by 1830: at the beginning of the period it was mainly rural, by the end nearly 50 per cent urban. Furthermore, according to Colquhoun's estimate of employment figures in 1803, only two million men, out of the total population, were in work: and 450,000 of those were in the lowest, poorest strata of society, living on family earnings of just over £1 a week. Captain Gronow, one of the most acute observers of his generation, considered that the years 1816 and 1817 were

a most dangerous period. The spirit of the people of England, exasperated by taxation, the high price of bread, and many iniquitous laws and restrictions was of the worst possible nature. In the riots and meetings of those troublous times the mob really meant mischief; and had they been accustomed to the use of arms, and well drilled, they might have committed as great excesses as the ruffians of 1793 in France.[16]

The Government's response to riots brought about by high prices, and the very real threat of starvation, was to order a large number of Dragoons to be posted all over the country, to be deployed in case of trouble. This, naturally, created a vicious circle: the peaceful section of society resented the presence of the army and linked forces with the rioters in protest.

Every time there was an election, too, the mob went wild, and again, dangerously so. Charles Greville, writing in 1818, thought that the behaviour of the crowds during the Westminster elections was as bad as anything seen in Paris during the Revolution. This may have been an exaggeration but it was a fact that the Tory candidate at the time was assaulted so violently that his life was in danger, and that when Lord Castlereagh, an arch-Tory, went to vote he was openly hooted, abused, pelted with stones, and only 'got off with some difficulty'.[17] The mob expressed its disapproval of an issue by smashing windows and stoning carriages. During one of the riots Lady Anne Barnard complained that she had had thirty-three of her windows smashed by the mob, and that some of the large ones cost 5 guineas each to replace. Anyone known to hold conservative views could expect their whole household, including their servants, to receive the same rough treatment. There were spontaneous fights in the streets and in several parts of London the Horse Guards were called in to prevent further violence by a show of force. During the election of 1820 Princess Lieven complained to Metternich that she was obliged to board up her house in Brighton and hardly dared go out of doors. She reported that the Whigs, led by 'the Cavendish gang', all wore pink ribbons and their opponents blue: the dangerous element was 'the pinks', furious at losing the election.[18]

It should be emphasized, however, that the manner in which the populace expressed their *approval* could be equally dangerous: the celebrations after the victory of Salamanca, for example, turned into a drunken saturnalia lasting for three days. Deprived of the Duke of Wellington himself, because he was still abroad, the mob managed to intercept his brother, the Marquess Wellesley, who was driving around looking at the illuminations all over the West End, dragged him out of his carriage and, much against his will, paraded him around the streets, finally dumping him at Apsley House. At this stage of the proceedings the crowd was still good-natured, but when the illuminations were turned out later that night they went berserk, smashing windows, letting off firearms and throwing fireballs into the crowds. Coaches were overturned, horses stampeded and several people were badly burnt:

In the Strand, at one time, three women were on fire, and one burned through all her clothes, to her thigh. Likewise in the Strand, a hackney coach, containing two ladies and two gentlemen, was forced open by the mob, who threw in a number of fireworks, which setting fire to the straw at the bottom of the coach, burned an eye of one of the gentlemen, his coat, and breeches; one of the ladies had her pelissè burned, and the other was burned across the breast. In St Clement's Churchyard, a woman, of respectable appearance, hearing a blunderbuss suddenly discharged near her, instantly dropped down and expired.

All this violence bred a certain insensibility, or, rather, a different set of sensibilities to those of the modern world. For example, in the weeks following Waterloo, according to one society lady, 'the great amusement at Bruxelles, indeed the only one except visiting the sick, is to make large parties & go to the field of Battle – & pick up a skull or an old shoe or a letter, & bring it home.'[19] These macabre relics were later put on display in the drawing-room, to the admiration of all, and this was considered neither ghoulish nor in bad taste. Public executions were always well attended, and not only by the rougher elements of society: George Selwyn, for example, would travel miles to see a good multiple hanging. (But then he was also suspected of necrophilia.)

When the Duke of Kent was given the command of Gibraltar he treated the troops with such gratuitous brutality that they mutinied: the Duke was also the only commander known to have sentenced a man to 900 lashes, a flogging tantamount to prolonged execution. Bear-baiting and cock-fights were theoretically illegal but carried on anyway all over the country and watched just as eagerly by members of the *haut ton* as the general public. But the most obvious testament to the paradox of Regency sensitivities was the cult of pugilism. The Regency was the golden age of boxing, when champions acquired the status of celebrities.

They were courted, fêted and emulated by a society conditioned to violence. The 'noble science' of pugilism attracted such diverse admirers as Hazlitt, Keats and Cobbett, while Lord Byron not only wrote about the ring but frequently put on the gloves himself. Though the Prince Regent withdrew his patronage, and refused to attend any further prizefights after a man he had promoted was killed in the ring, his brothers and friends had no such qualms: the Dukes of York and Clarence, the Earl of Barrymore and the Marquess of Queensberry, whose descendant clarified the rules of boxing, were all active patrons and regularly attended the fights.[20] News of a prizefight to be held in a country town, such as Grantham or Derby, would attract spectators from as far away as London or York and there was not a bed to be had in the inns for miles around.

It is no coincidence that the spectacular success of boxing, as a fashionable spectator sport, happened at a time when England was at war. The same aggression and cruelty were displayed in the ring as on the battlefield, but there was also the same glamour and excitement. The romantic young heroes of Salamanca and Talavera were the toast of the times: among those at home pugilism was the nearest expression of valour (or 'bottom', as courage was known colloquially amongst boxers). Sparring with 'Gentleman Jackson' at least provided a vicarious thrill. Jackson, a former champion, retired from the ring and started his own school at 13 New Bond Street. It was an instant success with the young men of fashion, who queued up for lessons from the Master and revelled in fighting each other under his auspices. This was, however, a peculiarly English phenomenon: there was no sudden craze for boxing among the European nobility. As Hazlitt wrote: 'Foreigners can scarcely understand how we can squeeze pleasure out of this pastime; the luxury of hard blows given or received; the great joy of the ring; nor the perseverance of the combatants.'[21]

At the same time it was also an age when men burst into tears on the slightest provocation, and thought nothing of crying in public. They cried about love, money and even politics, long and loudly and without embarrassment. Walpole reported that Fox was in floods of tears on the floor of the House of Commons over a political quarrel with Burke, who was so upset himself that he started weeping as well: Creevey, writing in 1815, said that 'there was not a dry eye in the House', adding that one minister sobbed so much that he was unable to speak. Sheridan was another one who always burst into tears when he failed to get his own way. On one occasion the Prince had just given Sheridan a particularly lucrative sinecure, worth £800 a year, but the latter wanted to pass it over to his son; when the Prince refused, pointing out there was little enough justification for giving the father the post and none at all for the son, Sheridan made a frightful scene and began to 'cry bitterly'.[22] Another time it was the Prince himself who 'cried long and loud' over some political dispute with one of his ministers. But then the Prince, too, was always in tears, usually over his love affairs. He had 'cried by the hour' over Mrs Fitzherbert, according to Mrs Armistead, later the wife of Charles James Fox, and 'testified the sincerity and violence of his passion and his despair by the most extravagant expressions and actions, rolling on the floor, striking his forehead, tearing his hair.' (This was in the early days of his courtship when Mrs Fitzherbert refused his advances because they were not married: after making endless scenes and bombarding the lady with appallingly senti-mental love letters – one is forty-two pages long – he threatened to kill himself unless she became his mistress. His suicide attempt caused a panic at Court because he was found moaning and covered in blood: in fact the Prince had almost certainly faked the whole incident, but it was enough to melt the heart of Mrs Fitzherbert.)

An excess of sentiment was thought to be so effective with reluctant ladies that it was common practice to spatter a love letter with fake tears. Brummell wrote, in his farewell letter to the young French girl he fell in love with at the end of his life, 'Adieu! I have yet sufficient command over my drooping faculties to restrain any tributary tears from falling over my farewell; you might doubt their reality; and we all know that they may be counterfeited upon paper, with a sponge and rose-water.'[23] Tears, during the Regency, were regarded as proof of an exquisite sensibility and a perfectly acceptable means of emotional blackmail. T. H. White writes that there was a certain jealousy of accomplished weepers, which 'came to a head in Fanny Burney, who became positively cattish about an unfortunate girl called Sophy Streatfield, because the latter was able to cry at will. It was because Fanny herself was probably the second-best weeper in the kingdom, and could not endure to be beaten.'[24]

The manners and mores of any society always fluctuate with succeeding generations, but the changes which took place during the Regency were almost revolutionary. During the eighteenth century the rules of etiquette and precedence were clearly defined, but by the beginning of the nineteenth they had become vague and elastic. The Prince Regent, for example, changed the accepted order whenever it suited him: at one of the Duke of Clarence's parties he went against all the rules of protocol by giving precedence to his brother's mistress, Mrs Jordan, over a Duchess. At the fête he gave in June 1811 to celebrate the advent of the Regency neither his legal nor his morganatic wife were invited. Mrs Fitzherbert had already been given her *congé*, and the Princess of Wales was not allowed anywhere near Carlton House. As one of the gossips said, 'the two wives are sitting at home'. Conversely, the rigid eighteenth-century code could be invoked as the perfect excuse whenever necessary. The Regent was besotted about Lady Conyngham, his final mistress, but society had reservations about her. Much to the Prince's annoyance his own sisters refused to accept Lady Conyngham, their argument being that, as he had insisted they ignore his lawful wife, Princess Caroline, they could not possibly speak to his mistress: what they meant, of course, was that they didn't like her. The royal princesses had had no such qualms about making friends with some of their brother's earlier mistresses, notably the Ladies Hertford and Jersey, both of whom were not only popular society hostesses, but received at Court. In 1796 a contemporary diarist wrote that Lady Jersey

was invited with the Prince's party to the Queen's House, and put to a card-table with the Princess Augusta and Lady Holdernesse. The Prince of Wales, in the course of the evening, repeatedly came up to her at table, and publicly squeezed her hand. The King sees and disapproves ... The Queen is won over to the Prince's wishes by his attention, and presents in jewels, etc.; the Princess says her father told her to observe everything and say nothing.[25]

The hypocrisy of the Court and society during the Regency could be breathtaking.

At the same time, society as a whole was becoming much more egalitarian and the criteria of acceptance less rigid. The eighteenth century's emphasis on breeding had fallen victim to the French Revolution. Blood alone was no longer enough and 'Who are her people?' mattered less than 'How much is she worth?', particularly in the matter of marriages. Nevertheless, snobbery was still endemic. The fifth Duke of Devonshire said of his cousin, the distinguished scientist Henry Cavendish: 'He is not a gentleman; he works.' Harriette Wilson, the leading courtesan of her day, agreed, defining a gentleman as a man 'who has no visible means of support'. But then Harriette, with the aims of her profession in mind, was prejudiced. She went on to explain that '... the system at White's Club, the members of which are all choice gentlemen, of course, is, and ever has been, never to blackball any man, who ties a good knot in his handkerchief, keeps his hands out of his breeches-pockets, and says nothing.'[26]

The Duke and Harriette were wrong, or at least in a minority. Poverty was no barrier to social success provided there was some other distinction to offer, be it brains or beauty, elegance or charm. The diarist Creevey, for example, lived on an income of no more than £200 a year but was invited everywhere and became almost a fixture at the Prince's parties. Henry Luttrell, too, one of the recognized 'wits' of the Regency, was not at all well-off but lived and moved in the wealthiest circles. Luttrell was the author of a long poem, originally titled 'Advice to Julia' but known by all as 'Letters of a Dandy to a Dolly'. According to one of the critics, it was 'full of well-bred facetiousness and sparkle of the first water', in other words snob-appeal. As for Lady Anne Barnard, she and her sister broke all the rules when they actually started their own 'business'. Short of money and with a natural talent for interior decoration, they took to buying or renting houses, doing them up, and letting them furnished for a considerable profit. One or two people had the bravery to see that this was an excellent idea, but others took the view of the lady who complained that 'she wished to God those two very agreeable women would leave off being upholsterers and begin to be women of fashion [again]'.[27] Inevitably, there were further complaints from the Old Guard about the new millionaires created by the Industrial Revolution. As usual, the *nouveaux riches* were blamed for any lapse in standards, and in particular for the extravagant entertaining with which they bought their way into society. As one peevish commentator put it, 'Commerce, contracts, loans and war prices have poured an influx of wealth into hands not hitherto in contact with the Corinthian pillars of society.' They were accused of inviting 'their noble friends to splendid dinners in apartments of Eastern magnificence', with the result that the aristocracy felt compelled to compete. And so 'The duke, the commoner, the contractor, all *entertain*, as it is called, in gay apartments, full of pomp and gold; "And one eternal dinner swallows all".'[28]

2

BUCKS, BEAUX AND 'PINKS
OF THE TON'

The Regency Beau, Buck or Dandy is an immortal character: urbane, elegant and yet totally masculine, he is the perfect hero of romantic fiction. He is not to be confused with his eighteenth-century predecessors, the Fop, the Fribble and the Macaroni, but it is still a genus with many variations. And to mistake a Corinthian for a Dandy would have been as insulting to both at the time as failing to differentiate between Mods and Rockers would have been in the 1950s, or between Sloane Rangers and Young Fogeys in the 1980s. Pierce Egan, the Regency sports-journalist and social commentator, defined the pedigree of a Dandy in his usual style, considered the height of wit at the time: 'The DANDY was got by *Vanity* out of *Affectation* – his dam, *Petit Maître* or *Macaroni* – his grandam, *Fribble* – his great-grandam, *Bronze* – his great-great-grandam, *Coxcomb* – and his earliest ancestor FOP . . .'[1]

Be all that as it may, it was these Regency beaux who set the tone of society. They were the new elite, the arbiters of fashion, the leaders of the *ton*: it is symptomatic of the period that the man who led them for so many years was the grandson of a valet.

George Bryan ('Beau') Brummell was one of the icons of Regency society, at least in the eyes of his peers. Lord Byron, with his usual affectation, pronounced that 'there are but three great men in the nineteenth century, Brummell, Napoleon and myself', and

Prince Puckler-Muskau,* who went to see the fallen idol in exile, thought England owed him a pension: 'And surely the English nation ought in justice to do something for the man who invented starched cravats! How many did I see in London in the enjoyment of large sinecures, who had done far less for their country!'[2] It is certainly true that Brummell, the ultimate Dandy, revolutionized masculine fashion and that his influence has lasted to the present day. He was the man who decreed that the outrageous dressing of the eighteenth century was vulgar: before Brummell arrived on the scene, velvets and silks, jewels and make-up were *de rigueur* amongst the peacocks of society, and the brighter and richer-looking they were, the better. For example, when the Prince of Wales first appeared in society, according to one report, 'His magnificence was such that the arbiters of fashion were compelled reluctantly to admit that a powerful rival had come upon the scene . . . His coat was pink silk, with white cuffs; his waistcoat white silk, embroidered with various coloured foil, and adorned with a profusion of French paste . . .'[3] Brummell took just as much time and trouble over his appearance but with a totally different effect in mind. He believed in absolute simplicity. As he said himself, 'If John Bull turns round to look after you, you are not well dressed; but either too stiff, too tight, or too fashionable.'[4]

Brummell's timing was right. By the beginning of the nine-teenth century the rules of fashion had already become more fluid, more democratic, in line with so many other aspects of Regency life. People were chary of extravagant dressing and though knee-breeches and crinolines were still mandatory at Court, for ordinary wear the younger men had begun to favour less elaborate clothes: pantaloons (which were in effect trousers) instead of breeches, plain riding boots instead of tasselled Hessians, and plain cloth coats. Brummell crystallized the style. He insisted that elegance was dependent upon the cut and style of a coat, not its ability to startle: it was during the Regency that English tailoring acquired a reputation for excellence which has

---

* Prince Puckler-Muskau was a German visitor who came to England in the 1820s and recorded his impressions in a series of letters to his wife.

lasted to the present day. For the first time the fit of a man's coat, rather than its materials or decoration, became the test of elegance. Brummell was said to have had his coat made by one tailor, his waistcoats by another and his breeches by a third, each a specialist in his own field. The coats often fitted so closely that it took considerable exertion on the part of a man's valet to get them on in the morning and the breeches could be so tight that it was impossible to sit down. And then there was the added restriction of movement imposed by the high, starched cravat. All in all men's dress during the Regency must have been thoroughly uncomfortable.

In the daytime Brummell always wore a perfectly fitting dark blue coat with brass buttons, leather breeches, top boots and a stiff white cravat, a uniform, incidentally, which became the trademark of the Whigs. It was considered a privilege in social circles to be allowed into Brummell's dressing-room and watch him 'making his toilette', a performance which took up several hours and became one of the legends of the period. Captain Jesse, a fellow dandy, recorded the ritual in detail: for a start the whole *batterie de toilette* was made of silver, including a silver spitting dish, since Brummell said that 'it was impossible to spit in clay'. After shaving, with the smallest possible razor, he spent two whole hours every morning in ablutions. 'He used to stand before the glass, not wearing his wig, in his dressing trousers, massaging his body with a stiff brush of bristle something like the trigil used by Petronius, to regenerate his epidermis; when he had done with it, as red as a lobster, he was ready for the camisole. But before dressing – or rather robing himself – Brummell took a dentist's mirror in one hand and a pair of tweezers in the other, and closely examined his forehead and well-shaved chin, and he did not lay the tweezers down till he had mercilessly plucked every stray hair that could be detected on the polished surface of his face.'[5] (This part of the proceedings, needless to say, was conducted in private and the public only allowed in when he actually began dressing: Jesse never confessed to Brummell that he had seen it all in the reflection of a mirror, when one of the doors had been left open by mistake.) According to another report when someone asked him the address of his hairdresser, Brummell replied, 'I have three: the first is responsible for my temples, the second for the front and the third for the occiput.' As for his boots, which were famous for their gloss, when asked for the recipe of his blacking, he replied, 'Blacking, my dear sir? Well, you know, I never use anything but the froth of champagne.' Of course, with Brummell it was always possible that he made these sorts of outrageous claims simply for effect, but there was usually an element of truth as well.

The high point of the whole performance was the moment when Brummell embarked on tying the enormous neckcloth, or stock, which was in fashion at the time and which had always in the past been made of limp cloth. Brummell had the brainwave of using starched muslin instead, an idea which created a sensation but was extremely difficult to copy without making a complete mess of the whole cravat. Brummell's dressing room was always thronged with fashionable spectators trying to see how he did it: they included the Prince Regent and the Dukes of Bedford, Beaufort and Rutland, all of whom were his personal friends. Brummell's actual method of tying the cravat was recorded thus by one of his disciples:

The collar, which was always fixed to the shirt, was so large that, before being folded down, it completely hid his head and face, and the white neckcloth was at least a foot in height. The first *coup d'archet* was made with the shirt collar, which he folded down to its proper size; and then, standing before the looking-glass, with his chin poked up towards the ceiling, by the gentle and gradual declension of his lower jaw he creased the cravat to reasonable dimensions.[6]

The slightest mistake ruined the whole effect and meant that he had to start all over again with a fresh cravat. One of Brummell's favourite maxims was 'clean white linen, and plenty of it'. He certainly lived up to it: yards and yards of starched muslin were tied and discarded every day. The valet referred to them as 'our failures'.

It was a life dedicated to style, in fashion, manners and mores; he had little interest in politics or current affairs, except in so far as they affected his friends. Brummell would have found nothing ridiculous in the remark, made by one of his successors, that 'the conduct of a cane is three-fourths of life'.[7] Max Beerbohm (a dedicated dandy in his youth) wrote some fifty years after Brummell's death that his hero had been 'in the utmost sense of the word, an artist' and went on to extol 'the costume of the nineteenth century, as shadowed for us first by Mr Brummell, so quiet, so reasonable, and, I say, emphatically, so beautiful; free from folly or affectation, yet susceptible to exquisite ordering; plastic, austere, economical.'[8] Beerbohm writes of the beau's 'fine scorn of accessories' and says that 'In certain congruities of dark cloth, in the rigid perfection of his linen, in the symmetry of his glove with his hand, lay the secret of Mr Brummell's miracles.' Yet another admirer referred to Brummell's dressing-room as 'a studio in which he daily composed that elaborate portrait of himself which was to be exhibited for a few hours in the clubrooms of the town.'[9] In modern parlance, his life was a daily 'happening', dedicated to style.

The leader of society for so many years had no pretensions to aristocratic breeding. Brummell came of strictly middle class stock: the family's rise in society began when his grandfather, an ex-valet, retired at the end of the eighteenth century, bought a house in Bury Street, St James's, and began taking in lodgers. Charles Jenkinson, father of the future Prime Minister, was one of them, and thanks to his patronage, Brummell's father was given a job as a clerk in the Treasury. From there he moved on to become private secretary to Lord North. Having acquired a number of lucrative government sinecures by means of his connections, he went on to consolidate his fortune by marrying a Miss Richardson, who was not only one of the prettiest girls of her day – and from whom Beau Brummell inherited his looks – but rich: her father was Keeper of the Lottery Office. Brummell senior moved up in the world, began mixing with the likes of Charles James Fox and the rest of the Whig grandees, bought an estate in the country and sent his son to Eton. The family had 'arrived'.

The Prince of Wales's first meeting with Beau Brummell took place in a farmyard in the middle of Green Park, at first sight a most unlikely venue for two such characters. It was, however, a decorative rather than functional farm, an English *Petit Trianon*. There was a pretty little pond surrounded by trees, a thatched cottage complete with rambling roses, and a few cows who grazed in the large adjacent field. The 'farmer' in charge of this rustic oasis in the middle of London was Brummell's aunt, a Mrs Searle, who pottered round her domain wearing full eighteenth-century dress, hooped skirts and powdered wig. It became the fashion during the Regency for the ladies of the Court to call on Mrs Searle when they went out for their daily constitutional, to watch her milking the cows. Some even played at being milkmaids themselves. On one such occasion, in 1793, Brummell was visiting his aunt when the Prince of Wales arrived, accompanied by Lady Salisbury. While the two women milked the cows the Prince talked to Brummell, at that date a good-looking boy of fifteen who had just left Eton and was about to go up to Oxford. When the Prince asked him what he wanted to do when he left college, Brummell, seeing an obvious opportunity, said that his one ambition was to go into the army, whereupon the Prince promised him a commission in the 10th Hussars. This regiment, as Brummell very well knew, was commanded by the Prince himself and therefore the most fashionable in the whole army at the time.

Brummell went into the army as a means of social advancement and because it offered the kind of life he wanted. He was not in the least interested in being a soldier *per se*. At the age of twenty he left the army, according to legend because the regiment was posted to Manchester, an unthinkable fate for a dandy. Having sold out, and also inherited some £30,000 from his father, Brummell bought a house in Chesterfield Street and began to hold court. By what means a young man, neither noble nor rich, nor particularly talented, managed to persuade society not only to follow his lead in fashion but to regard him as the ultimate authority remains unclear. But it is not in dispute that within a couple of years his good opinion was thought to be of more value than that of the Prince himself and his reputation was such that he could make or break a social aspirant with the lift of an eyebrow. A smile of approval from Brummell was thought to be worth more to a débutante than the most expensive ball, and his quizzing-glass was said to be the deadliest weapon in London. The Prince, one of his greatest admirers, once burst into tears because Brummell criticized the cut of his new coat – an apt comment on both of them, incidentally – and the young men of society wasted hours trying to emulate his style. Brummell was undoubtedly gifted with genuine taste and a natural elegance, of mind as well as of deportment, but then so were a number of other Regency beaux. The reason for his incredible success must be that he had charm, that indefinable quality which, allied to self-confidence, always works. Brummell was the supreme example of the dictum 'it's not what you do, but the way that you do it'.

His self-confidence bordered on plain arrogance, as some of his own quotes show. For example: 'It is my folly that is the making of me', or 'A life of leisure is a most difficult art ... boredom is as depressing as an insistent creditor.' He was known, too, as the 'master of the well-timed silence'; but then Brummell's whole life was dedicated to creating an effect. He knew by instinct every trick of the publicity game, the late entrance, the throw-away line or outrageous remark, sure to be repeated. Though young, strong and in excellent health he took a sedan chair rather than walk the length of Bond Street, for fear of getting dirt on his boots; and then made a mockery of the whole performance by starting a fashion for white tops to hunting boots, knowing quite well that if there was one place it was impossible not to get spattered with mud it was the hunting field. Brummell took a delight in such tricks. At parties, if he deigned to show up at all, he usually refused to dance, spoke only to his particular friends and left early. It seems odd that Regency hostesses were not only prepared to countenance this sort of behaviour but felt the evening had been a total flop if he failed to appear.

Furthermore, the stories which are always cited as examples of Brummell's wit seem nothing of the kind: in fact, they sound either feeble or just plain rude. Asked at a dinner party whether he liked vegetables, Brummell is said to have replied that he didn't know because he had never eaten them, adding, after what was no doubt meant to be an interesting pause, 'No, that is not quite true; I once ate a pea.' And he was reputed to have jilted a woman because she ate cabbage; although that particular story was almost certainly apocryphal since Brummell is not on record as ever having shown any serious interest in women. He was not homosexual, merely uninterested in sex, and far too much of a narcissist to be bothered with loving anyone else. Of course charm is an ephemeral quality which rarely survives repetition, but, even so, his conceit on occasion seems insufferable. It led indirectly to Brummell's fall from grace: the Prince Regent, a long-standing friend and admirer of Brummell's, began to grow weary of the latter's presumption. Like so many members of the royal family the Prince was touchy about his dignity, and though affable enough when it pleased him, took offence very easily. Brummell overstepped the line on several occasions, treating the Prince with far too much familiarity and an astonishing lack of respect. He obviously believed his position in society to be so secure that he could get away with anything. The crash came at a ball in London, in 1814. The Prince had arrived in the company of Lord Alvanley, and stood talking to him but openly ignored Brummell. The latter, furious at being cut in public, for once lost his habitual self-control, and called out in a loud voice the fatal words: 'Alvanley, who is your fat friend?' The Prince, whose vanity was legendary, never spoke to him again. It was the beginning of the end for Brummell, who was already on the edge of social ruin because of his debts.

From the start Brummell lived beyond his means. He filled the house in Chesterfield Street with exquisite Buhl furniture and Sèvres porcelain; began a collection of snuffboxes, a hobby with plenty of possibilities for expenditure; entertained, gambled and spent a fortune on clothes. When the money ran out he borrowed from his friends, eventually to a degree that bordered on fraud. He arranged a complicated deal, involving annuities, with the help of the Manners brothers, Lords Robert and Charles. The terms were unbelievable: in return for an immediate capital sum of less than £5000 the Manners brothers committed themselves to pay over £1000 a year for the rest of their lives. All three men were in their early thirties and Brummell must have known perfectly well that he would never have enough money to be able to pay them back.

Brummell was still only thirty-eight when the duns closed in and he fled to France. At that time peers were still exempt from arrest for debt but, for a commoner like Brummell, however fashionable he might be, the only alternative to prison was exile. Even then he remained as arrogant as ever and refused to give up his expensive tastes. One of his visitors, when he was living in lodgings in Calais, admired the various pieces of furniture and *objets d'art* with which Brummell had decorated his rooms but expressed surprise that, even though notionally bankrupt, he had yet again managed to acquire the trappings of gracious living. Brummell's reply is revealing: 'My friend, it is a truly aristocratic feeling, the gift of living happily on credit! One must, of course, be endowed with the gift of having no idea of the value of money.' The line between confidence-trickster and *poseur* is a fine one and not everyone appreciated the difference: when the sixth Duke of Devonshire met Brummell after the latter's fall from grace, he shook hands and said, 'Poor man'. . . we tolerate great swindlers in society.'

As an epitaph, however, the Duke's comment is not complete, for Brummell behaved outstandingly well in one respect. He refused point-blank to publish his memoirs. Rumour had it in London that he had been offered £5000 by John Murray to write his reminiscences and £6000 by the Regent to suppress them. At the time the ex-'King of the Dandies' was living in lodgings in Calais, on less than £100 a year, was in arrears with the rent, and yet again heavily in debt to the local tradesmen. Nevertheless, he refused all offers, explaining to his landlord, who had at last seen a hope of getting paid, that he would rather go to gaol than betray his friends. Brummell had his own code of honour.

Dandyism is a specific cult which has attracted as much adverse criticism as praise: and, once again, it illustrates the paradox inherent in the period. London society was ruled by a dandy, Beau Brummell, for more than fifteen years: yet the word at the time was more often used in a derogatory sense than as an accolade. The dandy was caricatured as a ridiculous figure in contemporary cartoons, and any aspirant to dandyism was liable to be mocked as a 'veritable tulip' or a 'pink of the *ton*': Regency prints show any number of these outrageously dressed characters. Similarly, a satirical booklet published at the time lists a number of styles for neckcloths, which though probably fictional, indicate the prevailing mood. There was the Oriental Tie (*couleur de la cuisse d'une Nymphe ennuyée*), the Mathematical Tie, the Osbald-ston, the American Tie, the Napoleon Tie, the Mail Coach Tie, also known as the Waterfall, the Trone d'Amour Tie (*couleur des yeux de jeune fille en extase*), the Irish Tie, the Ballroom Tie (*blanc d'innocence virginale*), the Horse-collar Tie, the Hunting-Tie (*couleur Isabelle*), and the Maharatta Tie (*couleur peau d'Ispahan*).[10] Keeping up with the various fashions could become a full-time occupation, and one which was fraught with problems. An anonymous extract from 'An Exquisite's Diary', published in 1819, mocks the tribulations of a dandy:

Took four hours to dress; and then it rained; ordered the tilbury and my umbrella, and drove to the fives' court; next to my tailors; put him off after two years tick; no bad fellow that Weston ... broke three stay-laces and a buckle, tore the quarter of a pair of shoes, made so thin by O'Shaughnessy, in St James's Street, that they were light as brown paper; what a pity they were lined with pink satin, and were quite the go; put on a pair of Hoby's; over-did it in perfuming my handkerchief, and had to recommence *de novo*; could not please myself in tying my cravat; lost three quarters of an hour by that, tore two pairs of kid gloves in putting them hastily on; was obliged to go gently to work with the third; lost another quarter of an hour by this; drove off furiously in my chariot but had to return for my splendid snuff-box, as I knew that I should eclipse the circle by it.[11]

A few of the more dedicated exhibitionists tore their clothes with broken glass before wearing them and went on to spend hours creasing and crumpling the garment in question. This, presumably, was intended to indicate romantic poverty or the lofty mind of an artist indifferent to fashion. Some things never change. Young men who carried a temporary craze to such extremes, however, were not 'true' dandies; they were fakes who had missed the whole point of the creed. In its purest form, dandyism can be classed as one of the decorative arts, and it has rightly been pointed out that the vanity of a dandy is a very different matter from the 'crude conceit of the merely handsome man ... the dandy cares for his physical endowments only in so far as they are susceptible of fine results. They are just so much to him as to the decorative artist is inilluminate parchment, or the form of a white vase or the surface of a wall where frescoes shall be.' Even the purists of the 'Dandy Set', as they came to be known, were not, however, exempt from attack. Captain Gronow, reminiscing in old age, is unusually vitriolic about the dandies:

How unspeakably odious – with a few brilliant exceptions such as Alvanley – were the dandies of forty years ago. They were a motley crew with nothing remarkable about them but their insolence, they were generally not high born, nor rich, nor very good-looking, nor clever, nor agreeable; and why they arrogated to themselves the right of setting up their own fancied superiority on a self-raised pedestal, and despising their betters, Heaven only knows. They were generally middle-aged, some even elderly men, had large appetites and weak digestions, gambled freely and had no luck. They hated everybody and abused everybody, and would sit in White's window weaving tremendous 'crammers' [tales]. They swore a good deal, never laughed and had their own particular slang, and had most of them been patronised at one time or another by Brummell or the Regent ... Thank heaven this miserable race has long been extinct! May England never look upon their like again![12]

(It did, of course. There was a renaissance of dandyism at the end of the nineteenth century, headed by Max Beerbohm and Oscar Wilde.) Gronow is usually a most reliable source of information on contemporary attitudes but, in this case, he may have been prejudiced. As a young man he had been a dandy himself, but a minor one, barely noticed by the leaders of society and never admitted to the Inner Circle, known as the 'Bow Window Set'. These privileged few spent their time sitting in the window of White's Club in St James's Street, passing judgement on everyone they saw; they had their own chairs which no other member would have dared to usurp.

Other admirers of dandyism have taken the view that it is a sociological phenomenon, the result of a society in a state of transition or revolt. Barbey d'Aurevilly, one of the leading French dandies at the end of the nineteenth century, explained:

Some have imagined that dandyism is primarily a specialisation in the art of dressing oneself with daring and elegance. It is that, but much else as well. It is a state of mind made up of many shades, a state of mind produced in old and civilised societies where gaiety has become infrequent or where conventions rule at the price of their subject's boredom ... it is the direct result of the endless warfare between respectability and boredom.

In Regency London dandyism was a revolt against a different kind of tradition, an expression of distaste for the extravagance and ostentation of the previous generation, and of sympathy with the new mood of democracy.

Lord Alvanley was a typical example of the new elite. He was a man in the same mould as Brummell but a much more sympathetic character. In Gronow's opinion, as has already been indicated, dandies 'were generally sour and spiteful', but Alvanley was the exception, 'combining brilliant wit and repartee with the most perfect good nature'. With a round face and a smiling expression he looked like 'one of those jolly friars one meets with in Italy'. Alvanley, like Brummell, came from the successful middle class, his family having only recently been ennobled. His father was a distinguished lawyer, Sir Pepper Arden, who made his own fortune and was rewarded with a baronetcy. Dandies such as Alvanley rarely left their rooms before noon, made 'morning calls' at 3.00 in the afternoon and would never have thought of dining as early as 6.00 in the evening, as was still the custom in the country and amongst the older generation.* They sat down to dinner at 8.00 and often lingered at table until midnight.

Alvanley was a tremendous gourmet, said to give the best dinners in London. On one occasion his friends offered a prize of a free dinner at White's for the member who devised the most expensive dish. Alvanley won with a *fricassée* made from the *noix* (the very best bits of the breasts) of three hundred birds of thirteen different kinds, including a hundred snipe, forty woodcocks and twenty pheasants. The ingredients alone cost £108 5s. It was Alvanley, too, who once enjoyed a cold apricot tart so much that he ordered his chef to have a fresh one on the sideboard every single day for a year, just in case he wanted it again. When his steward remonstrated about the cost Alvanley took absolutely no notice, saying, 'Go to Gunter's, the confectioner, and purchase all the preserved apricots, and don't plague me any more about the expense.' On another occasion Alvanley wanted to give a river party, so he asked Gunter's to hire the largest boat on the Thames, get it done up and furnished as comfortably as possible, with specially ordered carpets etc., hire a crew of twelve and provide a banquet – 'but Alvanley paid Gunter two hundred guineas for his folly'.

There is a story about Alvanley which illustrates the absurdity of some contemporary mores, let alone the touchiness of Regency dandies about their personal appearance. In middle age Alvanley grew distinctly fat, and Daniel O'Connell made the mistake of

---

* Henry Cockburn, who was born in Edinburgh in 1779, puts the dinner hour in Scotland as early as 2.00 if the family were alone. The usual hour was 3.00, which 'in time but not without groans and predictions, became four, at which it stuck for several years. Then it got to five, which however was thought positively revolutionary; and four was long and gallantly adhered to by the haters of change as "the good old hour". At last even they were obliged to give in. But they only yielded inch by inch and made a desperate stand at half past four. Even five however triumphed, and continued the average polite hour from (I think) about 1806 or 1807 till about 1820. Six has at last prevailed, and half an hour later is not unusual. As yet this is the furthest stretch of London imitation . . .' (*Memorials of His Time*, Edinburgh, 1856).

referring to him, in public, as a 'bloated buffoon'. This was not the kind of insult which could be ignored by a gentleman, even such a peaceable one as Alvanley, who smartly issued a challenge. O'Connell, however, had already killed one man in a duel and had sworn never to fight again, so he refused; but according to the prevailing code of honour this was an inadequate excuse and Alvanley remained unappeased. He threatened the Irishman with personal chastisement instead, whereupon O'Connell's son, rather than allow his father to be horsewhipped, offered to fight the duel on his behalf. Shots were exchanged at dawn on Wimbledon Common but no one was hurt. Alvanley's sense of humour returned, however, by the end of the day. When he tipped the coachman who brought him back from the duel a whole sovereign, the jarvey* exclaimed at the amount, and said, 'It's a great deal for only having taken your lordship to Wimbledon.' Whereupon Lord Alvanley replied, 'No, my good man. I give it you, not for taking me, but for bringing me back.'[13] Alvanley's career was typical of so many of his generation: he began life with a fortune and a first-class brain, but he wasted both. In the end the duns moved in on him; his horses and carriages were seized and the only tradesman left who would give him credit was the fishmonger.

London, of course, was the spiritual home of the dandies, most of whom subscribed to the philosophy expressed in a popular song, of which the last verse has become a common saw:

> In London how easy we visit and meet,
> Gay pleasure's the theme, and sweet smiles are our treat;
> Our morning's a round of good-humoured delight,
> And we rattle in comfort and pleasure all night.
>
> In the country, how pleasant our visits to make,
> Through ten miles of mud, for formality's sake,
> With the coachman in drink, and the moon in a fog,
> And no thought in our heads but a ditch or a bob.

* A jarvey was a Hackney cab driver.

In London, if folk ill-together are put,
A bore may be roasted, a quiz may be cut.
In the country, your friends would feel angry and sore –
Call an old maid a quiz, or a parson a bore!

Then in town let me live, and in town let me die,
For in truth I can't relish the country, not I;
If I must have a villa, in London to dwell,
Oh! give me the sweet shady side of Pall Mall.[14]

Eccentricity was never a bar to social success during the Regency, provided, of course, that the pundits approved of the taste of the eccentric in question. In fact it was positively fashionable; Lord Petersham, who was described by the Princess Lieven as the 'maddest of all the mad Englishmen', was one of the most popular figures in society. Petersham began his career as one of the military dandies at the age of fifteen, when he entered the Coldstream Guards as an ensign. By 1812, he had attained the rank of lieutenant-colonel, although still only just in his thirties, and decided to retire on half-pay in order to devote the rest of his life to the serious pursuit of pleasure. Petersham was generally recognized as a gifted and imaginative leader of fashion, even if some of his ideas were far too extreme for the purists. It was Petersham who introduced the ridiculous 'Cossack' trousers, which had nipped-in waists and ankles, with balloon legs in the middle, and were made of a particularly garish striped material. Petersham was a genuine eccentric, a dandy who dressed and behaved as he did because he felt like it, not because he was motivated by a childish desire to attract attention. He was a man of moods: for example, at one time everything in his life had to be a particular shade of brown. This affectation started off as a tribute to a widow called Mary Browne, with whom he was briefly in love, but it lasted long after the lady herself had faded out of his life, and the colour brown became his permanent trademark. At the time of his infatuation Petersham bought a brown carriage, brown horses, brown harness and brown livery for his servants. Even the top hat and spurs for his coachman and postillions were specially made to match. Finally, on finding

that he needed a new embroidered coat to wear at Court, Petersham ordered one to be made in brown silk embroidered with
dead leaves. As Princess Lieven wrote to Metternich, 'You can
see the kind of man he is.'

Lord Petersham had a passion for tea and snuff and he was a
connoisseur of both. His collections are described in a contemporary account of a visit to his apartments; it is an account, incidentally, which shows a preoccupation with expensive trivia which
was typical of the Regency dandy.

The room into which we were ushered was more like a shop than a
gentleman's sitting-room. All around the walls were shelves, upon
which were placed the canisters containing congou, pekoe, souchong,
bohea, gunpowder, Russian, and many other teas, all the best of their
kind; on the other side of the room were beautiful jars, with names in
gilt letters, of innumerable kinds of snuff, and all the necessary apparatus
for moistening and mixing . . . Other shelves and many tables were
covered with a great number of magnificent snuff-boxes; for Lord
Petersham had perhaps the finest collection in England, and was
supposed to have a fresh box for every day of the year. I heard him,
on the occasion of a delightful old light-blue Sèvres box he was using
being admired, say in his lisping way, 'Yes, it is a nice summer box,
but it would not do for winter wear.'[15]

In spite of his affectations, Petersham, unlike Brummell, was
not a narcissist and enjoyed the company of women. His affair
with the beautiful Lady Frances Webster caused a public scandal:
her husband tried to horsewhip him in the open street. In his
fifties Petersham succeeded his father as Earl of Harrington and
shocked society by marrying Maria Foote, a famous ex-courtesan.
The couple lived happily ever after, however, and Harrington
House became the scene of some of the jolliest parties in London.
It was true that a few sticklers refused to accept the new Countess,
because of her disreputable past, but her husband was far too
secure of his position in society to be bothered by such old-
fashioned prejudice, and his wife was far too secure of him.

Some of the other pretenders to dandyism, men who floated
around the edges of the Carlton House set, were much more

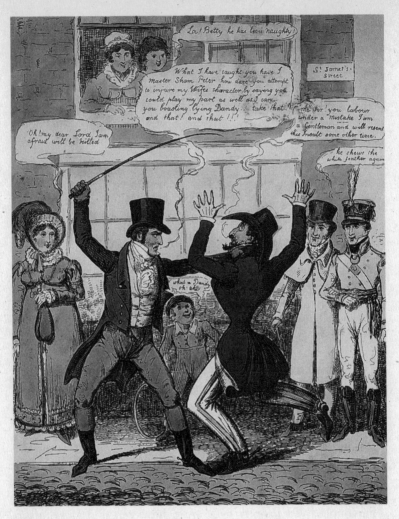

BY ST PETER THIS IS NO SHAM
Caricature by Robert Cruikshank, published by G. Humphrey, 1821.
James Webster Wedderburn (left) horsewhipping Lord Petersham, a celebrated dandy, for making advances to his wife.

vulnerable. Neither 'Golden Ball' Hughes nor 'Romeo' Coates was ever fully accepted by the *haut ton*, in spite of their great wealth. Money was never enough on its own; it was a fastidious society, neither to be fooled nor bribed by vulgar ostentation. Both Hughes and Coates desperately wanted to make their mark on the world and both got it hopelessly wrong.

There was some doubt about Golden Ball's antecedents. According to one source he was the son of a slop seller, but that sort of story was typical of Regency malice, and probably untrue. The generally accepted version is that he was the son of a Captain Ball in the navy, whose widow married an immensely rich admiral, Sir Edward Hughes, and that he inherited his enormous fortune from the latter on condition that he add the name of Hughes to his patronymic. He was said to have a cash income of £40,000 a year from investments alone, and that was without the encumbrance of an expensive country house to maintain. He was good-looking, generous and entertained lavishly, but, nevertheless, Ball Hughes never realized his social ambitions. The trouble was that he tried too hard: he was such an obvious snob, about fashions as well as people. As Lord William Pitt-Lennox, a rival dandy, said, 'Brummell set the fashion; Ball Hughes merely followed it.' Hughes disliked hunting, but kept a stud of hunters because it was the smart thing to do; cared little for music but kept a box at Covent Garden for the same reason (to be fair, so did a great many other people); knew little about racing but never missed Ascot or Goodwood. And so the indictment went on, through all the conventional amusements of a Regency beau, none of which, according to Lennox, Hughes actually enjoyed, wanting only to get back to his comfortable house in Brook Street. Finally, said Lennox, poor Hughes's 'manner in public was too coxcomb-ical; he screwed his mouth up, and lisped or drawled forth his words', while his manner of walking was so affected that he looked as if 'he was on stilts, and had swallowed the kitchen poker'. But then Lord William Pitt-Lennox was well known for his malice – which he mistook for wit.

Hughes, like Petersham, made a *mésalliance* in the eyes of the world when he married a young opera dancer, Maria Mercandotti.

For his honeymoon Hughes bought Oatlands Park, the Duke of York's country house near Weybridge, for £180,000, which was considered an exorbitant price at the time. However, a few years later there was a vogue for villas in the country, which started a property boom, and he was able to sell the house to developers for a considerable profit. Hughes and his dancer went to live in Greenwich, where they kept open house, and he played whist for five-pound points. In the end Hughes achieved the notoriety he sought as one of the greatest gamblers of his day; such was his addiction that he once spent a whole night in the garden gambling on battledore and shuttlecock. Eventually he lost most of his money, the marriage ended in divorce, and Hughes, faithful to fashion even in debt, 'retired' to France. Misfortune seems to have improved him, however. According to Scrope Davies, a fellow ex-dandy-in-exile: 'He is no longer "Golden Ball" but since the gilt is off, he rolls on much more smoothly.'

Scrope Davies, another dandy who came to grief over gambling, behaved beautifully in adversity – unlike Brummell, who spent his time whining and writing endless begging letters to his friends. Scrope Davies, apparently, 'bore with perfect resignation the loss of the wealth he had once possessed; and though his annual income was very limited, he made no complaint of poverty'. He, too, escaped the duns by going to France, where, according to the same contemporary account, he 'daily sat himself down on a bench in the garden of the Tuileries, where he received those whose acquaintance he desired.' It was possible at that time to live extremely cheaply in Paris and this *coterie* of bankrupt ex-dandies probably had rather a pleasant time together – certainly better than a stretch in the Fleet.* Among the other ex-dandies who went bankrupt and fled to the Continent were 'Kangaroo' Cooke, so-called because he once, as a practical joke, let a lot of kangaroos out of their cages in a public zoo; the Earl of Barrymore, the Prince Regent's hell-raising friend of his youth; and Viscount, better known as 'King', Allen. Allen was a pompous snob who referred to bankers and rich industrialists as 'trades-

* The Fleet was a debtors' prison.

men', and tried to blackball them from any club of which he was a member. Such tactics failed: when he ran into debt the bankers foreclosed on his estates and he left England for the Continent in a hurry. Unlike the majority of his fellow-bankrupts, Allen went to Spain, where he lived in dreary poverty, first in Cadiz and then in Gibraltar, which was even cheaper.

Lord de Ros came to grief in a different way. A scholar and a man of great charm, he spent much of his time playing whist and was considered an exceptionally fine player. He was a member of White's, Boodle's and Brooks's, but also of a much less reputable club called Graham's, where he was accused of cheating. The case became a public scandal, leaving de Ros no alternative but to sue for libel. The case was heard by Lord Denman and a special jury, with the Attorney-General leading for the plaintiff and an equally distinguished lawyer for the defence. Lord de Ros was found guilty and left London, forever dishonoured.

'Romeo' Coates became one of the joke figures of the Regency, much to his despair but thanks to his own incurable vanity. Coates was born in the West Indies and inherited not only a fortune from his father, a sugar planter, but also a large collection of diamonds – which he flashed around on every possible occasion, suitable or otherwise. He put diamond buttons on his coats, diamond buckles on his shoes and sprinkled diamonds all over his wigs. Coates, who arrived in England in 1807 and made Bath his headquarters, was lionized at first: a man of charm and intelligence who was also extremely rich and a bachelor, he seemed a gift to society. By the beginning of the nineteenth century matchmaking mothers were already beginning to see the advantages of solid cash over debt-ridden pedigree. Coates's passion in life, however, apart from his jewellery, was the theatre, and in particular Shakespeare, whom he used to recite with great dramatic flair in the drawing rooms of Bath. Such was his success as an amateur that the misguided dandy attempted to turn professional. He managed to persuade one of the local theatre managers to let him play Romeo on the public stage: posters announced that 'a Gentleman of Fashion would make his first appearance on February 9th in a *role* of Shakespeare' and the performance sold out in advance. 'Butlers and Abigails', it was reported by the local paper, 'were commanded by their mistresses to take their stand in the centre of the pit and give Mr Coates a capital, hearty clapping', and everyone wished him well. The dandy was unable to resist such a splendid opportunity to show off and, to the horror of the audience, Coates walked on to the stage dressed up like a clown, 'a mountebank, a monstrosity'. He was wearing scarlet tights, a sky-blue cloak, a Charles II wig, a top hat, an enormous cravat, masses of real diamonds and an idiotic grin. The whole performance was a ghastly joke: in the balcony scene, for example, he produced a snuffbox, and after taking a pinch himself, offered it to the bewildered Juliet, all the while grinning and bowing to the audience. Half the grand ladies in the boxes walked out, but the spectators in the cheap seats howled with laughter. Romeo's death was so ludicrous that the gallery called for an encore. Although the wretched man fled first to Brighton and then to London to escape his humiliation, the story preceded him, and he was known as 'Romeo' Coates ever after. He became one of the sights of the West End, driving around in a ridiculous, but gorgeous, carriage which he had designed himself, and which was drawn by a team of pure white horses. The carriage was shaped like a kettledrum, richly upholstered inside and embellished with a large golden cock, underneath which was painted his motto, 'While I live I'll crow'.

The case of Romeo Coates, however, illustrates one of the genuine problems inherent in Regency dandyism: there *were* no hard and fast rules as to what was permissible, and what was not, in the matter of dress. Many of the older generation carried on wearing the fashions of their youth throughout the Regency. Creevey, writing around 1810, reported that Lord Thurlow, the Lord Chancellor, who had been one of the great eighteenth-century dandies, was still 'always dressed in a full suit of cloaths of the old fashion, great cuffs and massy buttons, great wig, long ruffles, & . . .' The Marquis of Queensberry (known colloquially as 'Old Q.' or 'The Star of Piccadilly') was another relic from the eighteenth century who carried on well into the nineteenth. He used to sit under a scarlet umbrella on the balcony of his house in Mayfair, dressed in a green silk coat and white silk stockings, ogling all the pretty girls through his gold quizzing glass as they walked by. Then there was Sir Lumley Skeffington, 'who used to paint his face, so that he looked like a French toy; ... You always knew of his approach by an *avant-courier* of sweet smells; and when he advanced a little nearer, you might suppose yourself in the atmosphere of a perfumer's shop.'[16] He was a fop and a beau who had been one of the leading 'Macaronis' in his youth. The Macaroni's 'uniform' must have been the most ludicrous example of masculine fashion ever invented, as well as the most uncomfortable. It was a very specific style, copied from Paris, and entailed squeezing the figure into a very tight, very long-tailed coat with pastel-coloured breeches, a suffocating stock, wigs a yard high and high-heeled shoes, preferably studded with jewels. A jewelled quizzing glass, snuffbox, rings on their hands and plenty of make-up completed the effect of a painted puppet. Some even added a muff or a fan to the *ensemble*, and minced around sniffing at an enormous bouquet of flowers, carried in a carefully manicured hand. Not surprisingly, the fashion only lasted for about ten years in the 1770s. At the time, Skeffington's dandyism was the subject of many caricatures by Gillray and others. In spite of his affectations, however, Skeffington was one of the most intelligent and erudite of the dandies. A playwright and author of some standing, he wrote, among other things, *The Sleeping Beauty*, which was first performed at Drury Lane in 1805. Skeffington lingered on well into the nineteenth century but, in the end, he, too, 'was compelled to seek refuge for several years within the rules of the King's prison', for debt.

A variation of the beau who is equally attractive to the writers of romantic fiction is the Regency Rake, the villain who seduces the maiden and gallops off into the night with a devilish laugh. The Marquess of Hertford was certainly a rake, though he usually preferred married women to maidens. Hertford, who was known as 'Red Herrings' because of his ginger hair and whiskers, was one of the Prince's intimates, though fifteen years his junior. Like the Prince himself, Hertford was a self-indulgent volupt-uary: he was described by one of his contemporaries, albeit an exceptionally Puritan one, as 'a man without one redeeming quality in the multitude of his glaring, damning vices . . . the debauched sensualist, the heartless *roué*, the gamester – he who never evinced a latent spark of virtue among his glaring vices, revelling in crime even in his impotent old age and dotage.' He is said to have been Thackeray's model for the Marquess of Steyne in *Vanity Fair*: like Steyne, Lord Hertford kept a secret *garconnière*, where, according to Harriette Wilson, who was a regular visitor, he would entertain 'any fair lady who would honour him with a visit incognita, after his servants should have prepared a most delicious supper and retired to rest'. Hertford, incidentally, was one of the few men whom Harriette seems to have respected. She wrote that '. . . he is a man possessing more general knowledge than anyone I know. His Lordship appears to be *au fait* on every subject one can possibly imagine. Talk to him of drawing, or horse-riding; painting or cock-fighting; rhyming, cooking or fencing; profligacy or morals; religion of whatever creed; languages living or dead; claret, or burgundy; champagne or black strap; furnishing houses, or riding hobbies; the flavour of venison, or breeding poll-parrots; and you might see that he had served his apprenticeship to every one of them.'[17] Harriette was quite right: Lord Hertford was a highly civilized man and a serious *connoisseur*. He had inherited a fortune of at least £80,000 a year and lived in great style. He collected miniatures, snuffboxes and watches as well as paintings, and became a respected expert on art, often buying on behalf of the Prince Regent. Hertford's scandalous private life, however, obscured his intelligence and taste: he was, in fact, one of the truly cultivated characters of the Regency, one of those who helped to create the modern image of the period as the epitome of grace and style.

In conclusion, it would be wrong to assume that the beaux and the dandies conformed to a pattern, that they all possessed more or less the same characteristics and behaved, more or less, in the same manner. For example, it would be unjust to dismiss the whole race of dandies as effete: Captain Barclay was one of the most celebrated athletes of his generation. He once walked a thousand miles in a thousand hours for a bet. Nor were they all as vain as Tom Raikes, who, when challenged to a duel, said that it would be unfair if his opponent marked his face, because he, Raikes, was so beautiful, but it would be perfectly all right to mark his opponent's face because the latter was so ugly. Tom Raikes never moved without a gold dressing case which was so heavy that it took two men to carry it. And few were as gloriously fatuous as Lord Westmorland, one of the later dandies, who has gone down in history for his famous answer to some remark made to him by Louis XVIII: 'Je wouldrai si je couldrai, mais je cannais pas.'[18]

3

'THE SEVENTH HEAVEN
OF THE FASHIONABLE
WORLD'

The ladies of the Regency put a much higher premium on the distinctions of class than their menfolk. Whereas the latter were quite prepared to admit a man who had made his fortune in trade to their clubs, because he was amusing, or interesting or simply a friend, the *grandes dames* of society had no such tolerance with regard to Almack's, their particular domain. Almack's was considered the most exclusive club in London and regarded by many as 'the seventh heaven of the fashionable world'. Admittance was by a strictly controlled system of vouchers, in the gift of seven formidable ladies, known as 'patronesses': in 1814 these were the Ladies Castlereagh, Jersey, Cowper (later Palmerston) and Sefton, Mrs Drummond Burrell, Princess Esterhazy and Princess Lieven. According to Gronow, 'the most popular amongst these *grandes dames* was unquestionably Lady Cowper. Lady Jersey's bearing, on the contrary, was that of a theatrical tragedy queen; and whilst attempting the sublime, she frequently made herself simply ridiculous, being inconceivably rude, and in her manner often ill-bred. Lady Sefton was kind and amiable, Princess Lieven haughty and exclusive, Princess Esterhazy was a *bon enfant*, Lady Castlereagh and Mrs Burrell *de très grandes dames.*' (Not everyone agreed with Gronow's assessments: Harriet Cavendish, for example, thought that Lady Sefton was an 'odious and tiresome woman', spiteful and affected, who was always making faces and 'nodding her head about' like a Muscovy duck.)[1]

The patronesses of Almack's retained the right to blackball any-one they considered would lower the tone of the club, or was in any way undesirable, without explanation: they were known to have blackballed Lord March and a Mr Boothby, 'to their great astonishment'. These formidable dragons were ruthless, arbitrary and despotic but there was no appeal from their decision. Not even the Duke of Wellington was immune: on one occasion he was refused admittance to Almack's because he arrived at the club wearing black trousers instead of the regulation knee-breeches.

People went to ludicrous lengths to try to get an invitation to this 'exclusive temple of the beau monde'. One man challenged Lord Jersey to a duel because Lady Jersey had refused to give his wife a voucher.[2] (Lord Jersey declined to fight, saying that he could not be held responsible for his wife's decisions in social matters.) No one even remotely connected with commerce stood a chance of getting a voucher, and out of 300 officers of the Foot Guards not more than half a dozen names featured on the magic 'list'. As Henry Luttrell wrote:

> All on that magic list depends;
> Fame, fortune, fashion, lovers, friends.
> 'Tis that which gratifies or vexes
> All ranks, all ages, and both sexes.
> If once to Almack's you belong,
> Like Monarchs you can do no wrong;
> But banished thence on Wednesday night,
> By Jove, you can do nothing right.

The mystique of Almack's was based upon snobbery and social cachet alone, for there was nothing particularly attractive about the club itself, or the entertainment it offered. In the eyes of one foreign visitor, Prince Puckler-Muskau, the whole concept of Almack's was a confidence trick and a failure. After going there for the first time, in 1827, he wrote: '. . . it so little answered my expectations that I was perfectly astonished. A large bare room, with a bad floor and ropes around it, like the horses' enclosure in an Arab camp; two or three equally bare rooms where the most wretched refreshments were served; and a company into which, despite the immense difficulty in getting tickets, a great many nobodies had forced their way, and in which poor deportment and tasteless dress prevailed; in a word, a gathering fit for an inn – the music and lighting were the only good things. And yet Almack's is the pinnacle of the English fashionable world. The oddest thing is that one ticket, for which so many English men and women strive, actually costs only ten shillings* ... [it] forms a most ludicrous contrast with the general splendour and luxury of England.'³ But the German Princeling had not been brainwashed since birth into the subtleties of English snobbery; and at least had the sense to confine his criticisms to the privacy of his diary. He was far too canny to risk being banned himself.

Almack's membership fee, for those lucky enough to be accepted, was 10 guineas and the club premises were in King Street. There was a huge ballroom, about one hundred feet long and forty wide, decorated with gilt columns, classic medallions and enormous mirrors; and by the time of the Regency it was lit by gas, in elaborate cut-glass lustres. The committee of Almack's organized a ball and supper once a week for twelve weeks (i.e. throughout 'the season', from the beginning of March to early June). These may have been the most exclusive parties in London, but the mood of the evening was sedate to the point of boredom, at least as far as those members of society who were not interested in social climbing were concerned. Only the mildest drinks were served, light wines such as orgeat or ratafia,† and the food was negligible. Furthermore, before 1814, the only dances allowed at Almack's were traditional country dances, plus an occasional Scottish reel. It is hardly surprising therefore that the more amusing young men on 'the list' (i.e. eligible bachelors) found

---

* Approximately £25 today. To find an approximate cash equivalent in modern terms it is necessary to multiply by a factor of 50: rather less after the war. It should be noted, however, that the value of the pound fluctuated enormously during the Regency period and it is not possible to give exact figures or comparisons.
† Orgeat was a non-alcoholic drink made of barley or almonds and orange-flower water; ratafia was a very light liqueur, flavoured with fruit or almonds. Both were considered 'ladies' drinks.

evenings at Almack's unbearably flat and by the middle of the Regency, in line with the new spirit of freedom from convention, had started defecting in droves. This trend, if allowed to continue, would clearly spoil the whole point of the proceedings, since Almack's main function was to act as a showcase for the pick of the débutantes: these were the parties where girls were launched upon society by their mothers, and made to parade for inspection, however gauche and uncertain they might be, like so many fillies for sale. Almack's was rightly known as 'the Marriage Mart'. The concept of 'Hunt the Husband' and 'Debs for Sale' was captured in the following verse, published anonymously but thought to have been written by George Lamb, brother of the future Prime Minister. He certainly would have known the form since his mother, Lady Melbourne, was an arch matchmaker:

> . . . I chang'd a Misses trammel'd life
> For all the glorious license of a Wife;
> And every candid female here allows
> How hard a Miss's life, who seeks a spouse.
> At operas, plays and routs we never fail,
> Put up, alas! to everlasting sale.
> First in Hyde Park, sent by Maternal care,
> At noon we walk, and seem to take the air,
> Or Bond Street's gay resort, for game we try
> And call at many a shop and seem to buy,
> While, like a Dealer, the good Matron shews
> Our shapes, and paces, to the chapmen Beaux,
> Well skill'd th'unfitting Suitor to dispatch,
> And to allure the Eligible Match.
> At night again, on us all pleasures pall;
> Bid for by inch of candle at a ball –
> And e'en when fashion's toilsome revels cease,
> For us no pause, no liberty, no peace –
> Then when the Matrons speak of suppers small,
> 'A few choice friends besides ourselves – that's all,'
> This language in plain truth they mean to hold
> 'A girl by private contract to be sold.'[4]

In 1814 it was decided that something must be done to make Almack's more attractive to all these eligible bachelors: the patronesses agreed to sanction not only quadrilles, which had hitherto been banned as 'fast', although they had been danced at private parties for years, but also waltzes. Waltzing had been popular on the Continent for some years but London had been reluctant to adopt so daring a dance. However, once Almack's, the holy of holies, permitted it, waltzing became a fashionable mania: 'in course of time Lord Palmerston might have been seen describing an infinite number of circles with Princess Lieven', while 'Baron de Neumann was frequently seen perpetually turning with the Princess Esterhazy'. These two couples already knew how to waltz, of course, having danced it in Paris or Vienna, but most of the English needed lessons. A few years earlier the Duchess of Devonshire had very sensibly started a fashion for morning dances, followed by a breakfast, so that the girls could practise the complicated steps of the quadrille and avoid making fools of themselves when they 'came out'. The custom was resumed so the young could learn to waltz. These informal affairs were the Regency equivalent of teenage parties, and, though strictly chaperoned, doubled as an opportunity for vetting potential escorts. Débutantes at Almack's, however, were not allowed to waltz unless one of the patronesses had signified her specific permission, a favour granted only to those whose deportment was considered impeccable.

Almack's was a temple of insipid propriety: politics, the war, the riots in the streets outside, were all taboo as subjects of permissible conversation. Sex was obviously banned, talk about money was vulgar and the only permissible conversation seems to have been gossip, possibly rising to outright scandal. What makes this banal approach to conversation at Almack's so curious, and must have made it so difficult to sustain, was the dichotomy in the lives of the patronesses themselves, the contradiction between their public and private personae. On the surface, Almack's, with all that it implied, was the epitome of 'polite society' and its patronesses paragons of virtue and decorum. In fact most of these ladies had extremely dubious pasts, were

DOS À DOS — ACCIDENTS IN QUADRILLE DANCING
Caricature by George Cruikshank, after an amateur published by H. Humphrey, 1817.
The quadrille involved a number of complicated steps. The Duchess of Devonshire inaugurated morning dances so the girls could practise before they 'came out' officially. The custom was resumed when the waltz appeared in London in 1812.

surrounded by lovers, either ex or current in their private lives, and prided themselves on the skill with which they juggled their various intrigues, be they social, political or amatory. It must have been difficult for a débutante who had been brought up at Melbourne or Devonshire House, for example, to know which set of values to adopt. Even the marriage of that Queen of Almack's, Lady Jersey, had caused a major scandal at the time. The daughter of Robert Childs, a banker, she was a considerable heiress, and when both her family and Lord Jersey's refused their consent to the marriage, the couple eloped to Gretna Green — behaviour which would have been grounds for a lifetime of ostracism had she been less rich or he less well connected. As it was, she went on to become one of the outstanding hostesses of the Regency, holding court both at Osterley, her beautiful eighteenth-century house on the outskirts of London, and Middleton, the Jerseys' house in the country.

'Sally' Jersey was clearly a fascinating woman, but nobody seems to have liked her. One of the delights of the Regency period is the freedom with which people wrote about their friends, although, of course, they had no idea at the time that letters and diaries intended for a private audience would ever be published. Had the correspondents of the Regency been aware of any such future fate when they committed their private criticisms to paper, they would have been far more circumspect. Greville, for example, never expected his comments to be read by the general public when he wrote of Lady Jersey that 'She is deficient in passion and softness (which constitute the greatest charm in women), so that she excites more of admiration than of interest; in conversation she is lively and pleasant, without being very remarkable, for she has neither wit, nor imagination, nor humour . . .'[5] Moreover, he thought her intellectual pretensions were thoroughly false, based on second-hand opinions and prejudice. To complete this unamiable portrait Lady Jersey acquired the nickname of 'Silence', because she never stopped talking, a trait which was admirably satirized by one of her guests at Middleton:

She is like one of her numerous gold and silver musical dickey birds, that are in all the show rooms of this house. She begins to sing at eleven o'clock . . . she retires to her cage to rest, she sings till 12 at night without a moment's interruption. She changes her feathers for dinner, and her plumage both morng. and eveng. is the happiest and most beautiful I ever saw. Of the *merits* of her songs I say nothing till we meet.[6]

Lady Jersey and her ilk represented the shallowest side of the Regency, a mini-world with little on its mind beyond the latest crim. con.* or the set of a cravat. Some of the other patronesses

---

* 'Crim. con.' was short for 'criminal conversation': a conversation overheard by a third party indicating evidence of adultery could be used as grounds for divorce.

of Almack's, however, were of a different stamp, ladies of authority and intelligence with a real interest in current affairs: Lady Castlereagh was the wife of the Foreign Secretary at the time of the Congress of Vienna, and Lady Cowper's husband was the future Lord Palmerston.* Both men were committed Tories, the party in power throughout most of the Regency, and expected their wives to keep open house. And a political hostess during such a busy and traumatic period as the Regency was naturally in a position of considerable power. Emily Cowper, in particular, excelled at the job, having been brought up in political circles at Melbourne House. Gentle by nature and popular with everyone, she was also highly intelligent, well educated and tactful: by the time she became Lady Palmerston she was one of the most respected women of her generation.

Princess Esterhazy and Princess Lieven, as the wives respectively of the Austrian and Russian ambassadors, represented the diplomatic world among the patronesses. Princess Lieven was a clever, scheming *intrigante* who, as Metternich's mistress of many years' standing, was known to be a serious influence behind the scenes in politics throughout Europe, as well as in London. She loathed England but loved her position of power: 'I quite like Prime Ministers', she was once quoted as saying in all seriousness. In spite of her many prejudices Princess Lieven's letters to Metternich are full of brilliant comments on the Regency scene, and are well worth quoting in some detail. For a start, like many other visiting foreign grandees, she was shocked by the blatant immorality of English society, and in particular that of the women. At a grand ball she attended in the country, she told Metternich, so many couples wandered off into the bushes that by the end of the dance almost the only people left in the ballroom were débutantes, chaperones and the host. 'Englishwomen always astonish me, in spite of my long experience in the country,' she wrote. 'I should like to take their indiscretion for the height of naiveté; but, after all, they have husbands, and I confess myself

* Lady Cowper was born Emily Lamb, Lord Melbourne's daughter. After the death of her first husband, Earl Cowper, she married Lord Palmerston.

baffled.'[7] Furthermore, she found the English gauche and lacking in fundamental courtesy: 'Here black is always seen next to white; great regard for manners, beside great boldness of conduct. You cannot appear in front of a woman except in shoes and stockings, but you do not bother to offer her your chair ... What a strange country! I have been here eight years, and every day I find something to be surprised at.'

Princess Lieven was a brilliant but acid and dangerous woman whose wit was lethal. She always referred to old Lady Jersey – wife of the fourth Earl – who had been the Prince of Wales's *maîtresse en titre*, as 'the little leech', because of the way she tried to hang on to her lover long after he had moved on to Lady Hertford; and said of the next Lady Jersey, the notorious 'Silence', that when she came to call, 'she chattered so hard that she lost her voice'. But the Jersey ladies were treated lightly compared to poor Princess Esterhazy, whom most people liked but Princess Lieven held in contempt: 'what a mediocre person [she] is,' Princess Lieven wrote scornfully, 'and what pretensions to airs and graces! Do you know the kind of woman who always wants to be the centre of social interest? She is afraid of mice, she loves cats, she tumbles down, she burns herself, she upsets her tea on her dress – all this happened in her house the other day. In short, she must at all costs be the focus of interest and general attention.'[8] Finally, the Austrian princess was sentimental, not one of the qualities which appealed to Princess Lieven.

A handsome rather than beautiful woman, Princess Lieven was not averse to being the centre of attention herself. She was liable to appear at parties in what amounted to fancy dress. At one Court function, she turned up wearing a high-necked black velvet robe, with a huge Elizabethan ruff; her only ornaments were a long chain of very large diamonds, and a *picture*, which hung *on her back*. At a time when the prevailing fashion for women's hair was a cloud of curls and ringlets, Princess Lieven dressed hers flat on her head, thus completing the image of Mary Queen of Scots. A fellow guest described her as looking 'exactly like something walked out of its frame in an old picture gallery'.

All this affectation and bitchiness made Princess Lieven

thoroughly unpopular. Charles Greville was one of many who disliked her, writing that

She is beyond all people fastidious. She is equally conscious of her own superiority and the inferiority of other people, and the contempt she has for the understandings of the generality of her acquaintance has made her indifferent to please and incapable of taking any delight in society. Her manners are very dignified and graceful, and she is extremely accomplished . . . She carries *ennui* to such a pitch that even in the society of her most intimate friends she frequently owns that she is bored to death . . . she is not liked, and has made hardly any friends. Her manners are stately and reserved, and so little *bonhomie* penetrates through her dignity that few feel sufficiently attracted to induce them to try and thaw the ice in which she always seems bound.[9]

Almack's was one of the great institutions of the Regency but its limitations were obvious. In spite of the attractions of the waltz and the debs, the young men continued to be put off by the formal atmosphere of the club, and by the middle of the nineteenth century it had closed. Meanwhile, the young bloods discovered a compromise: after the ball at Almack's was over it became the fashion to finish the evening off with a tour of the East End pubs. It was considered 'a lark' to get drunk in plebeian company and one of the East End pubs, in Nightingale Lane, off Smithfield market, became so popular with this sort of young blood that it became known as 'All-Max in the East'. Here, according to one of their number, they could 'sluice their ivories with Blue Ruin' (gin), and fancy themselves involved in 'Real Life'. At 'All-Max in the East':

All was happiness! – . . . [and] The group motley indeed; – Lascars, blacks, jack tars, coalheavers, dustmen, women of colour, old and young, and a sprinkling of the remnants of once fine girls, were all jigging together . . . Heavy wet was the cooling beverage [porter], but frequently overtaken by flashes of lightening [a glass of gin].[10]

This sort of language, a mixture of thieves' 'cant' and Cockney slang, was brought to the notice of society by one of the most extraordinary literary phenomena of the Regency. *The True*

History of Tom and Jerry; or the Day and Night Scenes of Life in London by Pierce Egan was first published in serial form at the beginning of 1820, in monthly instalments costing 1/- each. It was an overnight, runaway success: Jemmy Catnach, 'the renowned Ballad-monger of Seven Dials', produced a pirate edition less than twelve hours after the first instalment appeared and sold it in the streets for two pence. The book of *Life in London* was published in July, illustrated with marvellous caricatures by Cruikshank and dedicated, with his permission, to the new King George IV. By the end of the year, according to Egan, sixty-eight separate publications appeared, all plagiarizing the original.

Life in London purports to tell the story and chronicle the adventures of 'Corinthian Tom', a London dandy, and his country cousin 'Jerry Hawthorn'. It is a wonderfully vivid (if appallingly written) picture of Regency bucks at their silliest and worst. The two young men visit the sights of London 'both among the high life and low life', do the rounds of the clubs and the pubs, take boxing lessons at 'Gentleman Jackson's Academy', ogle the debs at Almack's and the tarts in Piccadilly, run up bills at their tailor's, parade down Bond Street, drive down St James's, gamble, get drunk, get arrested and generally behave in a way which Tom assures Jerry is the acceptable London mode. Egan, who loved doggerel, wrote on the title page:

> LIFE IN LONDON, my boys, is a round of delight,
> In frolics, I keep up, both the day and the night,
> With my TOM and JERRY, I try to '*get the best*'
> Of the COVES in the *East* – and the SWELLS at the West! . . .[11]

There was a good deal more in the same vein, but the first verse gives the general idea.

The prudish element of society was shocked by *Life in London,* complaining as much about the racy language as the bawdy nature of some of Cruikshank's illustrations. Every generation invents its own slang, words and phrases which seem as dated to the next as the 'What Ho!' and 'Top-Hole' of the 1930s do today. Regency slang, in retrospect, seems glorious, evocative, descriptive and very funny. To go 'upon the strut' in Hyde Park, for example, says it all; so does the phrase a 'peep o'day boy' to describe a young blood about town. A 'swell cove' needs no explanation, though the uninitiated might have difficulty in realizing that a 'flash mort' meant an upper-class girl. The modern mind might well misunderstand the continual references to young men as 'roses', 'pinks' and 'tulips': they were an indication of breeding, not sexual preference, shorthand for saying that the young man in question was 'a member of the *ton*'. And when Tom says to Jerry that 'A man must have the *look* of a gentleman, if he has nothing else', he goes on to elaborate in language which is at least intelligible:

This cover-me-decently, was all very well at Hawthorn Hall, I dare say; but here, among the pinks in Rotten-row, the lady-birds in the Saloon, the angelics at Almack's, the top-of-the-trees heroes, the legs and levanters at Tattersall's, nay, even among the millers at the Fives, it would be taken for nothing less than the index of a complete Flat.

Some of the slang which enlivened the Regency, however, definitely needs the glossary which Egan thoughtfully supplied at the end of the first edition of *Life in London*, and which is a delight in itself. The words for cash included 'blunt', 'dibs' and 'rhino', while being able to 'flash the screens', 'post the pony', 'stump the pewter' or 'tip the brads' is translated as being rich. A 'snyder' is an excellent word to describe a tailor who doesn't mind waiting for years to get paid but charges a high rate of interest. Tom and Jerry's progress around the West End took the form of 'A *turn* or two in Bond Street – a *stroll* through Piccadilly – a *look-in* at Tattersall's – a *ramble* through Pall Mall – and a *strut* on the *Corinthian Path*' (i.e. a visit to Gentleman Jackson's boxing saloon). Later they cruise the Burlington Arcade, looking for girls, colloquially referred to as 'straw-chippers' or 'nob-thatchers': the slightly more expensive prostitute was 'a bit of muslin' or a 'fair Cyprian', and the serious courtesan a 'prime article'. 'A bolt to the Village' meant going to London, and when funds ran out they went into the country 'on a repairing lease'. That famous, all-embracing phrase 'the

thing', meaning acceptable, as opposed to unacceptable, behaviour
has passed into the vernacular.

Egan's glossary includes, amongst many others, the following:
'Ace of Spades' – a widow; 'Apartments to Let' – a widow on the
catch, also an empty-headed, or 'shallow cove'; 'Babes in the
Wood' – people confined to the stocks, or the pillory, also dice;
'Billy Buzman' – pickpockets who stole only silk handkerchiefs.
'Cant' was the generic term for the language used by beggars,
gypsies and thieves. A 'Dandiprat' seems an excellent word for
an 'insignificant or trifling fellow'; and a 'Demi-rep' for a woman
of doubtful morals. A 'Game pullet' or 'Bird of Paradise' meant
the same thing. To call a man a 'Flat' was to indicate that he was
honest, but a fool, easily taken in by a 'Captain Sharp', his opposite
number . . . To arrive at 'Point Non-Plus' meant having run out
of both money and credit, while a 'Nonesuch' or 'Nonpareil' was
a leader of fashion . . . 'ogles' were eyes, the head was a 'pipkin'
or 'pimple', and the stomach a 'bread-basket' . . . the 'lump' was
the workhouse, 'limbo' a prison and a 'Jerry Sneak' a hen-pecked
husband. A 'Snowball' was the rather silly name for a black man
or chimney-sweep but a 'Town Tabby' is perfect for an aristocratic
dowager.

A dramatic version of *Life in London* was produced at the
Adelphi the following year and was a smash hit at once, running
for ninety-three nights in succession, packed for every performance with cheering audiences. (This original production only
closed because the Adelphi season came to an end: at that date
theatres were run on a fixed, limited schedule, regardless of the
success or failure of the play.) Copycat versions appeared all over
town: during the season of 1821–2 it was performed at ten
theatres, in and around the metropolis, always to overflowing
houses. Other versions travelled all over the country and even
abroad: *The Adventures of Tom and Jerry*, in one form or another,
was produced on the stage in Brighton and Edinburgh, Dublin
and Paris. Sometimes it was turned into a musical or burlesque
and sometimes it was played straight. The success of the dramatic
version in Ireland led to the publication of *REAL LIFE IN
IRELAND; or, the Day and Night Scenes, Rovings, Rambles, and*

*Sprees, Bulls, Blunders, Bodderation, and Blarney of Brian Born, Esq.,
and his elegant friend Sir Shawn O'Dogherty.* In France it was
treated with more respect and became *The Diorama; or Picturesque
Rambles in London* but had an equal success, and a version was
even produced in the United States.[12]

Life in London was a Regency phenomenon of modern pro-
portions, but there was one outstanding difference: most of these
productions were, in modern parlance, 'pirated'. Copyright laws
were derisory at the beginning of the nineteenth century; the
unfortunate Pierce Egan, who was the author of the whole
concept, even if some of the words and scenes were changed in
different productions, received no royalties from these rogue
versions and had no legal redress against either the producers
or the authors. Tom Dibden, Farrell and Douglas Jerrold were
all well-known contemporary writers in their own right, but they
all stole the theme of *Life in London* (often referred to as 'Tom
and Jerry') and produced their own versions either on the stage
or in print. By 1825 Tom and Jerry had spawned a whole industry.
Moncrieff, the producer, summed up the phenomenal success of
Life in London in the preface to a performance at Drury Lane
dedicated to the Duke of York, who was considered something
of an expert on low life: '. . . the Piece obtained a popularity, and
excited a sensation, totally unprecedented in Theatrical History;
from the highest to the lowest, all classes were alike anxious to
witness its representation; Dukes and Dustmen were equally
interested in its performance, and Peers might be seen mobbing
it with Apprentices to obtain admission'. A sequel, brought out
some years later, was not nearly so successful. The vogue was
over. *Life in London* was an ephemeral craze, an apotheosis of
the Regency but pointless out of context.

Tom and Jerry, and their ilk, based their lives on the premise
that money fell from the sky and living in debt was not only
normal, but somehow rather chic. In later life it was more than
possible they would discover their mistake, as has already been
seen in the case of the large number of dandies who ended up
bankrupt. This attitude to money, so alien to the twentieth

century, needs to be seen in the context of its time. Historically, wealth in England derived from the land but, with the advent of the Industrial Revolution, the emphasis began to change. Scions of the great estates during the seventeenth and eighteenth centuries had some justification for their reckless extravagance: they were brought up to believe that they would inherit the earth, in a literal sense, and that land was a commodity which could not fail. They had been rich for generations and there seemed no reason why they should ever cease to be so. The new fortunes built upon commerce and industry were far more speculative. Furthermore, the success of these recent fortunes was usually due to the hard work and vision of one particular man, and, only too often, his heirs turned out to be men of a very different calibre. The aim of these new millionaires was always the same: to 'better themselves', to move up the social scale, to send their sons to public school, marry their daughters into the peerage and in every way possible emulate the ruling classes. Unfortunately one of the classic characteristics of the nobility at the time was a sublime indifference to economic reality. Debt was a way of life, a matter only of juggling credit. Deficit financing may not have been invented as a term during the Regency but they certainly knew the principle. The disastrous aspect of this attitude to money was that nobody thought it was wrong. Bankruptcy was bad luck but no grounds for ostracism; when Brummell's debts finally caught up with him, an extraordinary number of people helped to bale him out over and over again – proof enough of their friendship and lack of disapproval. Friends from the past who replied to his begging letters included the Duke of Wellington, the ever-loyal Alvanley, the Earls of Burlington and Pembroke, Charles Greville and even the Marquess of Worcester to whom he had already behaved disgracefully over money, and who was, in any case, always in trouble himself. Princess Lieven's story about the Worcesters illustrates perfectly the prevailing attitude to financial crises.

A few years after they were married, the young Marchioness of Worcester, 'who is so sweet, so pretty and so negligible . . . that if you were to dissect her, you would find nothing inside but a sweet little machine', was faced with disaster. When she got up one morning, she found the bailiffs in the house taking all their furniture away: her husband had contracted debts of more than £100,000, with no possibility of paying them. The bailiffs stripped the place, leaving her with only the clothes she stood up in. The Marchioness fainted and burst into tears but by the evening had risen above her woes and was seen laughing happily at Covent Garden.[13] After the opera she went off to the country to 'rusticate' until either her family or his could be prevailed upon to settle the debts, whereupon the Worcesters returned to London and started running them up again . . . (The tale of Lady Worcester got worse: a year later the blameless young Marchioness died and her incorrigible husband then eloped with his late wife's sister, which was against the law. Furthermore his new love was the Duke of Wellington's niece, so the scandal had endless ramifications.)

Friends borrowed from each other so frequently, and with such obvious lack of embarrassment, that it almost seems as though they regarded their money as communal, to be passed around on demand. Sometimes they tried to recoup, usually without success. Lady Spencer lent the Queen of Naples £1000 (which is in itself an odd concept by modern standards, comparable to the Queen of Holland borrowing money from an English visitor to The Hague). Lady Spencer never got the money back in spite of writing a number of letters, which she referred to as 'duns', and which the Queen simply ignored. 'Lost in the post' was the excuse, even then. Lady Spencer wrote crossly that 'I have had a letter this morning from the Queen of Naples, without a word about money. She only reproaches me for not writing, which, as my letters went by her own courier, must be all *fudge*. I am very angry, but it cannot be helped.'[14] The same thing happened to the money Lady Spencer was foolish enough to lend Mme Talleyrand during a visit to Paris. The English, at that time, were regarded as the plutocrats of Europe.

Occasionally, when the duns became too demanding, people tried to retrench. Lord Bessborough's idea of an economy drive, however, was to cut down on the number of gardeners at his country house. He was horrified to find there were twelve of them, costing half a guinea each, every week. This was at the same time as he was arranging to pay his wife and his sister-in-law's gambling debts, to the tune of £32,700; he had also just contributed £200 towards paying Charles James Fox's debts, again incurred at the tables. (Fox's friends organized a subscription in 1793, which had already raised the extraordinary sum of £33,000, with a further £10,000 promised.) But then any attempt to balance accounts in families where gambling was endemic was doomed from the start and Lord Bessborough's wife was one of the Cavendishes, the most notorious gamblers of their generation. When Georgiana, the fifth Duchess of Devonshire, died her son inherited over £100,000 worth of his mother's gambling debts, which he had to pay, even though her husband had settled others again and again during her lifetime. Thomas Coutts, the banker, who had lent both the fifth Duke and his Duchess enormous sums of money, pressed their son for payment. Unfortunately for himself, Coutts adopted an extremely snobbish and silly line of argument: knowing that debts of honour were the only kind that ever got paid promptly by aristocratic creditors he wrote to the new Duke, 'I can boast of as noble a descent from ancestors as Your Grace of any man in Britain.'[15]

Gambling debts, during the Regency, were sacrosanct and had to be paid at once: voluntary exile or even suicide were preferable to dishonour. The rationale behind this attitude to gambling debts seems to have been that interest was not involved between gentlemen: therefore it was obviously incumbent upon the creditor to pay them at once. Fox, attempting to repay Sir John Lade, noticed that the latter was doing sums on a piece of paper and asked Lade why. Lade answered that he was merely calculating the interest, as though this was a perfectly normal occurrence. 'Are you, by G—,' said Fox, as he put the money back into his pocket. 'Why, I thought, Sir John, that my debt was a debt of honour, but as you seem to look at it in another light, and intend making a trading debt of it, I beg to inform you I make it an invariable rule to pay my Jew creditors last. You must therefore wait a little longer for your money, Sir John.'[16] Tradesmen, in fact, were made to wait for their money for years during the Regency, even if their businesses went bankrupt in consequence. Thackeray's wonderful description of Rawdon Crawley is a scathing satire of a very real trend: 'He lived comfortably on credit. He had a large capital of debts, which, laid out judiciously, will carry a man along for many years, and on which certain men about town contrive to live a hundred times better than even men with ready money can do.'[17] And the fate of Raggles, the Crawleys' unfortunate landlord in London, may have been fictional but it was clearly based on fact:

This was the way, then, Crawley got his house for nothing: for though Raggles had to pay taxes and rates, and the interest of the mortgage . . . ; and the insurance of his life; and the charges for his children at school; and the value of the meat and drink which his own family – and for a time that of Colonel Crawley too – consumed; and though the poor wretch was utterly ruined by that transaction, his children being flung on the streets, and himself driven into the Fleet prison; yet somebody must pay even for gentlemen who live for nothing a year.[18]

It was a curious morality, and one which would be unacceptable today – as, indeed, it had already become by the time Thackeray wrote *Vanity Fair*.

4

RELATIVE VALUES:
THE COST OF LIVING

The emphases of wealth and expenditure were quite different during the Regency to those of today, which makes an exact translation of cash equivalents suspect. As a general guide, however, it is necessary to multiply by a factor of 50: if the cost of an item in 1812 was £200 it would be £10,000 today and an overall income of £600 a year would afford the same sort of lifestyle as someone with approximately £30,000. And the taxes, much as people complained about them at the time, were minimal by modern standards. The sixth Duke of Devonshire then, with an income of £100,000 a year from land alone, and a few others like him, lived on a scale comparable with that of the Arab potentates today. Yet even the richest noblemen lived on credit. Three years after Lord Hartington* had inherited the title his outstanding debts came to £593,000 and by 1829 he had become so accustomed to living in debt that he exceeded his income in that year alone by nearly £17,000. By the end of his life the Duke was more than £1,000,000 in debt. It was an attitude of mind, but one which had little to do with reality.

At the beginning of the nineteenth century the wealth of the Cavendish family seemed limitless, and the size of their estates unreal to the modern reader. When the sixth Duke came into

* The Marquess of Hartington is the courtesy title of the eldest son of the Duke of Devonshire.

his inheritance in 1811, it included not only Chatsworth, and its adjacent estate, but Hardwick Hall, the magnificent Elizabethan house built by Bess of Hardwick, founder of the Cavendish fortunes; two large estates in Yorkshire, Bolton Abbey in the West Riding and Londesborough Hall in the East Riding, both again surrounded by vast and valuable lands; and Lismore, a fabulously romantic castle in Ireland, along with a sizeable chunk of County Waterford. The Duke was known to have complained that he had too many houses – it was a question of juggling his time between them. When the Duke went to Lismore in 1844 it was only his second visit in twenty-two years. To give some indication of the amount of money involved Londesborough Hall was sold for £475,000 in 1844 to one of the new railway kings, George Hudson, who wanted an estate to enhance his social status. (Hudson later went bankrupt and lost the lot.) To continue the litany of Cavendish properties, one of the sixth Duke's favourite houses was his villa at Chiswick, an architectural gem designed by Lord Burlington, and, in London, he owned Burlington House as well as Devonshire House, both enormous mansions in the middle of Mayfair. Furthermore the Cavendishes built and owned for many generations large sections of the West End of London, no mean source of revenue even at that time, when the cost of renting a London house could be as much as a thousand guineas a year. Added to all this there was the income from lucrative mining interests in Derbyshire. All this wealth was, of course, unearned income, involving little or no effort on his part. For example, when the Duke wanted to know more about the workings of Grassington mine, he had a full-scale model made of it, which he said was 'the best piece of mechanical imitation I ever saw, entirely absolving me from any necessity of going to look at my subterranean property in the bowels of the earth.'[1]

As James Lees-Milne says, in his biography *The Bachelor Duke,*

The status of the 6th Duke of Devonshire on his succession in 1811 is to our eyes, although it was not . . . in those of the Prince Regent, little short of royal. In a way it was superior in that the responsibilities, although onerous to a man with a conscience, were lighter; and unlike a constitutional sovereign the Duke was his own master. He could behave as he pleased without the threat of forfeiting position and possessions.[2]

Fortunately the sixth Duke was a considerate and generous landlord, a highly cultured patron of the arts and a gentle, charming man. His sister, Harriet Granville, wrote that 'Hart is so good-humoured and *facile à vivre* that he makes everything *couleur de rosé*. One of the Duke's first acts on inheriting the title was to raise the wages of some of the senior servants employed in his various houses: at Devonshire House, for example, the Maître d'Hôtel's salary went up from £140 a year to £200, the butler's from £60 to £80, the footmen's from £25 to £35, the head coachman's from £50 to £60 and the second, third and fourth coachmen's from £25 to £35. Even the fourth groom got a rise from £15 to £25 a year and the junior housemaids from £11 to £16, which must have been *largesse* on a grand scale in their eyes. At Devonshire House alone thirty-one male and twelve female senior servants were employed, plus an unspecified number of daily helpers. The figures come from a memorandum headed 'Household Establishments', dated 25 December 1811, which lists increases in salary for ninety-three servants at his various houses.[3] Each residence had its own housekeeper, housemaids, porters, watchmen, steward and outdoor staff. Many of the staff, however, moved around the country with the family; cooks, confectioners, butlers, under-butlers, grooms of the chamber, footmen, valets, ladies maids, nursery staff, etc. would either be sent ahead to prepare the next port of call on the Duke's progress around his estates, or travel with him.

The Duke kept his own private orchestra at Chatsworth, on permanent stand-by. The pianist Charles Coote was paid £200 a year and stayed with the Duke until his death; Coote was also taken on trips, to Ireland, to play at Lismore, and to stay with friends in the country. Another notable musician on the staff was Edouard Schulz, a Hungarian immigrant who had been discovered by the Prince Regent and was poached by the Duke.

Schulz was more upper class than Coote and became something of a friend to the Duke. (Although musical parties and concerts were held in all the great houses, and were thus obligatory at Chatsworth, the Duke's interest and emphasis on musical excellence seems a trifle odd in his case since he was deaf.)

To give some idea of the extraordinary wealth which still existed in private hands during the Regency it is worth quoting a few more examples of the sixth Duke's lifestyle. Eighty gardeners were employed at Chatsworth alone, under the supervision of Joseph Paxton, who became one of the most famous botanists of the nineteenth century. The Duke sent emissaries to India, the Far East and South America with commissions to bring back interesting flora and fauna. One of them, a Mr Gibson, brought back from India such a splendid collection of exotica that the Duke and Paxton decided to build a special conservatory to house them. The 'Chatsworth Stove' or 'Great Conservatory', was the largest glass building in the world at the time. It was 277 feet long, 123 feet broad, and, at the highest point of the arched roof, 67 feet high. The conservatory was heated by seven miles of iron pipes fed by an elaborate system of eight furnaces supplied with coal brought by a specially built tramway. At Chiswick the Duke had his own zoo, with an elephant, giraffes and other animals wandering in the gardens. Sir Walter Scott conjures up a delightful picture of Regency society at its most elegant in his description of a breakfast party at Chiswick:

A numerous and gay party, assembled to walk, and enjoy the beauties of that Palladian demesne, make the place and highly ornamented gardens belonging to it resemble a picture of Watteau. There is some affectation in the picture, but in the ensemble the original looked very well. The Duke of Devonshire received every one with the best possible manners. The scene was dignified by the presence of an immense elephant, who, under the charge of a groom, wandered up and down, giving an air of Asiatic pageantry to the entertainment . . .[4]

Devonshire was one of the great collectors of his generation, of books, paintings, sculpture and many other artefacts which happened to have caught his eye. He bought Henry VIII's rosary, designed by Holbein, which had turned up unexpectedly at the jewellers Rundell and Bridges for £200, and the whole of John Kemble's collection of plays and manuscripts for £2000. The latter was generally considered to be the best collection of theatrical manuscripts in the world and included 7500 plays, 111 volumes of playbills or programmes, and one of the only two surviving first editions of *Hamlet*; and when the Bishop of Ely died the Duke bought his entire library of rare books for £10,000. Bibliomania was a part of the cultural creed of the Regency and an architect commissioned to build a new house would always be told to include a library. The library, the sculpture gallery and the art collection were regarded as essential status symbols, the Regency equivalent of the pool, the gym and the communications centre today. The Lower Library at Chatsworth held, in the sixth Duke's time, more than 5700 books. Some of the doors were covered with the leather spines of fake books, for which the Duke amused himself inventing titles such as:

'Johnson's Contradictionary'
'Boyle on Steam'
'Burnet's Theory of Conflagration'
'Minto's Coins'
'Macadam's Rhodes'
'Percy Vere, in forty volumes'
'Raffle's Lottery of Life'
and 'Cleopatra's Pearl, by the venerable Bede'.[5]

Those who could afford it thought nothing of buying vast objects abroad and paying for them to be shipped back to ornament their country houses. One of the sixth Duke's earliest purchases, when he went to Rome in 1819, was a series of five great slabs of Oriental granite, which were not even polished. The colour of the stone must have taken his fancy for he had them brought back to Derbyshire and placed in the middle of the floor of what was once the housekeeper's room at Chatsworth, making a granite carpet. He had a particular passion for marble and, every time he went to Italy, embarked on a serious bout of studio-crawling, visiting all the great contemporary sculptors. Canova, Lorenzo

Bartolini, Adamo Tadolini and Carlo Finelli were the leading Italians working at the time but the great Danish sculptor Thorvaldsen was also in Rome. There were even a number of English sculptors, whose studios in Rome the Duke patronized as well, notably John Gibson, Thomas Campbell and a Mr Locke of Norbury. The Duke's favourite sculptor was Canova, from whom he bought the famous statue of Napoleon's mother, Madame Mère, seated, Petrarch's Laura, and Hebe (bought from Lord Cawdor), as well as busts of Madame Mère and Napoleon. He also commissioned a statue of Endymion, which, when it finally arrived in London, caused an artistic sensation. Everyone rushed to Devonshire House to view and admire and Endymion became the rage. According to a contemporary witness, all the Mayfair dandies started practising the 'Endymion pose', draping themselves over the drawing-room sofas – a manoeuvre which met with little success since it is an extremely difficult position to sustain with grace.

Similarly, when one of the Russian officers brought a Cossack to London in his retinue all the ladies vied for his attention and there was a brief, disastrous craze amongst the dandies for copying his uniform: society was always eager for new blood and any excuse served to start a new fashion and create a new celebrity. The Cossack was considered such a noble and extraordinary figure that he was given the Grand Tour of London, taken to meet the Lord Mayor, written up at length in the *Morning Chronicle*, and finally exhibited to the public at the Royal Exchange. Numerous prints of 'Zemlanowhin, the Brave Russian Cossack', carrying the ten-foot spear with which he was said to have killed thirty-seven Frenchmen, were rushed off the presses: Ackermann, the leading print-seller, made so much money out of the Cossack that he gave him his choice of four beautiful swords as a present. Having chosen a Turkish scimitar, he was taken to Westminster and allowed to play with one of the large Crown swords, to the delight of the crowds who followed him all over town. Zemlanowhin seems to have taken it all in his stride and delighted in the attention. On his last night he was taken to visit the Exhibition Rooms at Spring Gardens, where he 'heard a new

ALEXANDER ZEMLENUTIN, KOSSACK OF THE DON REGIMENT
Illustration to Ackermann's *Repository of Arts, Literature, Commerce,* July 1813.
*In the summer of 1813 one of the visiting Russian officers brought a Cossack to
London in his retinue. He became a celebrity in society and launched a craze amongst
the dandies for wide 'Cossack' trousers.*

March played on an awful instrument called the Panharmonium.
On this fiendish invention the combined noise of 200 instruments
was ground out by machinery . . . The trumpets sounding victory,
and the bells, with the horns and kettledrums, rejoicing for glory,
gave joy to all present.' The Cossack, 'on being introduced to
the fair Albiness [i.e. leading lady] seemed, by the expression of
his countenance, to be much pleased.'[6] After shaking hands with

the lady, and saluting her, he asked for a lock of her hair as a souvenir. Needless to say such Continental grace paid off and he was given an elegant locket to contain the hair as well. Regency society was never mean about presents.

All grandees travelled with their own personal servants: on a trip to Constantinople the sixth Duke of Devonshire took his doctor, his chief valet and his dog with him in his own carriage, a 'britshka', which had been specially built for the journey. His retinue included two more sub-valets, a cook, a courier and his personal footman. On another occasion he took a party of fifteen on a tour of Italy and France which included his head gardener, Joseph Paxton, as well as his own personal artist: before the ubiquitous camera was invented, tourists who were rich enough took along a professional painter to record the various sights and treasures they encountered on their travels. When the Duke went to Italy for the first time, he hired a local artist, Raffaele Carelli, on the spot and kept him on the pay roll for years. The man's whole life was changed when he was taken up by the Duke; thereafter he trailed along in the wake of his employer all over Europe.

The size of the Duke's retinue, however, was no guarantee of comfort. In fact the upper classes during the Regency were prepared to put up with an appalling degree of discomfort in their pursuit of culture. In Sicily, for example, it was quite usual for four people to share one room, which probably had only one bed in it and no glass in the windows. Lesser members of the party often slept, fully clothed, on the floor, or, at best, on straw palliasses. Standards of hygiene and sanitation were often deplorable, involving a serious risk of disease and infection. It was often preferable to sleep and eat in the carriage, rather than in the accommodation available. Many of these travelling carriages were built to the owner's specifications and fitted up with all the comforts of a luxury mobile home. Nevertheless, most of the Regency grandees took the precaution of including a doctor in their retinue when they travelled abroad. The Duke of Devonshire was always accompanied by his own private physician, but he was expected to be much more than just a doctor – a cross between accountant, companion and secretary. The terms and status of the doctor were spelt out in advance and illustrate to a nicety the emphasis on social distinctions – however liberal the employer believed himself to be. According to a document in the Chatsworth Archives headed 'Arrangement with Physician':

The Duke of Devonshire offers to the Gentleman who accompanies him as his physician in travelling the sum of £50 a month.

He will be expected to undertake the superintendence of all travelling expenses and the examination of the courier's accounts, also transactions with the different foreign bankers when it may be necessary. The second carriage will always be appropriated to his use, even when the Duke is not accompanied by any other person.

The Duke cannot undertake to introduce him, or promise his introduction, to any of the courts which he may visit. Neither can he answer for it in private societies though it is likely that they will usually be open to all the party.

The Duke carries with him only the books with which he himself is occupied, therefore he requests that Dr — will be provided with any that he may want for his own use.

At large towns where the Duke may stay some time and where he is in the habit of dining out there will be no table provided for Dr — but his company will be very acceptable whenever the Duke dines at home.[7]

This contract was drawn up for the benefit of one Dr Eyre, who accompanied the Duke to Italy in 1819, but would have been equally applicable to most 'Travelling Doctors' at the time. In fact, the terms may have been too stringent for Dr Eyre since, on his next trip abroad, two years later, he was replaced by Dr Richard Verity. The Duke described Verity as 'the queerest man I ever saw, sometimes pleasant in society, but so absent and vain of his person & dress, gazing at himself in the glass that I sometimes think he is cracked.' (The Duke was fairly vain himself: when he decided to redecorate the state music room he had his own likeness incorporated in stamped leather which had been specially ordered for the purpose. His portrait is repeated eight times in the leather cornice of the room.) In Naples, Verity went around dressed alternately in fur and India rubber. Nevertheless he must have suited, or amused the Duke, since, along with the private artists and musicians, he remained in his employ for years.

The sixth Duke of Devonshire's parties were magnificent, almost as grand as those given by the Prince Regent himself and in much better taste. There were dinners and balls at Devonshire House in London, garden parties at Chiswick, shooting parties at Hardwick and Bolton, and huge house parties at Chatsworth and Lismore in Ireland whenever he was in residence. The style and scale of some of these parties, however, was too much for some of the guests. The poet Tom Moore, for example, felt he was just not rich enough for Chatsworth. In a letter to Samuel Rogers he explained:

I have no servant to take with me, and my hat is shabby, and the seams of my best coat are beginning to look white – and in short if a man cannot step upon equal ground with these people, he had much better keep out of their way. I can meet them on pretty fair terms at a dinner or a ball; but a whole week in the same house with them detects the poverty of a man's ammunition deplorably; to which, if we add that *I* should detect the poverty of *theirs*, I think the obvious conclusion is to have nothing to do with each other.[8]

The novelist Emily Eden was another who found Chatsworth a strain, but for different reasons. Miss Eden was a well-off and well-known member of society, and as such was invited every-where, but she was an intellectual and found the Chatsworth set too frivolous. Though flattered to be asked to stay, she always found herself making excuses after a couple of days:

I shall continue to think a visit to Chatsworth a very great trouble . . . We have now made a rule to accept one invitation out of two. We go there with the best dispositions, wishing to be amused, liking the people we meet there, loyal and well affected to the King of the Peak himself, supported by the knowledge that in the eyes of the neighbourhood we are covering ourselves with glory by frequenting the *great house*; but with all these helps we have never been able to stay above two days there without finding a change of air absolutely necessary – never could turn the corner of the third day – at the end of the second the great depths of *bore* were broken up and carried all before them; we were obliged to pretend that some christening, or grand funeral, or some pressing case of wedding (in this country it is sometimes expedient to hurry the performance of the marriage ceremony) required Robert's [her brother was with her] immediate return home, and so we departed yawning. It is odd that it should be so dull. The G. Lambs are both pleasant, and so is Mr Foster and Mrs Cavendish and a great many of the habitués of Chatsworth; and though I have not yet attained the real Derbyshire feeling which would bring tears of admiration into my eyes whenever the Duke observed that it was a fine day, yet I think him pleasant, and like him very much, and can make him hear without any difficulty, and he is very hospitable and wishes us to bring all our friends and relations there, if that would do us any good. But we happen to be pleasanter at home. However private vices may contribute to public benefit, I do not see how private bore can contribute to public happiness, do you?[9]

So much for the life of the seriously rich. But Emily Eden was a 'blue-stocking', one of that dreaded band of women who were not ashamed to parade their intelligence. Dreaded, at least, by most of society, including those one might have expected to appreciate them. Coleridge wrote, 'The longer I live, the more do I loathe in stomach and deprecate in judgement *all* blue-stockingism'[10] and Byron, though surrounded by clever women, was distinctly ambivalent about their brains. He referred to his wife, a mathematician, as the 'Princess of Parallelograms', and showed his feelings in *Don Juan* when he wrote: 'But Oh! ye lords of ladies intellectual,/ Inform us truly, have they not hen-pecked you all?'[11] All the same, he was proud of his daughter Ada's success as a scientist. She inherited her mother's interest in mathematics, taught herself geometry and astronomy, and was taken up by Charles Babbage, the pioneer of modern computers. She was a beautiful girl, with much of her father's charm, and remarkably clever. The wife of a fellow scientist described the reaction of Babbage's audience when he demonstrated one of his new inventions: 'While the rest of the party gazed at this beautiful instrument with the same sort of expression and feeling that some savages are said to have shown on first seeing a looking-glass or hearing a gun, Miss Byron . . . understood its working and saw the great beauty of the invention.'[12]

During the eighteenth century there seems to have been slightly less prejudice against brains in a woman than appeared later, or perhaps it was just less apparent. Wit, after all, was just as much at a premium during the Regency as amongst the previous generation, and the great Whig hostesses of both periods were all highly educated, clever women. The term 'blue-stocking', incidentally, derives from a club of the same name founded towards the end of the eighteenth century by Elizabeth Montagu. Basically it was a gathering of aristocratic ladies with literary leanings, and the only difference between Mrs Montagu's parties and those given by the other great hostesses was that the guests came for the conversation alone: there were none of the usual frivolous attractions, such as cards and dancing. Hannah More, who was one of the regulars, described the company in a poem with the title '*Bas-Bleu*', hence the nickname. A few men were allowed to attend, provided they were of sufficiently intellectual calibre. Edmund Burke, Joshua Reynolds and William Wilberforce were among those who qualified. Horace Walpole refers to the group as 'a charming poetic familiarity called *The Blue-Stocking Club*'.[13] As the nineteenth century progressed, however, with its inherent prejudice against the education of women, the term acquired a slightly pejorative connotation. It was felt that a display of brains was thoroughly unfeminine and therefore unattractive. The taint of being a blue-stocking was enough to frighten off any nice young man and the girl so accused destined to remain for ever 'on the shelf'.

Such was the ridiculous view of one element of society; others, of course, were only too delighted to find themselves in the company of clever women. The most famous literary salon of the Regency was that of the Misses Berry, in North Audley Street, where 'the blues and the wits were assembled', and as Sydney

Smith said, 'the conversation raged'. Mary Berry was born in 1763 and Agnes in 1764 and they were known as 'Elderberry' and either 'Blackberry' or 'Gooseberry', according to the benevolence or otherwise of the speaker. The sisters made their debut in London society during the early years of George III's reign and were still holding their own little court during that of Victoria. They were among the most entertaining women of their generation, exceptionally well educated and intelligent, and though neither aristocratic nor wealthy, lived all their lives at the epicentre of society. They were amongst the most celebrated and popular hostesses in London for more than fifty years, with a guest list that ranged from Horace Walpole (who was one of their greatest fans and lent them Strawberry Hill, his beautiful house at Twickenham, for years), via Fox and the brilliant Whig society of the late eighteenth century, to the Duke of Wellington.

The great appeal of the Berrys' salon was that it was informal, because they neither wished nor could afford to be otherwise, and that it was neutral ground: they made a point of being apolitical. As one regular remembered, 'It was no secret society which met there . . . there was perfect freedom of speech, and no fear of informers.'[14] They liked mixing people, the débutante and the dandy, the young and the old, artists and patrons, choosing their guests for their conversational worth alone. Other regulars at the salon included such diverse characters as Sydney Smith and Caroline Lamb, Brougham and Brummell, Thomas Moore and Sir Thomas Lawrence, Sir Lumley Skeffington and the Glenbervies. It must have been an oasis in a society which put so much emphasis upon status, and where social advancement was the motive for so many of the parties.

When Mary Berry was engaged to General O'Hara, she prepared an estimate for her fiancé of their future expenses. It should be emphasized that the Berry sisters were not rich, in comparison with the company they kept, and could only just afford to sustain their role in society. According to Mary Berry, her budget 'includes every comfort necessary to a small establishment in London.'[15] She feels that an income of just over £2000 a year is the absolute minimum upon which they could entertain 'agreeably all those friends who should prefer a neat plain dinner or supper, and *our agreeable society* to a French cook and dull company.' The budget allows her fiancé £800 a year to spend on himself, but she has cut off 'all *your* extravagancies, your Saddle Horses, your separate carriage, and one of your Men-Servants.' This is not as selfish as it sounds since she has allowed herself only £200 a year for personal expenses, including clothes – a fraction of the amount most women in their circle spent on dressing.

From a letter from Mary Berry to General O'Hara,
undated, circa *January 1796.*

	£	s	d
One pair of Job Horses inclusive of coachman's wages for 8 months of the year	125	0	0
Annual repairs to Carriage about	25	0	0
Two men servants at £20 apiece	40	0	0
An Upper Man at the wages of	55	0	0
Wages of 4 Women Servants, a Housekeeper, a Cook under her, a House maid and Lady's maid	58	0	0
Liveries for the 3 Men Servants and the Coachman	80	0	0
House rent and taxes	200	0	0
Coals	50	0	0
Candles	25	0	0
Beer	25	0	0
Wine	100	0	0
Housekeeping, at the rate of £10 a week or £40 a month	480	0	0
	£1263	0	0
To you	800	0	0
To me	200	0	0
	£2263	0	0

Translated into modern cash equivalents this means that a young couple living *modestly* in society during the Regency needed an income of well over £100,000 a year *after tax*. And this budget was prepared in 1796, when the economy was relatively healthy:

so, without venturing upon exact comparisons, it is fair to assume an even higher figure. To put these figures into perspective, the Prince of Wales at the time was £630,000 in debt (in the region of £30 million, in terms of modern money), and it had just been agreed that his allowance, when he married Princess Caroline, should be increased to £138,000 p.a. (approximately £7 million). Furthermore, the Duke of Devonshire was only one of several private individuals in possession of an income of several hundred thousand pounds a year at the beginning of the nineteenth century; others in the same financial bracket included the Duke of Buccleuch, who had estates in England as well as Scotland, the Duke of Bedford and the banker Nathan Rothschild. In a book on contemporary mores published in 1816 the author defines a rich man as one with an income of £5000 a year (£250,000 today), which he considers the minimum required to qualify as a man of fashion, and sustain a position in what he refers to as 'The Great World'. As far as the middle classes were concerned £400 a year (£20,000) as a parson's wife was an 'income hardly enough to find one in the common necessaries of life', according to Isabella Thorpe in *Northanger Abbey*,* and the thought of living on such a paltry sum was enough to make her switch suitors at once. And in *Sense and Sensibility* the dreadful Mrs John Dashwood, having condemned her sisters-in-law and their mother to living on £500 a year, points out exactly what such an income will, or rather will not, buy: 'They will have no carriage, no horses, and hardly any servants; they will keep no company, and can have no expences of any kind! Only conceive how comfortable they will be,' she tells her husband gleefully. On such an income the Dashwood ladies could exist, certainly, but hardly in the manner to which they had been accustomed. In the end Elinor and Edward married on £850 a year – just about enough for a young middle-class couple to live in reasonable comfort, in the country, in 1811. Finally, it must be remembered that amongst a large proportion of population, whole families existed on an income of

* Jane Austen's *Northanger Abbey* was published posthumously in 1818 and *Sense and Sensibility* in 1811.

£50 a year or even less, which equates with an income of about £2000 today and as such is well below the poverty line. The dichotomy between rich and poor was infinitely greater two hundred years ago than it is today.

Miss Berry's budget illustrates the great difference between the costs of various commodities during the Regency and their equivalents today. A house in Mayfair, large enough to entertain in and to house seven servants besides themselves, costs less than ten per cent of their income, but the servants' liveries cost as much as their wages for the whole year. The housekeeping is expensive, if multiplied by the relevant factors, and people like the Berrys lived on a fixed income. The greatest luxury in the budget is their carriage. Transport of any kind was enormously expensive, relative to modern costs: those who could afford to keep a string of hunters and several carriages were on a par with people who have their own helicopter and a fleet of cars today. *The Traveller's Oracle*, published in 1827, estimated the cost of keeping a single riding horse in London, inclusive of stabling and groom, at approximately £120 a year. The *Oracle* puts the total cost of keeping a family carriage in London at a minimum of £400 a year, nearly three times Miss Berry's estimate, which shows both the extent of inflation after the war and that the Berrys' budget was based on the strictest economy. The cheapest form of private transport was a vehicle with two wheels and a single horse, but even that, according to the *Oracle*, would have cost about £150 a year, all in (the equivalent of £6000 p.a. today). These were the sports cars of the carriage trade, the dashing vehicles favoured by the Regency 'bloods' and members of the 'Fancy', and included the tilbury, stanhope, cabriolet and curricle. A racing curricle, or other two-wheeled carriage, was much lighter, and faster, than the conventional four-wheeled coach, and was a much better vehicle for showing off the driver's skill 'with the ribbons'. John Thorpe in *Northanger Abbey* thinks 50 guineas for a curricle, complete with 'seat, trunk, swordcase, splashing-board, lamps and silver moulding' is an average price, but the blades of high society would have paid very much more and the cost of a showy horse to draw the curricle could be twice as much again. Two-wheeled carriages were referred to by a contemporary Chief Justice as 'Bankrupt Carts', 'because they were, and are, frequently driven by those who could neither afford the Money to support them, nor the Time spent in using them, the want of which, in their Business, brought them to Bankruptcy.'[16]

One horse and two wheels obviously cost less than two horses and four wheels, but even so a breakdown of expenses shows that the horse's food, at £30 a year, came to more than the groom's; hay came to another £20–£30 p.a. and a carriage horse was liable to get through 28 sets of shoes, at 5/- a set, in the same period. Moreover both horses and carriages were taxed, horses at around 30s a head and carriages, depending on size, several pounds each. Stabling in London during the Regency seems to have been as much of a problem as parking today, for those whose houses were not grand enough to include their own mews. The solution to transport in London was to rent – the horses, the carriage and even the coachman – on a long-term basis. The *Oracle* strongly recommends the principle of 'Jobbing' (i.e. renting), as opposed to setting up one's own stable, because it was much easier and half the price; the estimate for hiring a carriage and pair, with their own coachman, is given as between £200 and £250 a year (£10,000–£12,500). Once again a breakdown of the expenses shows that the cost of the labour is minimal: the wages of the coachman come to £26 p.a. and his board to £36 8s 0d. The cost of hiring the horses to draw the carriage, however, is given as £135 p.a. and the hire of a 'handsome new Chariot or Coach and Harness, from £70 to £84'.[17]

The coachman's livery, at just under £20, in both Miss Berry's and the *Oracle*'s estimation, seems inordinately expensive in relation to the other costs. It should include, according to the latter, 'Two handsome Suits of what is termed the best Second Cloth'. The author suggests a heavy light blue coat, edged with crimson, lined with matching light blue silk, with a gold-laced collar and buttonholes. The buttons themselves, of this 'rich but not gaudy' uniform, are to be gilt and stamped with the owner's crest. A blue waistcoat and plush breeches with gilt knee buckles and this second-best outfit is complete. However, he still needs 'A good full-made Box-Coat, with six real capes' for driving in the rain, which will cost another £7, including a matching silk lining, and a couple of hats, decorated with more gold lace binding at £2 10s 0d each. This expensive outfit is purely for display; another entry lists 'working dress' at £3 13s 0d. Livery was yet another way of demonstrating status.

As for travelling by 'post', i.e. in a private hired carriage, it cost a fortune in comparison with the expense of an equivalent journey today. The hire of a chaise and pair cost one guinea a mile, but that of a larger coach drawn by four horses, which would mean a much faster and more comfortable journey, was 2/6d per mile. No wonder only the rich could afford to elope to Gretna Green.

In the end Mary Berry never married the general but continued to live with her sister in London, both immersed in their social life and their salon. After the war, however, it became clear that they were increasingly worried about money and found it difficult to keep up with their richer friends. Dressing was a particular problem. Clothes were a major item of expense because contemporary mores in high society demanded so many different outfits during the Regency. Fashionable ladies needed morning dresses, walking dresses, riding habits, and afternoon dresses as well as evening dresses of varying grandeur, culminating in the court dress. Hats were obligatory and so were gloves, different for every possible permutation of the social scene. Then there were mantuas, pelisses and opera cloaks; reticules, parasols and scarves; boots, shoes, sandals and dancing slippers. It is not surprising that Mary Berry's letters, when she went on a visit to Paris after the war, are full of complaints about the prices. Nevertheless while she was there she went to the most fashionable and expensive milliner of the day, Mlle Phanie, and bought a bonnet known as a *capotte*; it was made of white crêpe and satin, trimmed with artificial flowers and cost 50 francs (2 guineas in English money: in 1816 the rate of exchange was approximately 25 francs to

£1). She fell in love with the French fashions, but wrote that everything was horribly expensive and she was spending much more than she could afford, buying such luxuries as embroidered stockings at 10s a pair. Even the *artificial* lace cost the iniquitous price of 6/2d a yard, but 'I really think so beautiful as to be not at all distinguishable from real on trimmings &.' However, at least the French silks were relatively reasonable, at 5s a yard, and she bought enough for two dresses, one of which could double as a morning and 'Theatre Gown'. Asked to execute a number of commissions for friends in England, Mary Berry warned them about the prices 'Lady Hardwicke says your morning-gown is beautiful. It ought to be so. It cost you exactly £3 . . . The women here *must* never pay their debts or *must* spend much more than we do.'[18] Mary Berry soon found a cheaper dressmaker in Paris, but still complained that she had 'been obliged to spend all my money in gauze trimmings, a trumpery which vexes me, but it was not to be helped in the way I happened to be living, and everybody at their dinners and evening parties look always as if they came out of a bandbox, so that one cannot wear the same things for ever.'[19] Even a blue-stocking was not above the familiar female moan. To be fair to Miss Berry, however, she was moving in a world where many women thought nothing of spending 100 guineas on an evening dress and served truffles at dinner parties, at 16s a pound.

Such problems were relative. The economic reality of the country as a whole was disastrous in the aftermath of the war. Huge amounts of money had been raised over twenty-two years, to pay for the war, more than a hundred million pounds in all: but all this was of no use to the working classes in their daily lives. As one economist wrote, 'not a penny was spent on the education of a labourer's children, or to any purpose that made the perils and difficulties of his life more easy to be borne.'[20] The slump in world trade, added to the problems caused by the return of thousands of soldiers, led to a frightening level of unemployment and poverty. A series of failed harvests, allied to the passing of the Corn Law in 1815, meant that the price of home-grown wheat rose out of all proportion to the economy as a whole, beyond the purse of the common man. According to Cobbett agricultural prices fell by at least 60 per cent after the war and hundreds of farmers were ruined. In 1813 a good cow would fetch approximately £15 at auction, but no more than £3 in 1822. A ewe which had sold for between 55s and 72s in 1812 raised only 25s fourteen years later. At the same time the average rural labourer's wages dropped from around 15s a week to 6s, if he was lucky enough to find work at all, and many families found themselves on the edge of starvation. 'The poor were daily crying out for food,' Thomas Dibdin, a contemporary diarist, wrote during the exceptionally harsh winter of 1816.

The great landlords, on the other hand, made large profits as a result of the war. The Corn Laws, which led to such hardship amongst the working classes, guaranteed their employers' income, and, at the same time, running inflation had a knock-on effect on the rents. Lord Egremont's gross rental from his Sussex estates in 1791 was £7950; in 1831, forty years later, it had risen to £14,770. The same pattern is repeated on his Yorkshire estates: an enormous jump from a total of £12,976 in 1791 to £34,000 in 1824.[21] In some cases the rents were increased five-fold between 1790 and 1830.

It was a time when the rich got richer and the poor got poorer – with the inevitable results. In 1816, at Brandon, near Bury, the first of a series of riots which were to erupt all over the country took place. Fifteen hundred rioters, armed with spiked sticks and carrying a flag, inscribed with their slogan 'Bread or Blood', went on the rampage. Their demand was for a fixed maximum price for both bread and meat, half a crown per bushel for wheat, and 4d a pound for best beef. In the course of this first great protest the rioters set the barns and ricks of their landlords on fire, but they stopped short of physical violence. Few of these men were revolutionaries: they simply meant what they said. And according to *The Times* the disturbances ceased and the men went quietly back to work when their demands were met a few days later. Not only was the price of flour reduced, but wages were increased for a couple of weeks – to two whole shillings a day. Rioting, however, is infectious. In the following weeks riots broke out in

East Anglia, and, inevitably, several became violent. On the Isle of Ely the disturbances ended in a straight battle, when the militia were called in. Two rioters had been killed, but seventy-five were taken prisoner and tried the following month by a Special Commission. Their sentences were regarded as horrific, not only by acknowledged Liberal politicians but by a large proportion of the educated classes: five men were hanged; five transported for life; and many others transported for between seven and fourteen years. By 1818 the agitation for repeal of the Corn Laws had spread and mass meetings were a common occurrence. Unfortunately, by this time, the meetings, if not the actual riots, were being orchestrated by the Radicals, led by the famous 'Orator' Hunt. The climax came on 16 August 1819, when a crowd of 80,000 people marched to St Peter's Fields, Manchester, to listen to Hunt's demands for political reform. The crowd was unarmed and included women and children. The most charitable explanation of the subsequent massacre was that the authorities lost their heads. The facts of 'Peterloo', as the massacre came to be known, were that the magistrates first sent in the yeomanry to break up the meeting and then the cavalry, who charged the crowd with drawn swords. Eleven people were killed, including two women and a child, and more than 400 were wounded, of which 113 were women. This unprovoked attack upon unarmed people conducting an orderly and peaceful protest meeting was greeted with almost universal outrage: even the Lord Mayor of London felt it incumbent upon himself to protest in a letter to the Prince Regent.

Tax, during the Regency, was minimal in comparison to modern rates – but it was considered iniquitous to have to pay any at all. Britain was actually the first country in Europe to enact income tax: in 1799 the government, desperate for money to pay the armed forces, imposed a personal levy of two shillings in the pound on all incomes in excess of £200 a year. A descending scale of rates was applied to lower incomes, with exemption below £60 p.a. In the euphoria which followed Waterloo income tax was temporarily abolished, but was later revived at 7d in the pound. By the end of the nineteenth century income tax had been accepted as a permanent levy. The window tax was another great cause of complaint, particularly, of course, amongst the landlords who owned whole villages as well as their various mansions. Although the window tax had been on the statute books since the seventeenth century, it was not until the end of the eighteenth that it became oppressive. In 1784 the tax on a house with ten windows was more than doubled, from 11s 4d to £1 4s 4d and by 1808 it had risen to £2 16s: a house with thirty windows paid £19 12s 6d annually, with corresponding rises according to the number of windows, and many of the new Regency houses were built with considerably more than thirty. It was thus an obvious economy to block up some of the windows, so people began to live and sleep in rooms which had neither natural light nor air, with inevitable results for the health of the community. This was not, however, a consideration which was obvious at the time since most people, including doctors, regarded fresh air as lethal.

It was indirect taxation which most affected the working and middle classes. Even the necessities of life were taxed. According to an agricultural magazine published at the time, indirect taxation during the post-war years cost the average labourer half his yearly income.[22] The figures quoted here are based on a yearly income of £22 10s, and include taxes on malt (by far the highest, at £4 11s 3d), sugar, tea and coffee (regarded as luxuries, and taxed accordingly at £1 4s), soap, housing, clothes and even food (£3). Admittedly the magazine in question was published by a philanthropic society which used such statistics as propaganda in their campaign against agrarian poverty, but that is no reason to doubt their accuracy.

Sydney Smith summed up the general feeling when he complained that Pitt, in his desperate attempts to finance the war, had made life a misery with his taxes on:

. . . every article which enters into the mouth, or covers the back, or is placed under the foot – taxes upon everything which is pleasant to see, hear, feel, smell or taste – taxes upon warmth, light and locomotion – taxes upon everything on earth, and the waters under the earth – or everything that comes from abroad, or is grown at home – taxes on the raw material – taxes on every fresh value that is added to it by the industry of man – taxes on the sauce which pampers man's appetite, and the drug that restores him to health – on the ermine which decorates the judge and the rope that hangs the criminal – on the poor man's salt and the rich man's spice – on the brass nails of the coffin and the ribands of the bride – at bed or board, couchant or levant, we must pay – the schoolboy whips his taxed top – the beardless youth manages his taxed horse, with a taxed bridle, on a taxed road – and the dying Englishman, pouring his medicine which has paid 7 per cent, into a spoon that has paid 15 per cent, flings himself back on his chintz bed, which has paid 22 per cent – and expires in the arms of an apothecary who has paid a license of £100 for the privilege of putting him to death. His whole property is then immediately taxed from 2 to 10 per cent . . .[23]

The last sentence of this diatribe puts death duties, at least, in proportion, considering the present rates on property and inheritance. Moreover, there is no doubt that, although the economic situation was indeed serious after the wars, England had still fared a great deal better than the rest of Europe. These alarms and complaints were regarded as risible by visitors from abroad. Frederick Lamb, writing to his mother from Munich, emphasized the point:

As to the distress among the people, it is nothing, it is not to be spoken or thought of in comparison to what exists over all the rest of Europe . . . Do you wish to know the impression England produces upon a Foreigner? Take the account of Mon. Berstett . . . who is a sensible impartial man, qui a beaucoup vu, but who never saw England before. He says that he never witnessed before such a state of incredible prosperity and activity, that Paris through which he returned, appears perfectly dead in comparison to London, that the alarm of popular commotion [a reference to the riots in England] is perfectly contemptible, but that [in England] liberty is carried to the greatest possible perfection, and that it would be impossible not to adore a country where every man is filled with the confidence and security of possessing it.[24]

5

LONDON: THE MOST PROSPEROUS CITY IN EUROPE

At the beginning of the Regency metropolitan London was confined within the limits of Oxford Street and Holborn to the north, the river to the south, the outer boundary of the City to the east, and Hyde Park to the west. But the acceptable residential area was confined to no more than a few blocks of Mayfair. Sydney Smith, a man not normally given to hyperbole, was overwhelmed by the West End of London when he arrived in 1803, and wrote that he believed the 'parallelogram between Oxford Street, Piccadilly, Regent Street and Hyde Park, encloses more intelligence and human ability, to say nothing of wealth and beauty, than the world has ever collected in such a space before.'[1] Kensington, Chelsea and Knightsbridge were country villages surrounded by open country; the houses of Westminster looked across the river to the hills of Surrey; Hampstead was a wild and empty heath, still harried by highwaymen; and Golders an uninhabited green. The site where Harrods stands today was part of Hans Town, a shabby, genteel suburb for those who lived on the fringes of society. Bloomsbury was colonized by respectable merchants and the professional classes, handsome houses but tainted by trade in the eyes of the elite. As the nineteenth century progressed, the Regency business men, or 'cits' as they were known in the vernacular, started building large family houses in the country villages closest to the City, from which they could drive in to work. Areas such as Clapham and

Camberwell south of the river, and Islington and Hackney to the north, became the first commuter suburbs, even then a concept regarded with dismay by the conservationists. The *Traveller's Oracle* was outraged by the growth of London, pointing out that 'instead of the Fields being come-atable with extremely pleasant facility, before you can put your foot upon a blade of *Verdant* Grass (there is *Black* Grass enough in the Squares), you must drag your Legs through a Grove of Houses of at least two or three Miles in length!'[2] The exclamation mark is the Regency author's: a modern commentator would feel a positive row of exclamation marks would be more apposite at the thought of a central London from which you could escape to green fields after only three miles.

Most of the great family mansions were situated in the middle of Mayfair: Grosvenor, Park Lane, St James's and Berkeley Squares were all lined with private houses. When the American minister Richard Rush came to London in 1817 and looked for a furnished house to rent, he was stunned by the luxury on offer, even amongst those which were not of the first rank.

From the basement to the attics, everything had an air of comfort. The supply of furniture was full. The staircases were of white stone. The windows and beds in servants' rooms had curtains. No floor was without carpeting. In many instances libraries made part of the furniture to be rented with the houses – a beautiful part. The rents varied from four hundred to a thousand guineas a year. In some of the *squares* of the West-end, I learned, that the rent of a furnished house was sixty and sometimes eighty guineas a *week*.[3]

He thought, however, that the houses in the West End were not grand enough for the 'residences of the richest people in the richest city in Europe'.

The daily life of the rich and great and grand, when they were in London, revolved around Mayfair and St James's, with an occasional shopping expedition to the larger warehouses of Covent Garden, the Strand and the City. Even within these limitations there were definite sociological distinctions. The St James's area was predominantly a masculine preserve, the side streets packed with bachelor lodgings and expensive shops, several of which have lasted to the present day. Locks, the fashionable hatters in St James's, which was founded early in the eighteenth century, has made everything from *chapeaux bras* and tricornes, to Panamas and bowlers. Similarly, Berry's, the wine merchants, have maintained a tradition of serving successive generations of the same families: it has been said that the long list of Berry's clients over the last 250 years reads like the pages of the peerage – or a list of the members of White's, which is much the same thing.

St James's Street itself, dominated by White's, Brooks's and Boodle's, was out of bounds to ladies of quality. It was felt that the bucks and the beaux who sat in the bow windows of their clubs ogling the passers-by with their quizzing glasses posed a moral hazard to the 'delicately nurtured', as girls were coyly referred to in contemporary women's magazines: and convention decreed that any lady seen driving along St James's Street in an open carriage, let alone walking, was guilty of impropriety. Europeans, needless to say, never saw the point of this peculiar attitude. 'Je déteste votre St James's Street,' one of the secretaries of the French embassy complained when he arrived in London, 'On n'y voit que des hommes!' Bond Street, on the other hand, was considered a perfectly acceptable promenade for women in spite of the prevalence of just as many bucks and beaux. One of the attractions of Bond Street was Hookham's circulating library, which specialized in novels, from the Gothic romances of Mrs Radcliffe and her ilk, to the latest Walter Scott, the most popular author of the Regency. The more discerning might even have asked for one of Jane Austen's novels: *Sense and Sensibility* was published in 1811, *Pride and Prejudice* two years later, *Mansfield Park* in 1814 and *Emma*, dedicated by permission to the Prince Regent, in 1815.

Sir Thomas Lawrence, the fashionable portrait painter, had his studio at 24 Bond Street, and people used to wander in off the street to admire the latest work in progress. When one of the Cavendish girls dropped in on Hoppner's studio nearby she was most annoyed to find that all the portraits of society ladies had been locked up for once, except for 'poor Lady G[eorge] Gordon', who 'stood dancing in the middle of the room without respite'.[4] Self-portraits were as popular amongst Regency society as studio photographs today, and artists such as Wilkie, Etty, Haydon, Phillips and de Wilde all received lucrative commissions. Lawrence, however, was by far the most sought-after because he specialized in flattering 'improvements' to those of his subjects who were past their prime or possessed of unfortunate features. For example, his portrait of the Prince Regent at the age of fifty-two was that of 'a well-fleshed Adonis of thirty-three',[5] according to Hazlitt, who went on to imagine 'the transports with which his Royal Highness must have welcomed this improved version of himself.' (In fact, at the time, the Prince looked gross and middle-aged.) Similarly, Lawrence's portrait of Wellington is an idealized version of the aristocratic hero and bears little resemblance to the man himself. For such a transformation people were more than willing to pay Lawrence's fee of 700 guineas per portrait, and there was always a waiting list.

'Gentleman' Jackson's boxing saloon was the main attraction of Bond Street to the young men about town, along with the premises of Mr Weston, the most expensive tailor in town: Weston's customers included Brummell, the Prince Regent and most of the dandies. Many of the shops in Bond Street had converted their top floors into bachelor lodgings, on a par with those in St James's or the new chambers in Albany. Originally the Duke of York's private house, Albany was transformed into a number of luxurious apartments in 1802 and became the first example of 'service' flats in London.

Another mandatory port of call was the window of Acker-mann's print shop, the 'Repository of Arts' at 101 the Strand (today the site of the Savoy Hotel). Ackermann was a publisher, print-seller and 'manufacturer of fancy articles'. According to the Repository, 'During the period when the French emigrants were so numerous in this country, Mr A was amongst the first to strike out a liberal and easy mode of employing them, and he seldom had less than fifty nobles, priests and ladies of distinction at work upon screens, card-racks, flower-stands and other ornamental works of a similar nature.'[6] But his main claim to fame, and contemporary popularity, was based on the shop's rapid turnover of topical prints and caricatures. The Regency was the 'golden age of caricature' when England led the world in illustrated satire. Encouraged by their publishers, often supplied with ideas by members of 'the *ton*' themselves, and allowed a licence to offend that astonished foreigners, they conveyed a vivid picture of the age which was often unrestrained by 'careless habits of accuracy'. The leading caricaturists of the period were Gillray, Rowlandson and Cruikshank, but there were many others, less well known today but almost as popular at the time. The London print shops not only drew great crowds to see the latest drawings displayed in the window, but did a flourishing export trade. Ackermann employed Rowlandson, one of the most gifted artists in the field, and they decided on the subject to be illustrated between themselves, often on a daily basis. Rowlandson also collaborated with another artist, Pugin (father of the Victorian architect) to produce the *Microcosm of London*, a large book in three volumes illustrated with 104 aquatint plates. This was followed, in 1812, by *The Tour of Dr Syntax in Search of the Picturesque*, a satire in verse, also illustrated by Rowlandson, which ridiculed the current fashion for the Gothic and pictur-esque, ruined castles, dank forests and haunted abbeys.[7] When the Napoleonic Wars came to an end some of the ferocity went out of political caricatures and artists tended to concentrate instead on social comment, ridiculing the absurdities of fashion and contemporary mores.

The daily promenade around Mayfair was an integral part of social life during the Regency, one of the ways to see and be seen, to show off new clothes and meet fellow members of the *ton*. Gunter's, the confectioners in Berkeley Square, had a room where exhausted shoppers could sit and eat ices. Friburg and Treyer, the 'Old Snuff House' in the Haymarket, was another social rendezvous. Customers would drop in to place an order and stay on to sample and criticize the latest consignment from Martinique, or wherever. London, during the Regency, was a shopping paradise, full of unexpected markets and arcades, an Aladdin's cave of beautiful and costly treasures. In a society which was as fashion-conscious as the Regency, and whose members had leisure as well as money, it is hardly surprising they turned shopping into a vocation.

The Prince Regent set a glorious example. Ludicrously vain, he spent a fortune on trying to improve his physical image by extravagant dressing and glitter. In 1783, when he first took his seat in the House of Lords, his costume made it quite clear that he was already bent on making a name for himself in the world of fashion. 'He wore a suit of black velvet this time, lined with pink satin and covered in pink and gold spangled embroidery, and tottered into the Chamber on shoes with pink high heels. His hair was frizzed and curled and fluffed up and out at the sides.' So it went on, for the rest of his life: the Prince revelled in splendid clothes and gorgeous accessories, and even Beau Brummell was unable to subdue his taste for exuberant dressing.

The *St James's Chronicle* reported with obvious awe on the Prince's outfits: in 1791 he appeared at the King's birthday wearing a

bottle-green and claret-coloured striped silk coat, a silver waistcoat, very richly embroidered in silver and stones, and coloured silks in curious devices and bouquets of flowers. The coat and waistcoat embroidered down the seams and spangled all over the body. The coat cuffs the same as the waistcoat. The breeches were likewise covered with spangles. Diamond buttons to the coat, waistcoat, and breeches, which his brilliant diamond epaulette, and sword, made the whole dress form a most magnificent appearance.[8]

It was the quantities of everything he bought which was so impressive (or monstrous, according to the point of view). John Weston, his favourite tailor, spoke of 'some hundred suits' hanging in the Prince's wardrobe even before he became Regent.[9] And Batchelor, the Prince's valet towards the end of his life, told Charles Greville that even a plain coat of his master's often cost £300 before it was finally approved. He bought more than 500 shirts in less than ten years and ordered at least eight full-dress field-marshal's uniforms. The wardrobe he ordered for a trip to Scotland, undertaken when he was already in late middle age, included such extravaganzas as astrakhan Polish caps, a silk bathing gown, white beaver morning gowns made 'extra wide and very long', 'rich gold marmaluke sword belts', 'rich Muscovy sable muffs', scores of new shirts, dozens of long white gloves, 'prime doe pantaloons', 'superfine scarlet flannel underwaistcoats lined with fine calico', and quantities of black silk drawers.[10] Around this time, Benjamin Haydon, the painter, described the King, as he had by then become, arriving in Westminster Hall looking like 'some gorgeous bird of the East . . . in full robes of great size and richness.'[11]

Accounts in the Royal Archives at Windsor list hundreds of extravagant fashion accessories. Did he actually wear 'a large sea otter muff',[12] or need 'six fencing masks lined with blue silk and nine fencing gloves bound with blue silk, to be sent to Brighton'?[13] The epaulettes on his coats were made of real gold and even the studs on his braces were made of silver gilt. Another order, from the linen draper, mentions '3 Rich Gold and Spotted Muslin Handkerchiefs', which at 12 guineas each (a total expenditure of approximately £1800 in modern money) were the kind of purchases which annoyed parliament. On one occasion he bought two pairs of gold-framed spectacles, reasonable enough, except that the order goes on to mention twelve different spectacle cases to contain them, all doubtless decorated and made of different materials to suit different occasions. Even his boots were embellished with gold or silver tassels.[14] In later life he was liable to loll around in expensive lingerie. Princess Lieven described what he referred to as his 'get-up' when she went to see him one day at Carlton House: he was 'lying at full length in a lilac silk dressing gown, a velvet nightcap on his head, his huge bare feet [he was suffering from gout] covered with a silk net.'[15] Another order, from Schweitzer and Davidson, includes '4 printed muslin dressing jackets and 5 white robes de chambres';[16] rather unsuitable gear, one might think, for such a portly prince.

The Prince was not only a compulsive shopper, often buying things on impulse that he would never even wear, but a 'squirrel', who hoarded his possessions and then forgot what he owned. After his death Charles Greville reported that 'five hundred pocketbooks' were found, 'of different dates, and in every one of them money', amounting to several thousand pounds. And this was a man who spent his life in a panic about ready cash. The same source reports that amongst the huge collection of clothes and accessories found in his wardrobes after his death there were three hundred whips, 'canes without number, every sort of uniform, the costumes of all the orders in Europe, splendid furs, pelisses, etc'; and a dozen pairs of new corduroy riding breeches which had been ordered years after he had given up riding.[17] Perhaps, rather sadly, he dreamt of one day becoming thin enough again to be able to make use of them. Considering that his last attempts to get on a horse had been by means of a specially built ramp in 1816, it seems unlikely that he would have succeeded. The sorry state of the Prince's condition at the time is implicit in a solemn account of the event in *The Times*:

It is true that the Prince has been on horseback, and has rode for some time about the Pavilion lawn. An inclined plane was constructed, rising to about the height of two feet and a half, at the upper end of which was a platform. His Royal Highness was placed in a chair on rollers, and so moved up the ascent, and placed on the platform, which was then raised by screws, high enough to pass the horse under; and, finally, his Royal Highness was let gently down into the saddle. By this means the Regent was undoubtedly enabled to enjoy in some degree the benefit of air and exercise; but the exercise implied little of spontaneous muscular power, and cannot, certainly, be considered as a criterion of renovated strength.[18]

By this time he was not only obese but almost immobilized by gout.

There were many more specialist shops during the Regency than there are today, small emporiums of craftsmen who had dedicated their lives to perfecting one particular skill. Messrs William and Son, of St Martin's Lane, made buttons to order, in ivory, leather, horn, silk, silver, gold and precious stones. There were shops which made only whips, or spurs, or swords; there were specialist linen drapers as well as more mundane haberdashers, cap makers as well as hatters, glove makers and hosiers. White silk stockings, embroidered with rich lace clocks, cost 30 shillings a pair and hand-sewn leather tan doe gloves 5s.[19] The Prince went to one tailor for his breeches, another for his uniforms and others for his coats. His collection of beautiful leather sabretaches and pouches were decorated with silver lace and silver spangles and finished off with a cluster of glittering Prince of Wales feathers made of gold wire. Plumassiers no longer exist today but they played a most important part in Regency wardrobes. Feathers were an essential, and expensive, feature of court dress. A single plume could cost as much as 16 guineas. The feathers of egrets, birds of paradise and peacocks were all popular as well as the more mundane ostrich plumes; and each came with its own specially made decorative case. The best perfumers at the time were a French firm, Bourgeois Amick and Son, with premises in the Haymarket. Both men and women wore scent as a matter of course, as well as cosmetics. The Prince used eau de Cologne, eau de Nile (*sic*), lavender water, Oil of Roses, Oil of Jasmine and Oil of Orange Flower as well as 'Bergamotte', another scented oil, and a cosmetic listed as 'Clouts d'Italie'.[20] Other items which feature regularly in the accounts include perfumed powder, almond paste and pots of pomatum, along with 'camphire wash-balls', which cost a shilling each, and toothpicks, which came in packs of 100.

The Prince was clearly unable to pass a jewellery shop without buying what he referred to as a 'trinket', meaning anything from a diamond tiara to a butterfly brooch with emerald eyes. Among the fashionable jewellers he patronized were Hamlet's – whose customers included the Duke of York, the Duchess of Gloucester and various foreign royals – Thomas Gray in Sackville Street and Phillips in Bond Street.[21] But his favourite by far was Rundell and Bridge, on Ludgate Hill, the principal goldsmiths and jewellers at the time. It is hardly surprising that Rundell referred to the Prince, in a letter dated 1 December 1807, as 'our greatest Patron & best Friend'. Over the years the Prince spent hundreds of thousands of pounds on plate and jewellery, most of it at Rundell's. They provided him with a never-ending supply of 'trinkets' which he gave away: rings, medals, fans, gold boxes and amulets as well as more serious jewellery. Bracelets, at the time, always came in pairs and were intended to be worn over long gloves. He ordered a whole series of jewelled butterflies, and another of brooches pierced by a diamond arrow for his various lady-friends. At one time amethysts came into fashion, particularly if set with diamonds, so the Prince, as usual, ordered several sets: one such, headed by a long amethyst necklace set with twenty-two 'brilliants', included both long and short ear-rings, two bracelets, three brooches of different sizes and an amethyst and diamond crescent hair comb.[22] The bill from Rundell and Bridge, for that month alone, October 1804, came to nearly £2000 and covered more than 30 pieces of new jewellery, including 8 bracelets and 4 brooches, plus various items of plate and several snuff boxes. Furthermore, it was the Prince's custom, on beginning a new affair, to present the lady in question with a portrait of himself, usually in the form of a miniature framed in diamonds or other bankable jewels: the alternative was a lock of his hair, in an equally decorative locket. Even though payment for all this finery often took years, Mr Rundell, when he died at the age of eighty, left between £1,400,000 and £1,500,000, most of it invested in the funds. During the financial panic after the war, Rundell offered to lend his own bankers money. Having started life as a penniless apprentice silversmith, he rose to become a partner in the firm during its most successful period, and by living as a miser all his life, amassed this incredible fortune. When his executors went to prove the will, they were told that it was the largest sum ever to have been registered at Doctors' Commons.[23]

The American minister's journal emphasizes yet again that, in the eyes of their visitors if not their own, the English, after the war, were regarded as the most prosperous nation in Europe, a status they were to maintain for more than a hundred years. Soon after he arrived, Richard Rush described a tour through the City:

Went through Temple Bar into the *city*, in contradistinction to the West-end of London, always called *town* . . . If I looked with any wonder on the throngs at the West-end, more cause is there for it here. The shops stand, side by side, for entire miles. The accumulation of things is amazing. It would seem impossible that there can be purchasers for them all, until you consider what multitudes there are to buy; then, you are disposed to ask how the buyers can be supplied. In the middle of the streets, coal-waggons and others as large, carts, trucks, vehicles of every sort, loaded in every way, are passing. They are in two close lines, reaching further than the eye can see, going reverse ways. The horses come so near to the foot pavement, which is crowded with people, that their hoofs, and the great wheels of the waggons, are only a few inches from them. In this manner the whole procession is in movement, with all its complicated noise. It confounds the senses to be among it all. You would anticipate constant accidents; yet they seldom happen . . . The Custom house, and black forest of ships below London Bridge, I saw by a glimpse: that was enough to show that the Thames was choked up with vessels and boats of every description, much after the manner that I beheld Cheapside and Fleet Street to be choked with vehicles that move on land . . .[24]

Others were less tolerant of the traffic, and complained that a walk round London was fraught with hazards. 'Then we wandered into the tumultuous City where you can get lost like an atom . . . and where, if you are not careful to look to right and left, you are in constant danger of being spitted by the shaft of a cabriolet which comes too near the footpath, or crushed to death by some diligence which has broke down and overturned.'[25] The *Traveller's Oracle* was much more indignant about traffic jams than accidents, particularly during what appears to have been the Regency rush hour. 'Never go into the City through the Strand, Fleet Street, and Cheapside, if you can avoid it, after twelve o'clock,' they advised, because, from that hour until five o'clock, they are crowded with Carriages and Carts ... If you go into the City on Mondays and Fridays, you will have to encounter *the most* BARBAROUS NUISANCE *that disgraces the British Capital* – droves of Oxen passing through its streets in the middle of the Day. That this is still suffered to continue in these times of universal improvement appears to us as wonderful as it is offensive.

The general confusion cannot have been helped by the craze for such contraptions as the 'Velocipede', or the 'Pedestrian Curricle'. The velocipede, commonly known as a 'Dandy Horse', was a progenitor of the bicycle but with no pedals, brakes or proper steering. Basically, the machine was a simple framework support-ing two wheels and a saddle, upon which the rider balanced and propelled himself along with his feet. It cost £8 and could be made to go at ten miles an hour – if the rider did not fall off or crash into someone else. The 'Pedestrian Curricle' was another fiendish invention which became the rage: it was a variation on the same theme, a cross between a hobby-horse and a bicycle. Young men dared each other to race down Piccadilly or St James's Street balanced on these machines, with obvious results. Harriet Granville describes yet another innovative form of transport, for which there was a craze in 1807. She thought it dangerous and wrote to her sister that she

was in a fever lest my grandmother should adopt it in London. It is the body of a sedan chair upon the legs of a Wheelbarrow, the two handles of which are strapped onto an unfortunate man's shoulders,* whose business it is to drag one from place to place, with this great inconvenience to oneself that when he has taken his first Spring, there is no possibility of stopping him if he was disposed to take one to the world's end. My grandmother is so enraptured with this safe conveyance that it is ten to one, by the time you arrive, you do not meet John Mathews wheeling her up St James's Street.[26]

---

* This sounds very like a bicycle rickshaw, which is still the most common form of transport in most Indian cities. Properly handled, it was quite safe.

The worst of London, in the unanimous opinion of visitors, was the notorious pea-soup fog which used to obliterate the city for days at a time. It was sometimes impossible to see more than a few yards ahead, so that all social life as well as commerce came to a halt. Foreigners, who had never encountered anything like this particular phenomenon, were particularly affected: Princess Lieven wrote that it 'gives a vivid picture of chaos and the void. There is something positively hellish in the effect exerted by the sight of that opaque atmosphere.' Another visitor complained that 'the fog was so thick that the shops in Bond Street had lights at noon. I could not see people in the street from my windows. I am tempted to ask how the English became so great with so little day-light?' In fact, these 'pea-soups' were not so much fog as smog, which was endemic in a city heated by coal. Furthermore, by the beginning of the nineteenth century most London houses had installed one of the new, closed kitchen stoves, in place of open fires, and these cookers, though much more efficient than their predecessors, burnt even greater quantities of coal. It was the emission of smoke from such stoves, added to that of the new factories, which combined to create the smog. A distinguished doctor, Sir Frederick Treves, writing at the end of the century when the problem had become acute, estimated that, during a London fog, a square mile of air contained six *tons* of soot, which killed people 'not by scores and hundreds, but by thousands'.

Nevertheless, Londoners made the best of their city whatever the weather. In 1814 when the Thames froze over, for the last time in its history, they held a fair on the solid ice. Within a few days the first tentative booths were put up on the ice and a wide thoroughfare, nicknamed 'Freezeland Street', spanned the frozen river from side to side. It was lined with booths and stalls selling all sorts of food and fairings: a slice of meat sold better when labelled as 'Lapland Mutton'. There was an atmosphere of carnival with swings, skittles, toy shops, gambling booths, bookstalls and even a dozen printing presses, churning out the latest satirical prints and drawings of the scene. Other attractions of the Great Frost Fair included 'The Wheel of Fortune, Pricking the Garter, and Te-Totums'; there were pedlars, hawkers and perambulating piemen, selling everything from ballads and prints to oysters and gin, brandy-balls and gingerbread. As usual, the Frost Fair triggered a spate of popular songs and doggerel, such as the following:

> All you that are curious downright,
> And fond of seeing every sight,
> If to the Thames you had repair'd,
> You might have seen a famous fair.
> Diversions of every kind you'd see,
> With parties drinking of coffee and tea,
> And dancing too, I do declare,
> Upon the *Thames*, they call FROST FAIR.
>
> It was really curious for to see
> Both old and young so full of glee,
> The drinking booths they enter'd in
> And call'd away for purl and gin,
> Some play'd at Thread my Needle, Nan,
> The lasses slipt down as they ran,
> Which made the men quite full of glee
> The young girls legs for all to see.[27]

As usual, there were several more verses in the same vein.

All the year round, Regency London revelled in noisy pleasure. Possibly the summers really were better two hundred years ago, or perhaps people were just hardier; whatever the reason, it is obvious from contemporary journals that those who could afford to do so spent far more of their time out of doors, even in London, than their descendants do today. Society loved all forms of entertaining alfresco: 'breakfasts', which began at noon and lasted all day, picnics and *fêtes champêtres*, river-boat parties and expeditions to watch a balloon ascent in Hyde Park, admire the flowers at Kew or to ride in Richmond Park. Nor was it necessary to go so far afield; central London at the time was dotted with unexpected greens and gardens, oases in the city which were open to all for the price of a few pennies.

There was a 'Tea Garden' on the site of King's Cross railway station during the Regency and another at Pancras Wells. At the 'Adam and Eve' tea garden they kept cows and sold syllabubs made from their cream. 'Harmony and Decorum', according to their own publicity, were the rule at Marylebone Gardens, where Handel was a regular visitor and would sit listening to his own compositions played by the band. An advertisement announced that

Mr Trusler's daughter begs leave to inform the nobility and gentry that she intends to make fruit tarts during the fruit season, and hopes to give equal satisfaction as with the rich cakes and almond cheesecakes. The fruit will always be fresh gathered, having good quantities in the garden, and none but loaf sugar used and the finest Epping butter. Tarts of a twelvepenny size will be made every day from one to three o'clock. New and rich seed and plum cakes are sent to any part of town.[28]

By 1826, however, Marylebone Gardens, and the fields around them, had disappeared for ever, giving way to Cavendish Square and Portman Place. Islington Spa was one of the most fashionable watering places during the eighteenth century and lasted well into the Regency: it was known as the New Tunbridge Wells, in deference to the supposed medicinal properties of its spring of 'chalybeate' water. One contemporary writer described the spa as 'a very pretty and romantick place', and another, after writing about the beauty of the gardens, adds that 'Pedestals and vases are grouped under some extremely picturesque trees, whose foliage is seen to much advantage from the neighbouring fields.' This was in 1803: by 1810, however, Charlotte Street, later renamed Thomas Street, had been built on part of the site and by 1840 these gardens had vanished as well, buried under rows of new houses.

The gentle charm of the tea gardens, however, was no match for the increasing splendour of Vauxhall, with all its lights and glories. By the end of the eighteenth century it was clear that spectacular entertainment was needed to draw the crowds: balloon ascents and firework displays, such as the Prince Regent organized for his many fêtes. Similarly, as the nineteenth century progressed, buns and ginger beer in Regent's Park took the place of Spanish *olio* and China tea in the Mulberry Gardens which once graced the area now dominated by Buckingham Palace. The heyday of Ranelagh Gardens was already over: they were thought to have become rather vulgar by the fastidious beaux of the Regency, too full of riff-raff and 'Cits'. Nevertheless the Pic-nic Society gave a breakfast there for 2000 people, which featured a balloon ascent by the French aviator Garnerin. The gardens at Ranelagh could be hired for private parties and the Spanish ambassador once gave a great ball there for 900 people. In 1803 a Peace Fête was held at Ranelagh, for which the booths were specially decorated with allegorical paintings, but a year later the buildings were demolished.

The gardens of Vauxhall, on the other hand, became ever more popular; 'Vauxhall . . . redolent of groves and nightingales and whispering lovers',[29] the venue for any number of fêtes, *ridottos al fresco*, masquerades, concerts and splendid entertainments. When the gardens were first laid out they were enclosed on the western side by a high brick wall, and on the other three by hayfields and open country. The whole area was designed on a grid, or parallelogram, with groves of trees divided by gravel walks which crossed each other at right angles. By the time of the Regency the gardens had become a maze of secluded alleys, groves and secret arbours. The names of the various walks indicate one of the main attractions of Vauxhall: the Dark Walk, the Druid's Walk and the blatantly named Lovers' Walk, for example. There was even an official, specially created, 'Wilderness', while another area of the garden was left open, to give a view of the river, and designated the 'Rural Downs'. Man-made caves, grottos and waterfalls represented the contemporary passion for the picturesque, and marble statues dotted throughout the gardens added the necessary classical dimension. There was a specially commissioned statue of Handel, whose music often featured in the concerts held regularly throughout the summer, and another of Milton, cast in lead and looking out over the downs.

The central square at Vauxhall was surrounded by temples, pavilions, rotundas, and a number of other specially built rooms, all dedicated to the arts. There was a large concert hall and a picture gallery as well as a dance floor, and rows of booths which sold fairings. The whole area was ringed by colonnades sheltering the supper boxes, each decorated and hung with paintings to illustrate a particular theme. Several of the boxes had been decorated by Hogarth, one of Vauxhall's earliest patrons. These paintings and murals included an original painting of Henry VIII and Anne Boleyn, copies of his series *The Four Times of Day*, and another original mural of popular sports, including *See-Saw, Leap-Frog, Sliding on the Ice* and *Milkmaids Dancing Round a Maypole*. (When the Hogarth paintings from Vauxhall were sold at auction in 1841 they were deemed too old and dirty to be worth serious money. One canvas, nailed to a board, of *A Drunken Man*, fetched 4 guineas, and another, of *A Woman Pulling out an Old Man's Grey Hairs*, only 3 guineas. *The Happy Family* went for £3 15s and *Children at Play* £4 11s 6d.) But the great innovation at Vauxhall was the lighting. The genius of the gardens, a Mr Tyers, who originally designed Vauxhall, was one of the first to appreciate the dramatic potential of the new gas lighting. More than a thousand lamps were concealed in the trees – coloured lamps, illuminated stars, chandeliers and lanterns reflected each other in revolving mirrors. Moreover they were linked together, so that, at a given signal, and accompanied by a crash of music from the orchestra, the whole garden would suddenly light up in 'a rich blaze of radiance'. Mr Tyers was an expert in creating special effects: when the management put on a particularly lavish pageant re-enacting the Battle of Waterloo, he lit the scene with an extra 20,000 lamps. Both the Prince Regent and the Duke of Wellington went to see it, along with several hundred thousand others during the course of the season. Everything at Vauxhall was carried to extremes: the food was as much a speciality of the gardens as the décor and lighting, particularly their delicious cold chicken and ham. The *Connoisseur* found the chickens no bigger than a sparrow while the wafer-thin slices of the ham were legendary. Patrons of the gardens declared that you could read the *Morning Post* or the *Chronicle* 'with perfect ease through the transparent medium of the delicate Vauxhall ham'.

Vauxhall Gardens were an immediate and lasting success, the most favoured alfresco haunt of Londoners for more than a hundred years. Several generations after they were built standards had not declined: from Dr Johnson's description of Vauxhall as 'that excellent place of amusement', to Thackeray's of 'the twinkling boxes in which the happy feasters made believe to eat almost invisible slices of ham', the praise was unanimous. As to the clientele, it appears to have ranged from royalty to chorus girls. According to another encomium, 'even bishops have been seen [there] without injuring their character.'

Originally, the price of admission was only a shilling, but in 1791 this was doubled and the tone of the gardens began to change. During the eighteenth century Vauxhall had relied on the charm of its surroundings, the excellence of its suppers and the weekly concerts to attract the customers; by the nineteenth the mood of the public had changed, particularly that of the rising new middle class, and people wanted more value for their money. Vauxhall gave it to them: there were balloon ascents, acrobats, panoramas of the Arctic, Indian jugglers, circus horses, tightrope dancers and terrific firework displays. A special tower was built for the fireworks, with a large platform and a sixty-feet-high mast from which the 'ethereal Saqui' descended, tiptoeing down on a tightrope 'in a blaze of blue flame and Chinese fire'.

The Prince Regent, always a glutton for extravaganza, adored Vauxhall and often entertained there. Not everyone, however, enjoyed the Prince's great parties: Harriet Cavendish was distinctly unenthusiastic about the crush and lack of organization at a fête in honour of the Prince's birthday which he gave at Vauxhall in 1802. Writing to her sister, Lady Georgiana, Viscountess Morpeth, she complained that

... we formed 8 of the 14,000 people assembled at Vauxhall ... and after having been nearly squeezed to Death, sat 2 hours and a half in a carriage without a possibility of moving one way or the other.

Mr Hare, Monsieur de Calonne and Frederick Foster were our only attendants and Mr Hare said he really could never have believed that any public amusement could have the power to make him so completely miserable. Frederick really *angry* and *affronted*, has been *sulky* ever since, and Lady Eliz, *nervous*, so you see our expedition was not very successful.[30]

The fête given by the Prince at Vauxhall to celebrate the victory of Vittoria in 1813 was a fiasco. It was billed as the 'most splendid and magnificent' fête ever to be held in England and began with a grand dinner for more than a thousand guests, including all the royal Dukes. However, as soon as the public began to arrive after the dinner, it was obvious that the organizers had wildly overestimated the number of people the gardens could accommodate, and the evening collapsed into an angry scrum. Although the original demand for tickets was such that the price rose to more than 15 guineas on the black market, many of those who had bought them never even got into the gardens. The Duchess of York had to wait in her carriage for two hours outside the gardens before the coachman could force a passage through the crowds to the gate; no places had been reserved for the ladies, who had been summoned to arrive at 9.00 p.m. (the gentlemen had dined at 5.00), and they ended up having to 'scramble for refreshments, and the hardiest were but ill-requited'. Colonel Torrens, who had been dragooned into organizing the fête, complained afterwards that he was 'half ruined by the expense, exclusive of having had my carriage broken to pieces in the scramble.' Even the *Gentleman's Magazine*, usually so sycophantic about the Prince's parties, admitted that 'The obstructions to getting in and retiring, after twelve o'clock, became almost impossible; and such a scene of confusion scarcely ever existed.'[31] To complete the Prince's discomfiture, at one point in the evening the Princess of Wales turned up, was refused a seat in the royal box, and departed in a rage.

An account written shortly after the gardens were closed in 1859 laments the slow decline of one of the great attractions of London:

Though Vauxhall Gardens retained their plan to the last, the lamps had long fallen off in their golden fires; the punch got weaker, the admission-money less; and the company fell in a like ratio of respectability, and grew dingy, not to say raffish, a sorry falling-off from the Vauxhall crowd of a century since, when . . . 'on its tide and torrent of fashion floated all the beauty of the time; and through its lighted avenues of trees glided cabinet ministers and their daughters, royal dukes and their wives, and all the red-heeled macaronis'. Even fifty years ago, the evening costume of the company was elegant: head-dresses of flowers and feathers were seen in the promenade, and the entire place sparkled as did no other place of public amusement. But low prices brought low company. The conventional wax-lights got fewer; the punch gave way to fiery brandy or doctored stout. The semblance of Vauxhall was still preserved in the orchestra printed on the plates and mugs; and the old fire-work bell tinkled as gaily as ever. But matters grew more seedy; the place seemed literally worn out; the very trees were scrubby and singed; and it was high time to say, as well as see, in letters of lamps, 'Farewell for ever![32]

Vauxhall was a democratic playground, open to one and all, but Hyde Park, during the Regency, had become the preserve of the upper classes. The cavalcade of carriages and horsemen which circled the Ring every afternoon was said to be the most splendid in Europe: Mary Berry, writing from Paris after the war, compared it to Longchamps,

where all the English received the consoling assurance that the worst Sunday that ever shone on Hyde Park produces twenty times more handsome equipages than this one day of Gala for all the Horses and Carriages of Paris. Longchamps was a thing of dirty Cabriolets and Hackney coaches, interspersed with here and there a clean Barouche and one or two foreign coaches and four.[33]

Captain Gronow confirmed her opinion, writing of Hyde Park with snobbish delight that:

The company which then congregated daily about five was composed of dandies and women in the best society; the men mounted on such horses as England alone could then produce . . . Many of the ladies

LEARNING TO DRIVE TANDEM
Caricature by Henry Alken, published by McLean, 1823.
Driving was a much-valued accomplishment and a matter of intense rivalry amongst the young men of fashion.

used to drive into the park in a carriage called a *vis-à-vis*, which held only two persons. The hammer-cloth, rich in heraldic designs, the powdered footmen in smart liveries, and a coachman who assumed all the gaiety and appearance of a wigged archbishop, were indispensable. The equipages were generally much more gorgeous than at a later period, when democracy invaded the parks, and introduced what may be termed a 'Brummagem society,' with shabby-genteel carriages and servants. The carriage company consisted of the most celebrated beauties; and in those earlier days you never saw any of the lower or middle classes of London intruding themselves in regions which, with a sort of tacit understanding, were given up exclusively to persons of rank and fashion.[34]

The Prince Regent used to drive himself round Hyde Park in a tilbury – one of the more dashing open carriages – with his groom sitting by his side (a practice which was thought most undignified by senior members of the Court). The Prince was an excellent whip in his youth, capable of handling even so difficult a vehicle as a high-perch phaeton drawn by a team of six horses, and both prided himself on his driving and enjoyed it. 'Skill with the ribbons', i.e. driving ability, was an accomplishment much admired and the subject of much ribald comment. Tommy Onslow, one of the dandies, always drove a black phaeton drawn by jet black horses, and was a master of the art: it was, however, his only claim to recognition, hence the popular ditty:

> What can little Tommy do?
> Drive a phaeton and two.
> Can little Tommy do no more?
> Yes – drive a phaeton and four.

The craze for driving themselves, amongst the young men of fashion (rather than depending on the services of a professional coachman), lent itself to all sorts of silly jokes: for example spoof advertisements, such as this one, in the *Gentleman's Magazine*:

FASHIONABLE DRIVING

AMOS PYEBALD begs leave to present his respects to the Nobility and Gentry, and to inform them that he intends opening an Academy for the instruction of Amateurs in the above branch of Polite Science. The Unicorn & Four-in-Hand will be taught by Masters of approved science; and the Tandem, Random, Harum-Scarum, Break-Neck, and Dead Certainty, by A.P. himself.

N.B. There will always be a coach with four sham horses in the Academy; so that elderly Gentlemen, and those who have families, or are constitutionally timid, may learn to mount and dismount the box, keep a firm seat, and handle the whip and reins before they turn out . . .[35]

Further affectations engendered by this particular passion included copying the dress and speech of the most vulgar and raucous of the professional coachmen, the men who drove the stagecoaches. Young men of fashion found it amusing to litter their conversation with the bawdy slang of the road and some even went to the trouble of having their teeth filed down so that they could whistle like the coachmen: one eccentric aristocrat paid 50 guineas to the driver of the Cambridge Telegraph coach, who was known as 'Hell Fire Dick', for lessons in spitting in the correct style of the professionals. Sir John Lade and Lord Barrymore, notable whips, were among those who indulged in this kind of behaviour. Lord Barrymore was one of the founders of the Whip Club as well as the ultra-exclusive Four-in-Hand Club, known as the FHC, to which only the very best drivers were admitted and whose members distinguished themselves by wearing bright yellow striped and spotted waistcoats. Gronow described his first sight of Barrymore, in Hyde Park one summer afternoon:

The weather was charming, and a great number of the *bon ton* had assembled to witness the departure of the 'Four-in-hand Club'. Conspicuous among all the 'turn-outs' was that of his Lordship, who drove four splendid greys, unmatched in symmetry, action and power.

It was said that few coachmen on the Great North Road could 'tool' a four-in-hand as well as Barrymore, and that his language while doing so was equally authentic.

If there had been a competitive examination, the prize of which would have been given to the most proficient in slang and vulgar phraseology, it would have been safe to back his Lordship as the winner against the most foul-mouthed of costermongers; for the way he blackguarded his servants for the misadjustment of a strap was horrifying.[36]

Byron ridiculed these noble coachmen in his poem 'The Devil's Drive':

> The Devil first saw, as he thought, the mail,
> Its coachman and his coat;
> So instead of a pistol, he cocked his tail,
> And seized him by the throat.
> 'Aha!' quoth he, 'what have we here?
> 'Tis a new barouche and an ancient peer!'

So he sat him on his box again,
And bade him have no fear,
But be true to his club, and staunch to his rein,
His brothel and his beer;
'Next to seeing a lord at the council board,
I would rather see him here.'

6

FROM THE SEASIDE RESORTS TO THE NORTHERN MEETING

London may have been the epicentre of the fashionable world, and the Mecca of the socially ambitious, but the priorities of the great families of the Regency were still firmly centred on their country estates. Their status as well as their wealth derived from the land; their primary obligations were to their tenants and dependants, and their principal homes were the castles and mansions built by the founding members of their dynasties. These were their roots, and it was to these that they would always return from whatever perambulations their particular lives dictated. Nevertheless, the beau monde spent much of the year on the move. As a general rule summers were spent in the country and winters in the nearest attractive town. Those in the North who did not aspire to a house in London would hire one in York, for example, for the winter months; in Scotland the lairds and their families moved to Edinburgh. Others migrated to the South – to Bath, or Cheltenham and similarly clement resorts to escape the harsh isolation of country winters.

The pattern of their lives varied, of course, according to the interests and duties of those involved. At the beginning of the nineteenth century the House of Commons sat for no more than four or five months in the winter,* which meant that even politicians were free to pursue their own inclinations for the rest

* Between October and March. The exact dates varied from year to year.

of the year. The sportsman's year revolved around the hunting and shooting seasons; the racing enthusiast's round the major race meetings; the health fanatic's round the various spas; and the dedicated socialite's round the fashionable resorts, each of which had its own particular attraction. The peak of the social year was the London season, which began in March and ended in June. (Princess Lieven, a woman who delighted in the pretensions of others, noted that those who remained in London after the season was officially over would disguise their presence at such an unfashionable time by closing the shutters on the street side of their houses and retreating to the rooms at the back.)[1] As the season in London ended, that of the resorts began, in particular those by the sea.

It is often assumed that Brighton was no more than a simple fishing village prior to the Regency but, in fact, it had been growing in popularity since the middle of the eighteenth century and was already established as a fashionable resort by the time of the Prince's arrival. It was the town's reputation as the centre of a smart, and slightly raffish, society which attracted the Prince in the first place. In his youth he was forbidden to go there. According to Horace Walpole, when the Prince was invited to Brighton by his disreputable uncle, the Duke of Cumberland, he replied, 'I cannot come to see you now without the King's leave, but in three years I shall be of age, and then I may act for myself. I declare I will visit you.'[2] This was in 1780, by which time the town had already accumulated a nucleus of regular visitors, including the Duke of Gloucester, who came for the first time in 1765, Dr Johnson, Fanny Burney and the Duke of Marlborough as well as the Duke and Duchess of Cumberland.

Initially, Brighton's popularity, particularly with the over-indulgent upper classes, was due to the eighteenth-century belief in the medicinal properties of sea water. A Sussex physician, Dr Richard Russell, was the man who could really be said to have 'invented' Brighton. He set up his practice in the town and published a treatise on the beneficial effects of salt water as a cure for almost everything, from 'fluxions of redundant tumours',

MERMAIDS AT BRIGHTON
Caricature by William H. Heath, published by McLean, 1828.
By the end of the eighteenth century the beneficial effects of sea water were firmly established. Treatments involved drinking it as well as bathing and rubbing the body with seaweed

via rheumatism, madness and consumption to impotence and rabies. The treatments involved drinking the sea water as well as bathing in it and rubbing the body with seaweed. It was also to be mixed with such ingredients as viper's flesh, crab's eyes, tar, snails and 'prepared wood lice' and taken as a pill, to be washed down by a pint of pure sea water. As a drink, it could be made more palatable by adding milk, in which case the two liquids combined 'became a noble medicine'. The sea was even bottled and sold to those living inland: an advertisement in a London journal announced that the genuine 'Oceanic fluid' from 'Brighthelmstone', as it was still called, could be bought at the Talbot Inn at Southwark. Dr Russell, who was well ahead of his time by the received ideas of the medical profession, realized the benefit of fresh air, particularly in the case of delicate children. 'I have had children sent to me,' he wrote, weak, pale, loaded with hair, their necks and throats wrapt up in flannel, and, in short, the whole texture of the body relaxed by too hot clothing, and night sweats; whom I have returned to their parents, bare necked, their heads shaved, the tumours of the neck cured, and their whole countenance healthy, after having strengthened them by bathing in the sea.[3]

By the end of the eighteenth century indoor bathing, in both hot and cold sea water, was possible as well for those too timid to venture into the sea. The new baths and the new Assembly Rooms, both designed by the same architect, were evidence of the town's growing prosperity. In the first decade of the nineteenth century the population of Brighton doubled and the number of houses increased nearly threefold.

Brighton may have been launched as a health resort but it very soon acquired an alternative reputation. It was the staid and serious Dr Russell's own son who first identified the town with love and pleasure:

> Brighthelmstone was confess'd by all
> T'abound with females fair,
> But more so since fam'd Russell has
> Preferred the waters there.
>
> Then fly that dangerous town ye swains,
> For fear ye shall endure
> A pain from some bright sparkling eye
> Which Russell's skill can't cure.

In 1784 the *Morning Herald* confirmed the image, writing that the town 'is the centre luminary of the system of pleasure . . . the women, the pretty women all hasten to see the Paris of the day.'

During the Regency there were two sets of Assembly Rooms in Brighton, one at the Castle Inn and one at the Old Ship. The ballroom at the Castle was designed in the style of Robert Adam, a double-cube eighty feet long and forty feet high and wide, beautifully decorated with classical mouldings, columns and a painted frieze: as for the suite of rooms* at the Ship, rebuilt in 1775, their splendour was described at the time as 'not to be excelled ... by any in England that of York excepted.' During the summer months the Castle held a ball every Monday night and the Ship every Thursday; on Wednesdays and Fridays there were card parties in the Assembly Rooms and on Sundays a Promenade and a Public Tea. A Master of Ceremonies organized the social schedule 'not according to the scale of morality, but that of aristocracy.' A most important functionary in the life of the town, he was also expected to vet the company, exclude undesirables and effect introductions: 'The Master of Cere-monies,' according to a contemporary source,

became Dictator, he promulgated laws, and all willingly yielded obedi-ence. Hence the first duty of visitors to Brighton was to pay their respects to him. Mothers with marriageable daughters were anxious to stand in his good places; the unprotected maiden of uncertain age, the lone dowager, reluctant to relinquish her waning opportunities of shining in society, each sheltered herself under his aegis; the portionless cons, or it may be needy adventurers, seeking prizes in the matrimonial market, assiduously sought his favour; the proprietors of the respective assembly rooms were content to do him homage; and as for the town authorities, such as they were at this period, they neither interfered, nor sought to interfere, in the domains over which the sway of the 'M.C.' extended.[4]

For those who found the atmosphere of the Assembly Rooms too formal, Brighton had plenty of other attractions to offer. In 1798 Sarah Siddons gave the first of many performances at the newly built theatre in North Street and Mrs Jordan appeared for a short season in 1800. Another celebrated actress of the day, Harriet Mellon, left the stage to marry Thomas Coutts, the banker, when he was in his eighty-sixth year; after his death she married the Duke of St Albans and became the leading hostess

---

* A ballroom, supper room and card room. This was the usual arrangement in all Assembly Rooms throughout the country. Some included a billiard room and extra facilities for private parties.

in Brighton, as well as a notable philanthropist. The theatre in Brighton, however – and despite the patronage of the Prince of Wales, Mrs Fitzherbert and the other influential members of society – was never particularly successful. The Brighton races, inaugurated in 1783 by a group of noblemen led by the Dukes of Cumberland and Queensberry, were a much greater draw. Within a few years booths and stalls lined the racecourse and a new stand had been built for the spectators, which 'For convenience and elegance . . . challenges any in the Kingdom.'* It was Brighton Camp, however, and the arrival of the Guards in 1793, which set the seal on the glamorous image of the town. As Jane Austen wrote in *Pride and Prejudice*:

In Lydia's imagination a visit to Brighton comprized every possibility of earthly happiness. She saw with the creative eye of fancy, the streets of that gay bathing-place covered with officers. She saw herself the object of attention to tens and scores of them at present unknown. She saw all the glories of the camp – its tents stretched forth in beauteous uniformity of lines, crowded with the young and gay, and dazzling with scarlet; and to complete the view, she saw herself seated beneath a tent, tenderly flirting with at least six officers at once.

The army was under the command of the Prince himself, acting as Colonel-in-Chief of his own regiment, the 10th Hussars. Most of the officers were his personal friends, including the smartest and most eligible young men in the country. It was a company dedicated to riotous pleasure, as *The Times* reported censoriously.

They [the 10th Hussars] associate with no one but their own corps. Most of them keep their own blood horses, their curricles and their girls. At one o'clock they appear on parade to hear the word of command given by the subaltern guard; afterwards they toss off their *goes* of brandy, dine about five, and come about eight to the theatre. *Vivent, l'Amour et Bacchus.*

---

* According to a cartoon by Rowlandson, made in 1791, this was not strictly true. The stand was only big enough to accommodate twenty-four people, in six boxes.

A local paper was equally sanctimonious on the subject of the camp-followers: 'The Cyprian corps* stationed in this town is now estimated to amount to over 300, exclusive of those at Brighton camp.' He feels that the situation whereby these 'good-natured but unfortunate creatures' are supported by the 'wages of prostitution casts a melancholy reflection on the increasing depravity of the age'.

The Prince of Wales's *modus vivendi* during his early years at the Marine Pavilion would have done little to set this particular writer's mind at ease. In 1785, after the Prince and his friends had spent a second summer in the town, the *Morning Chronicle* reported that:

The visit of a certain gay, illustrious character at Brighton, has frightened away a number of old maids, who used constantly to frequent that place. The history of the gallantries of the last season, which is constantly in circulation, has something in it so voluminous, and tremendous to boot, that the old tabbies shake in their shoes whenever his R — H — is mentioned.

The Prince of Wales came to Brighton to escape: from his father, from the formality of the Court and from the numerous restrictions on his liberty, imposed by the King. When he first arrived in the town, in 1783, he rented a house on the Steyne. Four years later he began to rebuild it, though still paying rent, and by 1793 had bought the house outright. The transformation of a relatively modest building† into the Pavilion as it stands today took more than thirty years and involved a series of architects, a commensurate number of different styles and a fortune. The first architect employed on the project was Henry Holland, who designed a simple classical villa, described by Horace Walpole as a 'chaste palace' of 'august simplicity'. Too

* 'Cyprian' was a Regency euphemism for a prostitute.
† Sydney Smith referred to the original building as 'a respectable farmhouse' and one of the Prince's early biographers called it 'a singularly pretty pictur-esque cottage in a small piece of ground where a few shrubs and roses shut out the road and the eye looked undisturbed over the ocean.'

simple for the Prince, however, and within a few years the Pavilion had begun to assume the aspect of an Indian mogul's palace, with various additions in the form of domes or columns. The Indian phase was mercifully short-lived and evolved, eventually, and via any number of modifications, into the conglomeration of Oriental styles represented in the finished product. The Pavilion is a supreme example of exotic folly, 'a paradigm of fairyland': at the time it was built it was also an important showcase for the latest technology. The Prince installed gas lighting, bathrooms, water closets, the latest kitchen gadgets and a form of central heating. One of the recurrent complaints about the Pavilion, however, was that the Prince insisted on keeping the rooms far too hot. As early as 1796 *The New Brighton Guide* compared the dining-room to 'a sort of oven', adding that 'when the fire is lighted the Inmates are nearly baked or incrusted'; and George Hanger, one of the Prince's friends, described it as 'Hot, hot, hot as hell.'

By 1818 the Pavilion was more or less finished although minor alterations continued for another four years. The building was an architectural sensation, but not everyone liked it. Sydney Smith, for example, wrote that it looked 'as though the Dome of St Paul's had gone down to the sea and pupped.' The radical Cobbett thought it was hideous and vulgar as well as a shocking waste of public money. He likened the Pavilion to a collection of large, sawn-off turnips or 'a parcel of cradle-spits: of various dimensions, sticking up out of the mouths of so many enormous decanters.'

As for the interior decoration of the building, for the first few years the Prince changed his mind with every new architect and every new vagary of fashion. The original designs, by Holland, were based on the French style of décor but with brighter colours, painted ceilings and an emphasis on gilt, mirrors and marble. The fittings were sumptuous: the Prince slept in a suitably gorgeous bed, lined with green and white checked silk, with a white satin mattress and white satin sheets. (At Carlton House his bedroom must have been even more daunting to the elderly ladies who joined him in it: the royal couch stood on a dais, draped with masses of gold satin brocade, and crowned with waving ostrich feathers.) The Oriental theme which dominates the interior of the Pavilion to the present day dates from 1802, when the Prince was presented with several rolls of particularly beautiful Chinese wallpaper. The paper was used to decorate a room specially created for the purpose, the Chinese Gallery. *Chinoiserie* was, of course, already well known in England but had gone out of fashion by the beginning of the nineteenth century. Such was the impact and success of the new Gallery, however, that the Prince decided to re-introduce the Oriental style throughout the building. Furniture and artefacts of all kinds were imported from the Far East. There were Japanese lacquer cabinets and bamboo sofas; Ming porcelain, delicate ivory models of Chinese junks and pagodas decorated the tables; Chinese lanterns hung from the ceilings and life-size imitation fishermen, dressed in real Chinese robes, stood in the niches of the corridors. The effect was delightful: 'Today I have been going all over the Pavilion, which is really beautiful in its way,' Lady Bessborough wrote in 1805. 'I did not think the strange Chinese shapes and columns could have look'd so well. It is like Concetti in Poetry, in *outré* and false taste, but for the kind of thing as perfect as it can be.'

Lady Bessborough, unlike some of the Prince's guests in later years, enjoyed staying at the Pavilion. 'His way of living is pleasant enough,' she continued,

especially if one might chuse one's society. In the Morning he gives you horses, Carriages etc., to go where you please . . . he comes and sits rather too long, but only on a visit. Everybody meets at dinner, which, par parenthèse, is excellent, with the addition of a few invitations in the evening. Three large rooms, very comfortable are lit up; whist, backgammon, Chess, trace Madame – every sort of game you can think of in two of them, and Musick in the third. His band is beautiful. He has Viotti* and a Lady who sings and plays very well.

The Prince kept his own private orchestra at the Pavilion, on full salary all the year round, and brought the best opera singers

* Viotti was a leading violinist and his daughter, usually referred to as Mademoiselle Viotti, a popular soprano.

and musicians down to Brighton for the night to perform at his private parties. The Prince was in his element, either singing along with the star or conducting the band himself. When he was not actively joining in with the orchestra he would sit for hours on end beating his thighs in time to the music. As one habituée of these evenings wrote: 'It was a curious sight to see a Regent thus employed, but he seemed in high good humour.' Another letter from Brighton reports that 'the Regent was again all night in the Musick Room, and not content with presiding over the Band, but actually singing, and very loud too.' There was a continuous house-party at the Pavilion whenever the Prince was in residence, with thirty or forty people for dinner every night, and about the same number coming in afterwards. Everyone wore full evening dress, with the glorious uniforms of the military taking the honours: the officers of the Prince's own regiment looked like 'very ornamental monkeys in their red breeches with gold fringe and yellow boots'. Around midnight the pages and footmen served iced champagne punch, lemonade and sandwiches. The Prince was at his happiest and most benevolent on such occasions.

Some of his other guests were unimpressed, if not openly critical of the Pavilion. Princess Lieven, though no radical, disapproved as strongly as Cobbett of such an example of conspicuous consumption. She wrote to Metternich that a single chandelier had cost eleven thousand pounds,* and that the Pavilion had already – by 1820 – cost £700,000 and was 'still not fit to live in'. The Princess found the whole atmosphere stifling:

I do not believe that since the days of Heliogobalus, there have been such magnificence and such luxury. There is something effeminate in it which is disgusting ... One spends the evening half lying on cushions; the lights are dazzling; there are perfumes, music, liqueurs.

* To light the three rooms used by the family when they were alone cost 150 guineas an evening, according to one guest's computation. When the apartments were fully opened up for a party the cost was at least double.

Charles Greville, too, disliked staying there. He wrote that 'the gaudy splendour of the place amused me for a little and then bored me', and went on to complain that the food was cold and the company composed of bowing and smiling sycophants.

The Princess Lieven and Charles Greville, however, were describing the tenor of life at the Pavilion in the closing stages of the Regency period, the 1820s, when the once-glamorous Prince had disintegrated into an elderly, querulous and infirm recluse who refused to be seen in public, and whose only companions were a handful of courtiers and his mistress, Lady Conyngham. Thirty years earlier, in the heyday of the Pavilion, complaints against the Prince's house parties were of a different nature: the emphasis was on drink and practical jokes, and the guest list included some of the Prince's most dissolute friends, men such as George Hangar, 'Cripplegate' Barrymore and their like. There was 'Jockey', the drunken old Duke of Norfolk, 'Old Q', Tommy Onslow, and Sheridan, who could always be relied on to spice up the evening. On one occasion Sheridan roared into the drawing room disguised as a policeman bent on arresting the Dowager Lady Sefton for illegal gambling, and on another, when they were all sitting in the dark, watching a phantasmagoria,* he deposited himself on the lap of a particularly haughty Russian *grande dame*, who 'made row enough for the whole town to hear her'.[5] Brummell was one of the more respectable regulars, until he was forced into exile, and so were the Creeveys. A letter from Mrs Creevey to her husband, written in 1805 (by which time the host was in his forties) is full of complaints about the late hours and drunkenness of the Prince's parties at the Pavilion: 'Oh, this wicked Pavilion . . .' she wrote despairingly, knowing she would have to go there yet again. An invitation to the Pavilion amounted to a subpoena, but the Prince did not even have the courtesy to let his guests know they were wanted until the last minute. According to Mrs Creevey, who, with or without her husband, was on permanent 'stand-by' whenever the Prince was at Brighton, the invitation would never arrive until 9.00, which

---

* A phantasmagoria was a form of magic-lantern show.

threw her into a panic that they would be late: and that, she knew, would be an unforgivable solecism in the eyes of such a petulant and paranoid host. In the event, the Prince did not even appear in the drawing room until 11.00, when it was clear that 'he had got more wine than usual', while the chief guest, a German baron, was 'extremely drunk'. Later on, the Prince decided to show off his skill at shooting with an air gun, taking pot shots at a target set up in the map room, and insisted on the ladies having a turn as well, whereupon 'Lady Downshire hit a fiddler in the dining-room, Miss Johnson a door and Bloomfield the ceiling'.[6] No wonder the cartoonists loved the Prince.

The pattern of life at Brighton was repeated, with minor variations, at resorts all over the country. Margate, Ramsgate, Eastbourne and Weymouth all had their own clientele, who returned year after year to paddle in the sea, drink the waters, attend the assemblies and gossip or flirt. Inland, there were the spas, Cheltenham, Harrogate and Tunbridge Wells, to name but a few, all renowned for the healing property of the water from the local spring. Each had its master of ceremonies, particular patrons and established routine. In the evening there were the usual dances and card parties; in the afternoons the company took their daily 'constitutional', walking on the promenade or driving out to view the neighbouring beauty spots and on wet days they repaired to one of the new circulating libraries. Subscription libraries came into fashion towards the end of the eighteenth century and by the time of the Regency had become an integral part of the social scene. Most provided a set of communal rooms where people could meet and read the newspapers and magazines, drink coffee or just pass the time in relative peace and quiet. The more sophisticated offered their customers collections of the latest topical caricatures and prints to browse through on the premises, even to take out on loan, as well as all the latest novels. The cartoons, or 'squibs', were bound into large, loose-leafed books and laid out on round tables so that people could view them at leisure. Margate had one of the finest libraries on the coast and Sidmouth one of the most famous – it specialized in educational toys as well as children's books. By the turn of the century every provincial town of consequence had at least one public library and often two or three.*

All summer long, itinerant entertainers toured the resorts all over the country. Jugglers, magicians and fortune tellers followed in the wake of the seasonal fairs; there were circuses and magic-lantern shows, concerts, pantomimes and puppet shows – as well as all the best London productions. The Italian opera and the Drury Lane repertory company, with their star performers, spent every summer on tour. Madame Catalini was reported singing in Exeter, and Mademoiselle Viotti in York. Mrs Jordan's itineraries over the years illustrate the success and popularity of local theatres all over the country. In the south of England, she performed to ecstatic audiences in Margate, Ramsgate, Deal, Canterbury and Brighton, amongst other towns: in one season alone she moved from Exeter to Portsmouth to Gosport, South-ampton and Salisbury. In Cheltenham, where she spent several weeks, the royal family came to see her in *The Merry Wives of Windsor* before she moved on to the Worcester Theatre for a few days; on her northern tours she played to packed houses in Leicester, Liverpool, Preston, Chester and York. Several winters were spent in Bath, where she starred at the Theatre Royal.[7]

Bath was already on the decline as a fashionable resort at the end of the eighteenth century. One set of critics dismissed it as old-fashioned and too staid: another took the opposite stance, and thought that the society had become indiscriminate and vulgar. The town was certainly a well-known hunting ground for adventurers and fortune-hunters. Nevertheless it had its adherents amongst the *haut ton* of the Regency, mainly descend-ants of the great families who had patronized Bath in the days of Beau Nash. After all, the main attraction of the city had

---

* The new industrial towns prided themselves on their cultural facilities and built some of the largest and finest libraries in the country. The Athenaeum, in Liverpool, which opened in 1799, cost £4400, housed 6000 books and had 450 subscribers, each paying 2 guineas a year. Some of the London libraries housed huge collections, even by modern standards: Fancourts, for example, held more than 40,000 volumes.

remained the same for two thousand years – the medicinal properties of the local spring. Generations of invalids had claimed
miraculous 'cures' from both drinking and bathing in the warm,
sulphurous waters. By the beginning of the nineteenth century,
however, there was a new emphasis on hygiene, and it was
realized that the baths were run on such insanitary principles
that they were likely to cause more problems than they solved.
The King's Bath consisted of a large tank of warm water, the
size of a small swimming pool, in which the patients sat side by
side. There was no discrimination of either sex or class, or, more
seriously, of disease. This principle of communal immersion
meant that people with infected wounds and running sores shared
the same water as those with contagious diseases. Everyone was
fully dressed, the men in special brown linen suits and the ladies
in suitable garments of the same material.[8] Little copper bowls
filled with scented oils and pomanders floated on the water,
presumably in an attempt to purify the air. The Queen's Bath
was smaller, and filled with cold water, but was managed in the
same way. Drinking the water, as opposed to bathing in it, was
slightly less hazardous but even so the glasses were often not
washed between patients, and, in any case, it tasted revolting.

For the dedicated minority who continued to patronize Bath,
however, there were plenty of alternative attractions. Life began
early, with the first customers arriving in the Pump Room at
eight or nine in the morning to drink their daily dose. The
orchestra would already be in position and played background
music throughout the day. Dancing began at noon every day
except Sunday and there were formal balls twice a week, starting
at 6.00 in the evening. The programme was inviolable: minuets
only for the first two hours. The country dances, which were
much more fun and much more energetic, started at 8.00. (The
eighteenth-century rules specified that 'No Lady dance country-
dances in a hoop of any kind and those who choose to pull their
hoops off will be assisted by proper servants in an apartment for
that purpose.' By the time of the Regency, of course, only the
most old-fashioned dowagers would have appeared in public in
a hoop, so the ban was irrelevant.) At 9.00 the company adjourned

to the Tea Room for refreshments and the evening ended at 11.00 sharp. It is not surprising that the Prince Regent and his friends preferred the free and easy life of Brighton.

During the Regency there was a boom in tourism. An alternative – or, indeed, a complement – to spending the summer at one of the seaside resorts was to go on a walking or sketching tour. The most popular destinations were the Lake District and the Scottish highlands, the former introduced to the public by the Romantic poets and the latter through the medium of Walter Scott's novels and poetry. *The Lady of the Lake* was responsible for the sudden interest in the Trossachs and Loch Katrine. It was published in 1810, and caused a furore even before it was finished.

James Ballantyne read the cantos from time to time to select coteries, as they advanced at press. Common fame was loud in their favour; a great poem was on all hands anticipated. I do not recollect that any of all the author's works was ever looked for with more intense anxiety, or that any one of them excited a more extraordinary sensation when it did appear. The whole country rang with the praises of the poet – crowds set off to view the scenery of Loch Katrine, till then comparatively unknown; and as the book came out just before the season for excursions, every house and inn in that neighbourhood was crammed with a constant succession of visitors. It is a well-ascertained fact that from the date of the publication of *The Lady of the Lake* the post-horse duty in Scotland rose to an extraordinary degree, and indeed it continued to do so regularly for a number of years, the author's succeeding works keeping up the enthusiasm for our scenery which he had thus created.[9]

Wordsworth's *A Guide Through the District of the Lakes* was published the same year as *The Lady of the Lake*, and performed the same office for the scenery of Cumberland. The discovery of the highlands and the northern lakes not only brought the tourists but also provided the inspiration for some of the greatest English poets. Keats, who had never been to the North of England before, set off on a walking tour in the summer of 1818 and was overwhelmed by the mountain country. Writing to his brother Tom from the Lake District, he describes the scenery and its effect on his philosophy, but he also deplores the influx of fashionable tourists.

This morning we arose at 4, and set off in a Scotch mist; put up once under a tree, and in fine, have walked wet and dry to this place, called in the vulgar tongue Endmoor, 17 miles; we have not been incommoded by our knapsacks; they serve capitally, and we shall go on very well.

June 26 – I merely put *pro forma*, for there is no such thing as time and space, which by the way came forcibly upon me so seeing for the first hour the Lake and Mountains of Winander – I cannot describe them – they surpass my expectation – beautiful water – shores and islands green to the marge – mountains all round up to the clouds . . .

There are many disfigurements to this Lake – not in the way of land or water. No; the two views we have had of it are of the most noble tenderness – they can never fade away – they make one forget the divisions of life; age, youth, poverty and riches; and refine one's sensual vision into a sort of north star which can never cease to be open lidded and stedfast over the wonders of the great Power. The disfigurement I mean is the miasma of London. I do suppose it contaminated with bucks and soldiers, and women of fashion – and hat-band ignorance. The border inhabitants are quite out of keeping with the romance about them, from a continual intercourse with London rank and fashion.

On reaching a series of waterfalls Keats writes that, though the space and magnitude of the mountains and waterfalls may be imagined in advance, the reality of their

countenance or intellectual tone must surpass every imagination and defy any remembrance. I shall learn poetry here and shall henceforth write more than ever, for the abstract endeavor of being able to add a mite to that mass of beauty which is harvested from these grand materials, by the finest spirits, and put into etherial existence for the relish of one's fellows. I cannot think with Hazlitt that these scenes make man appear little. I never forgot my stature so completely – I live in the eye; and my imagination, surpassed, is at rest.[10]

In Cumberland the two young men went to a country dance, which Keats wrote was 'indeed "no cotillon fresh from France". No they kickit & jumpit with mettle extraordinary, & whiskit, & fleckit, & toe'd it, & go'd it, & twirld it, & wheel'd it, & stampt it, & sweated it, tattoing the floor like mad'. By the end of the week they had walked 114 miles and were 'merely a little tired in the thighs, & a little blistered'.[11]

The poet Southey was less impressed by all this devotion to nature and passion for romantic scenery. 'Within the last thirty years', he wrote in 1807,

a taste for the picturesque has sprung up; and a course of summer travelling is now looked upon to be as essential as ever a course of spring physic was in old times. While one of the flocks of fashion migrates to the sea-coast, another flies off to the mountains of Wales, to the lakes of the northern provinces, or to Scotland ... all to study the picturesque, a new science, for which a new language has been formed, and for which the English have discovered a new sense in themselves, which assuredly was not possessed by their fathers.

Two years later the cartoonist Rowlandson collaborated with William Combe to produce *The Tour of Dr Syntax in Search of the Picturesque*, satirizing the whole trend. It tells the tale of a poor schoolmaster-cleric who sets off on a tour of the country, hoping to make his fortune by writing about it and sketching the scenery. He is well aware of the market value of ruins and the charm of decay:

> Whose eye the *picturesque* admire
> In straggling bramble and in brier;
> Nay, can a real beauty see
> In a decay'd and rotten tree.[12]

He is particularly pleased to be told of a nearby castle which has fallen into decay:

> A sad and ruinated scene,
> Where owls, and bats, and starlings dwell, –
> And where, alas! as people tell,
> At the dark hour when midnight reigns,
> Ghosts walk, all arm'd, and rattle chains ...
> 'A castle, and a ruin too, –
> 'I'll hasten there and take a view ...'[13]

In Cumberland his host invites him to join the hunt but Dr Syntax declines:

> Your sport, my Lord, I cannot take,
> For I must go and hunt a lake;
> And while you chase the flying deer,
> 'I must fly off to Windermere.
> Instead of hallowing to a fox,
> I must catch echoes from the rocks.
> With curious eye and active scent,
> I on the *picturesque* am bent.
> That is my game: I must pursue it,
> And make it where I cannot view it.'[14]

Edinburgh at the beginning of the nineteenth century was one of the intellectual centres of Europe, birthplace of the movement known as the Scottish Enlightenment and home to some of the most gifted and brilliant minds of their generation. The famous *Edinburgh Review* was founded in 1802 by the leader of their group, Francis (later Lord) Jeffrey, a Scottish lawyer. It was both a political (Whig) and literary magazine and contributors to the early issues included such men as Sydney Smith, Henry Brougham, John Murray (the publisher) and Sir Walter Scott – though the last-named later defected and founded a rival Tory magazine, the *Quarterly Review*. The Edinburgh intellectuals were passionate advocates of universal education: the standard of knowledge they expected from their own children proves the point, even if it does seem somewhat excessive in the case of one of their number. Elizabeth Grant of Rothiemurchus was the daughter of an Edinburgh lawyer and politician. The summer she 'came out', Elizabeth's father decided to take advantage of a brief break in her social life 'to take me through a short course of mathematicks. We went regularly over the first three books of Euclid, applying all the rules and some of the problems as we went on.' She admits that this was a 'then unusual science' for a girl, but explains that her father thought her too addicted to the 'poetick or portraitick style of writing' and 'judged the wisest thing to be done with so imaginative a brain was to square it a bit by rule and compass.'[15] In her memoirs Elizabeth recalls her early education. It appears to have been subliminal, absorbed through the intellectual atmosphere of her daily life: 'It is curious that I have no recollection of learning anything from any body except thus by chance as it were, though I have understood that I was a little wonder, my Aunts having amused themselves in making a sort of show of me.' She 'read well at 3 years old', 'had long ballads off by heart' and was taught to count by her aunt 'with a general notion of the first four rules of arithmetick by the help of little bags of beans, which were kept in one of the compartments of an immense box full of all sorts of *tangible* helps to knowledge.' The nursery was full of educational toys and children's books.

My books had very gaudy paper backs, red and green and all manner of colours, with dashes of gold dabbed on ... paper coarse, printing thick and the contents enchanting! Puss in boots, Riquet with the tuft, Blue Beard, Cinderella, the geni and the fishermen; and in a plain marble cover on finer paper, full of prints, a small history of Rome, where one print so shocked me – Tullia in her car riding over the body of her father – that I would ne'er open that classic page again.[16]

She was five years old at this stage.

Later on, when the family were living in Edinburgh, the house was filled with a procession of private tutors:

Six masters were engaged for we three girls, three every day; Mr Penson for the pianoforte, Mr Elouis for the Harp, M. L'Espinasse for French, Signor Something for Italian, and Mr-I-forget-who for Drawing, Mr Scott for writing and cyphering. And oh, a seventh! I was near forgetting, the most important of all! Mr Smart for Dancing.

The boy's tutors included three of the most distinguished professors in Edinburgh at the time: Thomas Hope, professor of chemistry; John Playfair, one of the leaders of the Scottish Enlightenment and successively professor of maths and natural philosophy; and Thomas Brown, metaphysician, who was awarded his chair in 1810.

Life was not all lessons, however. Elizabeth's description of her first appearance in Edinburgh society, in 1814, concentrates largely on her clothes.

This spring I was furnished with a new occupation. My mother told me that my childhood has passed away; I was now seventeen, and must for the future be dressed suitably to the Class young lady into which I had passed . . . I was so extremely pleased; I was always fond of being nicely dressed, but when the various things ordered arrived, my feeling rose to delight.

She was given a whole new wardrobe and 'I retained none of my old attire but my bonnets, my cloke and my habits.' The outfits sound charming:

Two or three gingham dresses of different colours very neatly made with frills, tucks, flounces, etc. Two or three cambrick muslins in the same style with embroidery upon them, and one pale lilac silk, pattern a very small check, to be worn on very grand occasions. My first silk gown . . . A pink muslin and a blue muslin for dinner, both prettily trimmed, and some clear and some soft muslins, white of course, with sashes of different colours tyed at one side in two small bows with two very long ends. In the bright, glossy, pale auburn hair no ornament was allowed but natural flowers . . . The best bonnet was white chip trimmed with white satin and very small, very pale, blush roses, and the new spencer was of blush rose pink. Then there were pretty gloves, neat shoes, silk neckerchiefs, and a parasol – just fancy my happiness . . .

The main event of the social year in Scotland was the Northern Meeting, held in the middle of October, at Inverness. It was inaugurated at the turn of the century by the Duchess of Sutherland, 'who was the Life of all circles she entered . . . There were dinners and balls in the evenings; the mornings were devoted to visiting neighbouring friends and the beautiful scenery abounding on all sides.' Elizabeth was one of the débutantes at the Meeting:

New dresses had come for my decoration, and beautiful flowers . . . There was white muslin with blue trimmings, shoes to match, and roses; white gauze, pink shoes and trimmings, and hyacinths; pearl gray gauze and pink, and a bacchus wreath of grapes and vine leaves, for we had three balls, dinners before the first two, and a supper after the last. With what delight I stept into the Barouche and four which was to carry us to this scene of pleasure. I had no fear about partners, Pitmain had set me quite at ease on that score. We went through the ford at Inverdruie, everyone we met bidding us Godspeed, and looking after us affectionately, for it was an era in the annals of the family, this coming out of Miss Grant.[17]

Her story, however, ended sadly, for Elizabeth fell in love with a young man whom her father refused to allow her to marry – merely because he had quarrelled with the young man's father. For all their vaunted liberality the Edinburgh intellectuals could be autocratic when their daughters were involved.

7

'A MISTRESS HAD A BETTER DEAL THAN A WIFE'

The role of the mistress during the Regency acquired a cachet which was positively respectable. This was largely thanks to the example set by the royal princes, nearly all of whom had lived openly for years with ladies to whom they were not married but who were treated by society with all the deference due to a wife. In the case of Mrs Fitzherbert, the Prince's morganatic 'wife', such an attitude was certainly justified, for she was a woman of far greater moral calibre than his legal wife, Caroline. William IV, on his brother's death, offered to make Mrs Fitzherbert a peeress, an honour which she declined, saying that she had never brought disgrace upon the name of Fitzherbert and saw no reason to abandon it. Largely thanks to the insistence of the Duke of York, she was given an allowance of £5000 a year for the rest of her life. She continued to live at Brighton, where the Prince had bought her house, respected by all and still regarded by many as having been the Prince's real wife, or the late King's widow. Madame St Laurent, too, the Duke of Kent's mistress for twenty-seven years, was impeccable in her behaviour: faithful, supportive and loyal throughout their liaison. When the Duke was dragooned into giving her up in order to marry and beget an heir to the throne,* Mme St Laurent was so shattered that rather than carry on alone, or take up with someone else, she

* He married the Princess of Leiningen, mother of the future Queen Victoria.

retired to a convent for the rest of her life. Not many society wives would have shown such constancy. When Mrs Jordan began her liaison with the Duke of Clarence in 1791, the affair was such public property that the *Morning Post* reported the preliminary negotiations: '... Her terms are a £1200 a year annuity, an equipage, and her children by all parties provided for.'[1] Mrs Jordan was in a rather special position at the time, since she was already a very successful actress and earning a considerable amount of money. In the end the Duke paid her 200 guineas every quarter for twenty years, but even so, Mrs Jordan often ended up out of pocket and having to pay most of the bills for the whole household out of her earnings.

Royal mistresses and their bastard children had a status of their own. The sons were even given titles. Mrs Jordan's eldest, George FitzClarence, for example, was created Earl of Munster. (Unlike Charles II, however, George IV never made his mistresses duchesses.) Mrs Jordan was the Duke's official hostess, even when other members of the royal family were present. At one of the Duke's dinner parties the Prince of Wales and all the royal dukes as well as the Lord Chancellor and other assorted grandees were present: nevertheless, the *Courier* reported that when dinner was announced, 'the Prince took Mrs Jordan by the hand, led her into the dining-room, and seated her at the top of the table. The Prince took his seat at her right hand, and the Duke of York at her left ...'[2] She was, in fact, accorded the status of a wife and, in this case, took precedence over both the Duchess of Bolton and the Countess of Athlone, much to their fury. (*The Times*, however, which was even then prone to attacks of puritanism, not to say pomposity, complained a few years later, when Mrs Jordan had fallen out of favour, that she was: '... a woman who ... had been admitted into the secrets of harems and palaces, seen their full exhibition of nude beauty and costly dissoluteness; the whole interior pomp of royal pleasure, the tribes of mutes and idiots, sultans and eunuchs, slavish passion and lordly debility ...')[3]

In the eyes of the Regency, therefore, the official mistress was an established figure, with her own position in society. An attractive, well-turned-out mistress, who kept a good table and was able to amuse her keeper's friends, could become a positive asset to a man of fashion, regardless of his marital status. Such an asset, or accessory, however, was expensive, particularly if exclusive rights were in question. The etiquette of setting up a mistress was clear: while the principals confined themselves to talk of love, friends were employed to negotiate the terms, rather in the role of seconds in a duel. It was said that '£2000 a year and £800 down' was the price of an opera dancer who had taken the fancy of one of Earl Grey's grandsons.[4] Captain Gronow was the 'broker' for that particular deal, which, translated into modern money, comes to £100,000 a year for as long as she stayed with him. Breach of promise was a genuine threat: when Maria Foote, an actress and courtesan who later married the Earl of Harrington (formerly Lord Petersham), brought a successful action for breach of promise against one of her previous lovers, her lawyer set the price of her disappointment at £10,000. The jury, however, put it at £3000. As for the sixth Duke of Devonshire, he set his mistress up in a London house in Dorset Square, gave her another at Brighton, an allowance of £1600 a year, carriages, jewels, furs and innumerable other presents, including an aviary because she liked birds.[5] Nevertheless, Harriette Wilson considered him mean.

Harriette Wilson was the courtesan *par excellence* of the Regency: sexy, charming and deeply avaricious. It was said of her that she changed her lovers as easily as her shoes and that she always went straight to the point on hearing of a potential customer, saying that 'a fifty pound note will do as easily as an introduction'. This was a hefty sum at the time, and one which only guaranteed that she was prepared to listen to a proposition: the terms of the contract could be negotiated later. Walter Scott described Harriette as 'far from beautiful . . . but a smart saucy girl with good eyes and dark hair, and the manners of a wild schoolboy.'[6] She was born Harriette Dubochet in 1786, one of fifteen children, whose father was a Swiss clockmaker with a small shop in Mayfair. Her elder sister Amy was the first to take an aristocratic lover and found her new life such fun that her sisters, Harriette, Fanny and Sophia copied her example as fast as they could. Harriette followed suit at the age of fifteen, with Lord Craven, about whom she had scarcely a civil word to say in later life.[7]

The list of Harriette's lovers reads like a roll-call of *Debrett's* and includes enough eldest sons to justify the panic she caused amongst their fathers. She had no brief for fidelity, finding it far more lucrative to keep several lovers competing for her favours at the same time. The most consistent were the Marquess of Lorne, son and heir of the Duke of Argyll; the Marquess of Worcester, son and heir of the Duke of Beaufort; Lord Frederick Bentinck, son of the Duke of Portland; and Frederick Lamb, son of Lord Melbourne. But, if young men were more attractive, old men were richer, and Harriette was a professional: thus, much as she preferred the attentions of the young Marquess of Worcester, he was kept waiting in the wings while she had a lucrative affair with his older cousin, the Duke of Leinster. The list of her alleged lovers includes such very different characters as John Wilson Croker, the politician and diarist; Lord Alvanley, a gourmet dandy; and Henry Brougham, the eminent lawyer and Liberal MP. Byron refused her advances but, even so, remained a friend and, on occasion, lent Harriette money – which, needless to say, she never repaid. Her only real failure appears to have been the Prince of Wales himself. She wrote proposing a meeting and the Prince replied that he would be happy to see her if she would come to London. Harriette was living in Brighton under the protection of Lord Craven at the time, and such was her conceit that she felt the Prince should come to her rather than vice versa. She wrote him an impertinent letter to this effect, which he never bothered to answer, so she moved on to Lord Melbourne's son instead.

Harriette was always impressed by success, particularly if it was accompanied by fame: she had a running affair with the Duke of Wellington for years even though she said he looked like a rat-catcher and that she found him a bore. One of her most revealing anecdotes concerns her first encounter with the great Duke. The meeting was apparently effected by a well-known

VENUS AND MARS! '*HE LOOKED VERY MUCH LIKE A RAT-CATCHER*'
Illustration by J. Findlay for *The Interesting Memoirs of Harriette Wilson*, 1825
Harriette Wilson, the notorious courtesan, and the Duke of Wellington. When she
wrote her memoirs she tried to blackmail her ex-lovers, offering to leave them out for
a price: it was in this context that the Duke replied, 'Publish and be Damned'.

procuress, one Mrs Porter, who ran her business from a house
in Berkeley Street. The Duke offered this lady 100 guineas for
an introduction to Harriette Wilson and suggested the same fee
for Harriette herself, if it was successful. At the time she was
having an affair with the Duke of Argyll, whom she needed to
pay her mounting debts; however, in her own words 'what was
a mere man, even though it were the handsome Duke of Argyle
[*sic*], to a Wellington!!!!' She goes on to describe their first
meeting:

. . . most punctual to my appointment, Wellington made his appearance.
He bowed first, then said,

'How do you do?' then thanked me for having given him permission
to call on me; and then wanted to take hold of my hand.

'Really,' said I, withdrawing my hand, 'for such a renowned hero
you have very little to say for yourself.'

'Beautiful creature!' uttered Wellington. 'Where is Lorne?' [Wellington was referring to Harriette's current lover, the Duke of Argyll, by his former, courtesy title.] 'Good gracious,' said I, out of all patience at his stupidity – 'what come you here for, Duke?'

'Beautiful eyes, yours!' reiterated Wellington.

'Aye man! they are greater conquerors than ever Wellington shall be; but, to be serious, I understood you came here to try to make yourself agreeable?'

'What, child! do you think that I have nothing better to do than to make speeches to please ladies?' said Wellington.

Nevertheless, he stayed, paid her bills, got rid of the bailiffs and remained one of her part-time lovers for many years. According to Harriette the Dukes of Argyll and Wellington vied for her favours at the same time and were liable to collide on her doorstep. One of her stories relates that Argyll, arriving early one evening, found his hostess already in bed with a cold and was about to grasp her in his arms, crying, 'for this night, at least, I will be a match for the mighty Wellington', when the latter started banging on the front door. A nice image, even if apocryphal; Harriette was a wonderful storyteller.

Harriette, her sister Fanny and their friend Julia Johnstone were known as the 'Three Graces'. Julia was a deb who had fallen from grace: the daughter of one of the Queen's Maids of Honour and a niece of Lord Carysfort, she was brought up at Court but slipped up in her first season with a married man, Colonel Cotton. She was rejected by her family but went on to live more or less happily with the colonel, by whom she had five children. She and her fellow-courtesans were known as demi-reps, or the 'Fashionable Impure', but there was nothing secret or shifty about their role in life. The girls were invited to all the smart parties – provided they were given by men. For example, Harriette and her sisters were taken to the fashionable masquerade given by the members of White's Club to celebrate the Peace in 1814, where they danced side by side with all the *grandes dames* of the day. And when Harriette was living with Frederick Lamb, in Yorkshire, where his regiment was quartered, she was received by the general and invited to all the regimental parties as well as dining on a regular basis in the officers' mess. Later, when she had moved on to Lord Worcester, who installed her in a house in Brighton, she ordered an exact copy of the glamorous uniform* of the 10th Hussars and rode out with him early every morning when he went on parade. She said it was the only way of getting him out of bed on time.

Any mistress worthy of the title had her own box at the opera and at Drury Lane, paid for by one of her lovers, where she held court openly. Even married men wandered in and out during the intervals, in full view of their wives and families, who were sitting in *their* boxes across the auditorium. Opera nights at Covent Garden, on Tuesdays and Thursdays, provided a splendid opportunity for the courtesans to show off their wares to the *haut ton*, including, of course, potential customers. A successful mistress lived a life of luxury and leisure, and, moreover, could do what she liked with her own money, unlike a wife, all of whose property, on marriage, passed into her husband's control. She could, and did, insist on the best of everything: when Harriette's sister Fanny fell ill she was attended by Sir William Knighton, who was not only the King's own doctor but the most expensive practitioner in London. They could afford, too, to be choosy about their lovers and touchy about their dignity. Harriette turned down Prince Esterhazy because, in accordance with Austrian custom, he kept his hat on in her presence. She always insisted that the first meeting with a potential lover should be in the open air, so that she could vet him before committing herself and escape if she wanted to. The appointed rendezvous was usually Mary-le-bone Fields or Regent's Park, where she would arrange to be walking at a certain time. These girls,

---

* A feminine version of military uniforms became the fashion in 1814. A Scottish débutante recalled that she 'walked out like a hussar in a dark cloth pelisse trimmed with fur and braided like the coat of a Staff officer, boots to match, and a fur cap set on one side, and kept on the head by means of a cord with very long tassels. This equipment was copied by half the town, it was thought so exquisite' (Elizabeth Grant of Rothiemurchus, *Memoirs of a Highland Lady*, vol. 2, ed. A. Todd, Canongate Classics, 1988, p. 10).

however, were no common prostitutes. They were educated, elegant, amusing and skilled in the art of pleasing men. The Wilson sisters both spoke and read French and took an active interest in current affairs. Harriette had occasional bursts of worrying about her relative ignorance, and, on one occasion, went off to rusticate in the country for a couple of weeks to study Voltaire and Roman history, staying all by herself at an inn. 'The Greeks employed me for two whole days,' she remembered, 'and the Romans six more.' She dipped into Rousseau, Racine and Boswell's *Life of Johnson*; but, after wading through a long speech by Fox, and another by Pitt, decided to admit defeat when it came to politics, and returned to town. Harriette was still only eighteen at the time.

Nevertheless, there were limits to society's tolerance, all the more cogent for being unwritten. For example, when Berkeley Craven became so besotted with his mistress, Harriette's sister Amy, that he cut his wife and family in public, they were both ostracized for a while. The Duke of York refused to receive Craven at Oatlands, even on 'public nights' (the Regency equivalent of a Buckingham Palace garden party). Harriette was outraged on behalf of her sister, but had a point when she wrote in her diary that: '. . . beyond all doubt, a man ought to be of royal blood before he presumes to commit adultery, except in private . . .'

At the age of thirty-four Harriette was 'bought off' by the Duke of Beaufort, desperate to break up her affair with his heir, the Marquess of Worcester. Worcester was infatuated with Harriette and begged her to marry him – in writing, unfortunately for the Duke. Harriette showed the letters to a solicitor and was advised they were worth at least £20,000 if she brought a case for breach of promise. The Duke haggled, so Harriette sought the counsel of Henry Brougham, the most celebrated defence lawyer in London and one of her ex-lovers. Brougham confirmed the value of the letters and a huge scandal threatened. In the end the Duke offered her £500 a year for life provided she retired to Paris, to which, rather surprisingly, Harriette agreed. Perhaps she felt she had used up London. In Paris she lived in style in the rue de la Paix, where all her old flames came to call on her, including the Duke of Wellington, even after her memoirs were published. Far from being ostracized, Harriette not only continued to circulate in the best society but was allowed by the British embassy to send her letters in the diplomatic bag. Such was the status of a courtesan during the Regency.

If the Duke of Beaufort's aim was to hush up his son's affair with Harriette, he failed completely. As soon as his heir married, the Duke reneged on the deal he had made with Harriette and stopped paying her allowance. Harriette retaliated by selling her story and the memoirs were published in 1825. The book was an instantaneous bestseller and Stockdale, her somewhat seedy publisher, sold thirty editions within the first year. (Murray, and several other respectable publishers, had rejected the manuscript on grounds of taste.) The book caused an uproar, particularly as most of her victims had long since turned respectable. She had canvassed most of those mentioned in the book before publication, offering, in return for a handsome settlement, to leave them out. Most refused to be blackmailed, including the Duke of Wellington, who replied succinctly, 'Publish and be Damned'.

Harriette Wilson's memoirs are often inaccurate and, in the case of those who refused to meet her demands, motivated by malice. To be fair, she had few illusions about herself and, though vain, was not pretentious. Apropos of her memoirs, she wrote: 'I have one advantage over other bad female writers and prosing ladies, which is, that I do not think myself agreeable . . .' The memoirs prove her point, but the bitchy gossip has the flavour of truth and gives a unique insight into the habits, morals and characters of many contemporary heroes. Thus, the wealthy dandy Lord Lowther goes down in history, according to Harriette, as having the filthiest comb she had ever seen; in his dressing-room she found 'a set of vile, dirty combs, brushes, towels and dressing gowns. Lowther, who always has a pain in his liver and knows not how to take kindly to his bottle.' Nor was this all. Lowther was notoriously mean, according to Harriette, and served such bad dinners and such cheap wine that Lord Hertford, though continuing to accept his invitations, felt free to complain about the 'scanty courses' and tell the host to

1. *A DANDY*
Caricature by Charles Williams, published by Fores, 1818.

2. *DR SYNTAX WITH A BLUE-STOCKING BEAUTY*

Illustration by Rowlandson to *The Third Tour of Dr Syntax, in Search of a Wife*, by W. Combe, 1821. 'The Blue-Stocking Club' was founded towards the end of the eighteenth century by Elizabeth Montagu. It was a gathering of aristocratic ladies with literary leanings and derived its name from a poem, *Bas-Bleu*, by Hannah More.

3. *THE GARDEN TRIO*

Illustration by Rowlandson to *The Third Tour of Dr Syntax, in Search of a Wife*, by W. Combe, 1821. Open air concerts were a regular feature of country-house life. At Chatsworth and other great houses the owner often employed his own musicians on a permanent basis.

4. *ART OF SELF-DEFENCE*
Illustration by Robert and George Cruikshank to *Life in London*, by Pierce Egan, 1821. 'Tom and Jerry receiving instruction from "Gentleman" Jackson in his Rooms'.

5. *FENCING*
Illustration by Robert and George Cruikshank to *Life in London*, by Pierce Egan, 1821.

6. *THE CONSERVATORY AT CARLTON HOUSE*
Illustration to Ackermann's *Repository of Arts, Literature, Commerce*, September 1811.

7. *THE PAGODA IN ST JAMES'S PARK*
Illustration to Ackermann's *Repository of Arts, Literature, Commerce*, October 1814. In 1814 the Prince Regent organized a series of spectacular fêtes culminating in 'The Grand Jubilee'. The Chinese Pagoda caught fire, and collapsed into the lake – to roars of approval from the crowd, who thought it was part of the entertainment.

8. *ACKERMANN'S REPOSITORY OF ARTS, 101 STRAND*
Illustration by Pugin and Rowlandson to Ackermann's *Repository of Arts, Literature, Commerce,* January 1809. Rudolph Ackermann was a publisher, print seller and 'manufacturer of fancy articles', e.g. screens, card racks and flower stands.

9. *MESSRS PELLATT AND GREEN, ST PAUL'S CHURCHYARD*
Illustration by Pugin and Rowlandson to Ackermann's *Repository of Arts, Literature, Commerce,* May 1809. One of the huge show rooms at Pellatt and Green, glass-makers to the King.

10. *HUMMING-BIRDS — OR — A DANDY TRIO*
Caricature by George Cruikshank after J. Sheringham, published by G. Humphrey, 1819.

The Year (1740) a Lady's full dress of Bombazeen ___ The Year (1807) a Lady's undress of Bum-be-seen.

11. *THE FASHIONS OF THE DAY OR TIME PAST AND PRESENT*
Caricature by Charles Williams after Woodward, published by Walker, 1807.

12. *THE BISHOP AND HIS CLARKE OR A PEEP INTO PARADISE*

Caricature by Rowlandson, published by Tegg, 1809. The Duke of York, Commander-in-Chief of the army (and titular Bishop of Osnabrück) being solicited by Mary Anne Clarke to obtain promotions for her friends. As a result of the subsequent scandal he was forced to resign.

13. *BLIND MAN'S BUFF*
Caricature by Robert Cruikshank, published by Tregear, *c.* 1825.

14. *HIGH LIFE BELOW STAIRS*
Caricature by Robert Cruikshank, published by Tregear, *c.* 1825.

his face that his claret was 'not worth a d——n'. Frederick Lamb was also accused of being mean, but considering how free Harriette had become with her favours by the time Lamb came into her life, he may well have felt some of the other men could contribute to her keep. A more curious complaint about Lamb was that he was too passionate and the violence of his love-making, Harriette told his successor, somehow disgusted her: but then promiscuity is often the reverse of true sexuality. No considerations of loyalty hamper the memoirs: she remembers, in print, for all his friends and descendants to read, that her very first lover, Lord Craven, drove her mad with boredom, droning on night after night about his cocoa trees in the West Indies. Anyway, she disliked the sight of him in his moth-eaten night-cap.

Harriette was a dedicated gold-digger and those of her victims whom she considered to have undervalued her charms bore the brunt of her revenge. The sixth Duke of Devonshire, for example, whom everyone else found easy and pleasant, was accused of being affected and stingy. The wretched Duke was clearly a little naive in his idea of a present with which to ingratiate himself. He sent round an 'ugly old red pocket handkerchief', which he thought she would treasure for its sentimental associations because he had worn it as an under-waistcoat on the occasion of his visit to her the day before, i.e. next to his heart: Harriette gave it to her footman and told the Duke she had done so. His other offering was a thin gold ring which she dismissed as worth no more than a shilling. But Lord Deerhurst was the meanest of the lot. He lived in squalor, albeit in Mayfair, and refused to afford anything but tallow candles, 'stinking butcher's candles'; seduced her sister Sophia at the age of thirteen and then palmed her off with shabby lodgings, currant wine and a paltry £300 a year – and that only after litigation. Moreover, when he invited the girls to drive out of town and have dinner at an inn, Deerhurst took them to a common village inn where there was nothing to eat except eggs and bacon, tried to cheat the tolls on the way back, and finished the evening by having a fight with the turnpike keeper. Harriette was furious.

Harriette's lovers often came on to visit her after they had been at some ball or Court function, which meant they were wearing full evening dress: black satin knee-breeches, powdered wigs, jewellery and high heels. The Marquess Wellesley, a nephew of Wellington's, was a confirmed dandy whose passion for finery was a gift to Harriette's malicious sense of humour: 'His Lordship appeared . . . in superfine elegance. Such cambric, white as driven snow! Such embroidery! Such diamonds! Such a brilliant snuff-box! Such seals and chains! . . . It was too much, too overpowering for a poor, honest, unaffected Suissesse like me .,. .' (Incidentally, Harriette must have lost some of her arrogance by the time she met Wellesley, since she was prepared to share him with that other well-known Regency courtesan, Moll Raffles. Perhaps they were both somewhat past their prime.) Having demolished the Marquess's clothes she went on to complain about men's make-up in general. Powder, pomatum and rouge were still used by any aspirant to fashion but, according to Harriette, whenever the men got overheated the thick make-up ran, falling down their faces in great globs.

One of the few men Harriette seems to have liked was Colonel Berkeley, another of Sophia's lovers: she found him 'lively and agreeable', and 'polite and attentive', but, even so, cannot resist pointing out, somewhat sanctimoniously, that 'the man bears an indifferent character, and perhaps with some reason . . .' Colonel Berkeley, it appears, pounced on girls in his carriage on the way home from parties. The colonel, complained Harriette, 'attacks both young and old, virtuous and wicked, handsome and ugly, maid, wife and widow'. There was only one man in her life whom she would never criticize: Lord Ponsonby. He was said to be the 'handsomest man in England' and Harriette was madly in love with him for three long years. Needless to say, he married someone else, leaving Harriette in despair; needless to say, too, she recovered and moved on to others.

Harriette Wilson and her fellow courtesans were paid for love and knew the price of their chosen career. But illicit sex between members of the same upper class was a far more complicated issue. High society during the Regency was caught between two very different sets of morality: between the licentious formality of the eighteenth century and the growing puritanism of the nineteenth. As a result it dithered between the two and conformed to neither. Although it was true that in most of the aristocratic houses adultery was taken for granted, a minor matter of no importance, always provided the affair was conducted with discretion, in others the taint of sin could never be overcome. It was often impossible for a lady of doubtful virtue to forecast the criteria of acceptance, or to force the issue to a favourable conclusion. As a result several of the most notable hostesses of the period, successful as they were in their own way, hovered on the brink of ostracism, or were forced to confine their ambitions to mixing with those who lived on the fringe of society. It was a situation guaranteed to cause terrible frustration amongst those who cared about that sort of thing; the Margravine of Anspach, for example, suffered for years. She spent much of her life as well as a fortune in pursuit of recognition by the Court.

The Margravine, born Lady Elizabeth Berkeley, was a romantic beauty with literary pretensions and a fine disdain for convention.[8] She married Lord Craven at the age of sixteen and caused a major scandal almost at once by having far too blatant an affair with a French duke, her first lover but by no means her last. Furthermore, after the duke she raced down the social scale and even had affairs with men who were working class. According to one report: 'When Lord Craven perceived . . . that she was become democratic in love, and had shown marks of *complaisance* to the *canaille*, he was surly, and indignant, and advised her to *take herself off . . .*' Lady Craven, by then, was happy to oblige, feeling that she was bored with London in any case, and went off to Paris to see what life had to offer in a less censorious city. She struck gold almost immediately in the person of His Serene Highness, the Margrave of Brandenburg, Anspach and Bayreuth, an immensely rich, and married, German princeling. His wife, a harmless Saxe-Coburg princess, was soon despatched, along with the Margrave's official mistress, a French actress, and Lady Craven set herself up as the resident Margravine. Such open adultery was acceptable on the Continent; the King of Prussia even lent them one of his palaces to live in when the Margrave sold his own. But in England the couple were ostracized, to their mutual rage and despair. His Serene Highness wrote to Lady Craven's brother, the Earl of Berkeley, explaining that it was a recognized custom in his own country 'to take a wife with the left hand', as the euphemism went, and added that he would marry her 'with his right hand as well' as soon as they both were free of their respective spouses. Lord Berkeley was not impressed: he took the view that his sister was married already to an English peer and therefore could not possibly marry anyone else. Disconsolate, they returned to the Continent again, where the courts and society had more sense than to ostracize a couple with so much money: the Margrave's income was estimated at £100,000 a year.

Eventually, both the real Margravine and Lord Craven died and the lovers got married in Paris, thinking all their troubles were over. It was said that Lady Craven heard the news of her husband's death on a Friday, went into weeds on Saturday, and into 'white satin and *many* diamonds' on the Sunday.[9] Legal at last, they returned to England, only to find that she, at least, was still *persona non grata*. Her own daughters refused to visit her, 'out of respect for their father', and the Queen sent an insulting message to the Margrave to say that his wife would not be welcome at Court.

This time, however, the Margrave and his lovely wife refused to accept defeat. They bought an enormous London house, on the banks of the Thames, christened it 'Brandenburg House', with typical ostentation, and set about entertaining on a mammoth scale. The Margravine knew perfectly well that society was fickle, particularly if the bait was attractive enough. If the Queen refused to recognize her, the Prince of Wales did not; and if the *grandes dames* of society stayed away from her parties, the demi-monde adored them. Her guests may have been confined to those who came from what one referred to as 'the gay world of both sexes', but the Margravine was at last content. Her breakfasts, dinners, receptions, masquerades, concerts, river-parties and balls were a riotous success. Anyway, as she knew perfectly well, the demi-monde was much more fun than the Court.

Marguerite, 'the most gorgeous Lady Blessington', was another great hostess of the period who fell victim to a dubious past.[10] Born Margaret Farmer, she was the daughter of an Irish spendthrift who virtually sold her into marriage with an elderly drunk. She ran away and lived in sin with a young lover by whom she had two illegitimate children: according to rumour, he, too, sold her on, for the magnificent sum of £10,000, to Lord Mountjoy, a rich Irish peer who was later created the Earl of Blessington. The Marguerites of the Regency, however, could expect none of the tolerance shown to the Duchess of Devonshire and her ilk. The great ladies of the Regency would never lend their countenance to an Irish girl of common stock who had behaved in a similar fashion to themselves, even though she had the excuse, unlike them, that it had been against her will. And so, though the lovely Marguerite finally married her peer, though her behaviour thereafter was faultless, though she was rich, intelligent, charming and held court in one of the grandest houses in London, her position in society was precarious.

However the ladies may have felt about Marguerite, the men adored her. She was a natural hostess and her salon became one of the most popular in London: the food and drink were excellent, the rooms sumptuous but comfortable, and, because the guests were almost exclusively male, sustained intelligent conversation was possible. Her parties attracted the best brains of her generation; writers, politicians and artists added a tone to her salon which was not to be found in more 'respectable' drawing rooms. Castlereagh, Canning, Brougham and Earl Grey were regular guests, along with Lawrence, Wilkie, Moore and Rogers. It was Dr Samuel Parr, the great classical scholar, who first called Marguerite 'the most gorgeous Lady Blessington', and from all accounts it was an apt description. One admirer said of her portrait by Lawrence, which was shown at the Royal Academy, that he had seen 'no other so striking instance of the inferiority of art to nature as in this celebrated portrait of Lady Blessington. As the original stood before it, she fairly "killed" the copy, and

this no less in the individual details than in the general effect.'
He went on to say that she was

perhaps the loveliest woman of her day . . . There was about her face,
together with that beaming intelligence which rarely shows itself upon
the countenance till that period of life [i.e. the late twenties, her age
at the time], a bloom and freshness which as rarely survive early youth,
and a total absence of those indefinable marks which thought and
feeling still more rarely fail to leave behind them. Unlike all other
beautiful faces that I have seen, hers was . . . neither a history nor a
prophecy . . . but an end and a consummation in itself, not a means to,
or a promise of, anything else.[11]

All these nuances of morality and immorality provided hours of
happy gossip: the period embracing the Regency was, after all,
known as the Age of Scandal. If the ladies who snubbed the
Margravine of Anspach and Lady Blessington hoped that their
example would induce the rest of high society to behave with
discretion and propriety, they must have been sadly disappointed.
The annals of the period abound with scandals caused by the
aristocracy: elopements, infidelities, duels, bankruptcies, suits for
breach of promise and cases brought on the curious charge of
'criminal conversation' (commonly known as 'crim cons'). This
was a euphemism for adultery, in the legal sense, and could be
used as the basis for a divorce.

Gretna Green was a spectre in many a wealthy Regency
household, particularly those which contained romantically
minded young heiresses; and the prospect of a daughter running
off with one of the dreaded fortune hunters, 'half-pay officers', or
even the dancing master encountered at school, was a constant
threat. By the beginning of the nineteenth century the marriage
of a minor without parental consent was illegal in England, but
there was no such barrier in Scotland. As a result many a young
couple, thwarted in love, raced north through the night in a
coach and four, with a furious father galloping after them in
pursuit. Sometimes the lovers won and were married over the
anvil, sometimes the parents won and the girl was dragged home
in tearful disgrace. Some of these elopements seem to have been

quite unnecessary, such as that of Lady Mary Beauclerck and Lord Coventry in 1811. Lady Mary, the daughter of the Duke of St Albans, was only sixteen at the time and an heiress, but Lord Coventry came from the same world and was rich enough in his own right: the objection appears to have been that he was already a widower at twenty-six and something of a playboy. On one occasion, at least, there was a reversal of roles and it was the children who did the chasing. After thirty-five years of marriage, followed by thirteen years of loneliness, the Lord Chancellor of England, Lord Erskine, fell in love with his young housekeeper, Sarah Buck. The girl became pregnant and Lord Erskine announced his intention of marrying her in order to legitimize the baby they were expecting – whereupon the grown-up sons of his first wife, realizing their inheritance was in jeopardy, tried to stop the marriage by getting their father committed to a lunatic asylum. Lord Erskine outwitted them, and disguising himself as an old woman, fled north of the border with Sarah, pursued all the way by his own sons. The couple were married in 1818 but the scandal ruined Erskine and he died only five years later.

One of the most sensational scandals occurred in the spring of 1809, when Lady Charlotte Wellesley eloped with Lord Paget. She was the Duke of Wellington's sister-in-law and the mother of four young children; he was the eldest son and heir of the Earl of Uxbridge and a leading cavalry officer, while his wife, born Lady Caroline Villiers, was the daughter of Lady Jersey, the Prince Regent's ex-mistress. There was an absolute uproar, with Lady Charlotte's family blaming Paget and *his* family blaming *her*. Harriet Granville wrote that no one could talk about anything else:

London is full of impenetrable fog and horror at Lord Paget's elopement – he went off the day before yesterday with Lady Charlotte Wellesley. It is in every way shocking and unaccountable. He has left his beautiful wife and 8 or 9 children and she a husband whom she married about five years ago, for love, and who is quite a *Hero de Romance* in person and manner, with 4 poor little children.[12]

Paget made matters worse by leaving a letter in which he explained that he had 'a great esteem and affection' for his wife 'but he could not resist taking the step he had done'. Harriet Granville admitted that Lady Paget was 'a very great fool', but thought his behaviour 'inexcusable and detestable' and Lord Paget's family retaliated by telling everyone that it was all Lady Charlotte's fault, calling her a 'nefarious damned Hell-hound' and a '*maudite sorcière*'. The Duke of Wellington felt that Lady Charlotte's brother, Lord Cadogan, should have been able to stop her living 'and performing' with a divorced man, and concluded that 'poor Henry will again be dragged through the Mire, & will marry this blooming Virgin as soon as she will have been delivered of the consequences of her little amusements.' The Muddle dragged on for years: 'What a complication of infamy and vice,' the Duchess of Wellington wrote angrily, as the two divorces were set in motion.[13] The scandal ended, however, with a typical twist: Lady Paget, the supposed victim in the case, turned out to have been having an affair for years with the sixth Duke of Argyll. There was a double divorce, with Lord Paget marrying Lady Charlotte, and Lady Paget marrying Argyll, and everyone settled down again – until the next explosion in high society.

Lady Caroline Lamb was the daughter of Lady Bessborough, the woman whom Byron describes as 'the hack whore of the last century';[14] she was brought up largely at Devonshire House where all the grown-ups in her young life had lovers, and her playmates were their illegitimate children. She was hardly out of her teens when she married William Lamb, the second son of Lady Melbourne, another of the Whig grandees whose attitude towards marriage did not include the concept of fidelity. Her mother-in-law was reported to have told a young bride that her duty to her husband was to provide one male heir, and that after that she was free to amuse herself as she pleased. It was advice which Lady Melbourne herself had followed without a qualm throughout her marital career: her eldest son, Peniston, was certainly her husband's, but at least two of her five children, including William, the future Prime Minister, were fathered by Lord Egremont, and her other lovers included such eminent men as the Duke of Bedford, Lord Coleraine and the Prince of Wales himself* – who also had a brief affair with Caroline's aunt, the Duchess of Devonshire. On the other hand, her grandmother, Lady Spencer, with whom Caroline also spent large parts of her childhood, and who maintained a strong influence over her all her life, was a zealous Puritan. With such an inheritance Lady Melbourne should have known better than to be surprised when her daughter-in-law went off the rails. Caroline's first major transgression, after she married William Lamb, was an affair with Sir Godfrey Webster, which neither of them took much trouble to conceal. Why should they? Caroline must have thought, bearing in mind the example of her mother, aunt and uncle. Her mother-in-law, Lady Melbourne, however, thought otherwise; one of the most socially and politically ambitious women of her generation, Lady Melbourne cared only for appearances. It was not the fact of Caroline's infidelity which shocked her, but the openness of it. Her furious letter about the affair, in which she washed her hands of Caroline, is a masterpiece of hypocrisy: '. . . Yr. behaviour last night was so disgraceful in its appearance & so disgusting from its motives that it is quite impossible it should ever be effaced from my mind. When anyone braves the opinion of the World, sooner or later they will feel the consequences of it . . .'[15] Of course her real fear was that Caroline's behaviour would harm her beloved son's political career, as she went on, in effect, to admit: 'A Married Woman should consider that by such levity she not only compromises her own honor & character but also that of her Husband . . .' Lady Melbourne was a cruel, manipulative and selfish woman, who dismissed her daughter-in-law as a spoilt and thoughtless beauty, a silly exhibitionist who revelled in melodrama. In fact, Caroline may have been all these things, but she had many other qualities which

---

* It was generally accepted that the Prince of Wales was the father of Lady Melbourne's third son, who was even christened George (L. G. Mitchell, *Lord Melbourne*, OUP, 1997, pp. 5–6).

account for her legendary charm. Lady Morgan, the novelist and poet, both liked and admired Caroline:

One of her great charms was the rapid transition of manner which changed to its theme . . . Lady Caroline was a woman gifted with the highest powers, an artist and a poetess, a writer of romance, a woman of society and of the world, the belle, the toast, the star of the day. She was adored, but not content. She had a restless craving after excitement. She was not wicked, not even lax, but she was bold and daring in her excursions through the debatable land between friendship and love. If she never fell, she was scarcely ever safe from falling.

Eventually, of course, she fell with a crash which finished her for ever in the eyes of society.

Lord Byron, in 1812, was already a celebrity, as famous for his love affairs as his poetry. He was the epitome of the romantic hero, but 'mad, bad and dangerous to know' as Caroline herself wrote, with unusual acumen, after meeting him for the first time. Nevertheless, a violent affair was inevitable considering their mutual dispositions and by May of that year the Duchess of Devonshire was busy reporting that 'Lord Byron continues to be made the greatest fuss [of] . . . Your little friend, Caro William, as usual, is doing all sorts of imprudent things for him and with him.' A few days later Harriet Granville confirmed that 'Lord Byron is still upon a pedestal and Caroline William is doing homage': the romance had begun which was to become the scandal of the decade. The situation was further complicated by the fact that Byron was a friend of Lady Melbourne's and a frequent visitor to Melbourne House. He admitted that, if she had been a few years younger, 'what havoc she might have wrought in my affections' – which must have been extremely galling to Caroline, barely on speaking terms with her mother-in-law, even though they were all living together in the same house. Caroline and her husband had the upstairs floors of Melbourne House while the older generation lived on the ground floor, but they all shared the same entrance: so each woman knew exactly when Byron called on the other one. It is amazing that he could face either of them under the circumstances.

As the affair progressed, Caroline became increasingly 'wild and improvident', haunting Byron all over town and making terrible scenes in public, much to his annoyance. On one occasion she disguised herself as a page in order to gain admittance to his rooms when he had refused to see her. He became afraid that she was making him look ridiculous and tried to break off relations, at first fairly gently. Having complained about her 'total want of conduct', he softened the criticism by saying that her heart was a little volcano which poured lava through her veins, and finished, cravenly, as follows: 'You know that I have always thought you the cleverest, most agreeable, absurd, amiable, perplexing, dangerous, fascinating little being that lives now, or ought to have lived 2000 years ago.' Caroline, naturally, interpreted this as a love letter, which was hardly Byron's intention. The final break was suitably dramatic. At a grand party given by Lady Heathcote on 6 July 1813, Byron arrived at the party with Lady Oxford and, in front of everyone, ignored Caroline completely. She collapsed screaming and then tried to commit suicide, first by breaking a glass and cutting her wrists with the shards and then stabbing herself with a pair of scissors. A contemporary letter describes the scene:

I am perfectly horror-struck, my dear Lady Holland, at the account I have received from town, of the scene at Ly. Heathcote's . . . I have been told that poor Ly. C[aroline] L[amb] not only wounded herself in several places, but at last was carried out by several people actually in a straight waistcoat.[16]

Poor Caroline Lamb: she was a classic victim of the double standards of morality prevalent at the time. In revenge she wrote *Glenarvon*, a novel in which she was able to vent her spleen on society. The plot is absurd, however, and the thinly disguised characters are for the most part malicious caricatures of the originals: the heroine is called Calantha and is, of course, Lady Caroline herself; both the villain, Glenarvon, and the soppy hero, Vivian, are Byron, a portrait intended to convey both the best and the worst of her lover; Lady Holland is satirized as the Princess of Madagascar; Lady Mandeville was Lady Oxford;

Lady Augusta a combination of Lady Jersey and Lady Collier; Buchanan was Sir Godfrey Webster (Caroline's ex-lover); Sophia was Lady Granville; and the vulgar, pompous and prejudiced Mrs Seymour was easily identifiable as Lady Melbourne, Caroline's disapproving mother-in-law. The book was an overnight best-seller, thanks to its gossip content rather than its literary merit, and ran into several editions in the first year. It is a silly novel, virtually unreadable today, but the satire contained enough veri-similitude to cause great offence. Creevey wrote that he was 'sorry to see the Melbourne family so miserable about it. Lady Cowper is really frightened and depressed, far beyond what is necessary.'[17] Byron himself, however, could not have cared less. When Madame de Staël asked him what he thought of his portrait in the book, he replied: '*Elle aurait été plus ressemblante si j'avais voulu donner plus de séances.*' The perfect snub.

Lady Caroline and her affairs were matters of no importance beyond her own immediate, and limited, circle: but at the same time a far graver scandal was causing a national sensation. In 1809 it came to light that the Duke of York's mistress, Mary Anne Clarke, had been accepting bribes to procure commissions in the army behind the back of the War Office; and the assumption was that she could have done so only with the connivance of her lover, the Duke, who was Commander-in Chief at the time.

Mary Anne Clarke was pretty, bright and pert. She became an actress of sorts and at the age of eighteen married a Mr Clarke, having already given birth to two illegitimate children. The Duke of York first met her around 1805 and promptly set her up as his mistress, with a large house in Mayfair and all the usual luxuries. From the start Mary Anne was outrageously extravag-ant and insisted on living in a style and splendour she could not possibly afford: the Duke gave her an allowance of £1000 a year, no mean sum at the time but not nearly enough to sustain Mary Anne's expensive tastes. She spent several times that amount on furnishing her house, including £2000 on the kitchen alone, and what would have been a small fortune, had she ever paid the bill for it, on the Duc de Berri's silver dinner service. As it was, she pledged the Duke's credit. Later, she cajoled him into providing her with an additional house in the country, near his own at Oatlands, so they could meet there as well as in London. The Duke was infatuated and never seems to have queried her expenditure. For several years Mrs Clarke managed to juggle her accounts more or less successfully, but by what means nobody was quite sure. In 1809 they found out: Mrs Clarke had been financing her lifestyle by the secret sale of commissions in the army. The Duke, as Commander-in-Chief, was the ultimate authority on promotions, for which there was both a waiting list and a fixed tariff. Mary Anne had created a black market which bypassed both. She guaranteed to secure commissions for applicants ahead of the queue in return for a payment to herself, the prices for her intervention ranging from £2600 for a majority to £400 for an ensigncy. It was said that she got hold of the War Office lists of pending commissions and added a few names before it was presented to the Duke for signature: the cartoonists drew her pinning the Army Lists above their bed. It looked as though the Duke must not only have known about her illegal deals but connived at them, and the government saw no alternative but to conduct a full-scale investigation in the House of Commons. The Duke denied all knowledge of the transactions and insisted that he had signed the papers without checking them. He was brilliantly defended by Sir Vicary Gibbs, the Attorney General, but the proceedings dragged on for seven weeks and the Duke had to bear the humiliation of having his love letters to Mrs Clarke read out to a packed House and published in every scandal sheet in the country. The House roared with laughter day after day as they heard the whole sorry story of his passion, and as Mrs Clarke, a consummate comedienne, played to the gallery from the witness stand. It was the biggest scandal there had been for years and a gift to the popular press. The scandal sheets and print shops sold out as fast as they could reprint and by the second week of the trial, according to one disappointed customer, there was not a print on the case to be had for love or money. The case was known as that of the 'Duke or Darling', a phrase which became so popular people used it instead of 'Heads or

Tails' when spinning a coin. 'Peter Pindar' was not exaggerating the mood of the public when he wrote this 'Epistle to Mrs Clarke':

> Heavens, what a dire confusion beauty makes!
> The Horse Guards tremble, and old Windsor shakes.
> Like bees, the mob around St Stephen's swarms;
> And every street and alley feels alarms;
> Men, women, coaches, gigs, each other jostle
> And *thou* the cause of all this horrid bustle!
> Hotels and tap-rooms sound with mingled din,
> And every coffee-house is on the grin.
> From morn to eve, from eve to midnight dark,
> Naught strikes the ear but 'Duke and Mistress Clarke!'
> Nay, too, the parrot and the simple starling
> Cry from their cages naught but 'Duke and Darling'.[18]

In the end, though it was proved that Mrs Clarke had indeed taken bribes, there was no evidence that the Duke had been involved. He was acquitted, by 278 to 196 votes, but public feeling was still so strongly against him that he resigned.

8

CLUBS AND TAVERNS:
GAMBLING AND
GLUTTONY

A man of means during the Regency divided his time between his wife, his mistress and his club, and often spent most of it in the latter. The concept that men were accountable to their womenfolk on the subject of their whereabouts had yet to be invented, and, in any case, clubs provided the perfect sanctuary. The role of club-widow was an accepted fact of married life, however much the wives may have disliked it: their plight was an obvious target for satire, such as the following poem, which appeared in the *Comic Annual*.

CLUBS,
TURNED UP BY A FEMALE HAND

Of all the modern schemes of Man
    That time has brought to bear,
A plague upon the wicked plan
    That parts the wedded pair!
My female friends they all agree
    They hardly know their hubs;
And heart and voice unite with me,
    'We hate the name of Clubs!'

One selfish course the Wretches keep;
    They come at morning chimes;
To snatch a few short hours of sleep –
    Rise – breakfast – read *The Times* –

> Then take their hats, and post away,
>   Like Clerks or City scrubs,
> And no one sees them all the day, –
>   They live, eat, drink, at Clubs! . . .[1]

Another point of view, however, held to the opinion that clubs were an excellent institution inasmuch as they acted as catalysts in marriage: if the couple were having a row it was better for the husband to take his bad temper out on his friends at the club than his wife and children at home.

Providing an escape from feminine society, however, was but a minor aspect of the attraction of clubs. The great clubs of the eighteenth and nineteenth century played a major role in contemporary life, and many a career was made, and many a cabinet decided over a lengthy dinner at one or another of them. (Most men belonged to several clubs and rang the changes between them according to mood.) Men could meet and talk 'off the record' in the clubs, be it about politics, art or love. The atmosphere in the clubs was, by and large, democratic, based on mutual interests rather than wealth. The ambitious young politician could make the acquaintance of the party leaders, artists could meet patrons and poets publishers. On a less elevated level the aspiring dandy could feast his eyes on the accredited beau, sportsmen could gamble, gluttons indulge and gossips chatter. Scandal, of course, was particularly virulent in this purely masculine society, as the betting book at White's proves. One of the records shows that Lord Alvanley bet a certain Mr Talbot a 'hundred guineas to ten guineas that a certain person understood between them does not marry a certain lady understood between them in eighteen months from this day. January 5, 1811.' There is a postscript to the effect that Talbot paid. A week later he was placing bets that one acquaintance would outlive another, or that so-and-so 'does not die a natural death'.

The great clubs of St James's were an integral part of English life, sacred institutions in their own right, governed by their own immutable rules of conduct and honour. As one foreign observer pointed out, 'the peculiarity of English customs can be much

15. *PUBLIC BATHING AT BATH OR STEWING ALIVE*
Illustration by Robert Cruikshank for *The English Spy*, by C. Westmacott, 1826. At the King's Bath the principle of communal immersion meant that patients with infected wounds shared the same water as those with contagious diseases.

16. *DR SYNTAX SKETCHING THE LAKE*
Illustration by Rowlandson for *The Tour of Dr Syntax in Search of the Picturesque*, by W. Combe, 1812. *Dr Syntax* satirized the contemporary passion for wild and romantic scenery.

17. *PUSH-PIN*

Caricature by Gillray, published by H. Humphrey, 1797. The Duke of Queensberry, an aged *roué*, playing a table game. The fat woman is probably 'Mother Windsor', a well-known bawd.

18. *TWO-PENNY WHIST*

Caricature by Gillray, published by H. Humphrey, 1796. The woman in spectacles is Gillray's publisher and landlady, Miss Humphrey; her maid 'Betty' is winning the trick.

19. *A SLEEPING PARTNER*

Caricature by Charles Williams, published by Walker, 1809. Mary Anne Clarke, the Duke of York's mistress, reclines amidst his love letters, at the height of the army promotions scandal.

20. *TALES OF WONDER!*

Caricature by Gillray, published by H. Humphrey, 1802. A satire on the contemporary fashion for Gothic novels.

21. *LA WALSE*
Copy by Gillray of a French caricature, 1810. The waltz was not accepted in London until 1812 because it was regarded as indelicate.

22. *KING'S COLLEDGE*
Caricature by T. H. Jones, published by Fores, 1829. The Earl of Winchilsea and the Duke of Wellington fought a duel in 1829 over the question of Catholic Emancipation. The Duke missed and Lord Winchilsea fired wide.

23. *A MAN OF FEELING*
Caricature by Rowlandson, published by McCleary, 1811.

24. *QUITE WELL AGAIN*
Caricature etched and published by J. L. Marks, 1820. The new King George IV, who had been seriously ill, between the Duchess of Richmond (*left*) and Lady Hertford (*right*).

25. *POSTING IN SCOTLAND*
Caricature by Gillray, published by H. Humphrey, 1805. A satire on the inconveniences of travel in Scotland.

26. *SPORTS OF A COUNTRY FAIR*
Caricature by Rowlandson, published by Tegg, 1810.

27. *THE SALUTE*
Caricature by Gillray, published by H. Humphrey, 1797. A satire on the Foot Guards. The officer taking the salute is supposed to be General Davies, an amateur caricaturist despised by Gillray.

28. *MILITARY ORDERS*
Caricature by Rowlandson, published by Tegg, 1807. Another joke about the sexual voraciousness of women.

better observed here [i.e. in a club], at first glance, than in the great world which is always more or less the same, for the same individuals which in part make it up reveal themselves here entirely without restraint.'[2] Although each of the clubs retained its own particular flavour, the facilities on offer were more or less the same, with the accent on comfort and privacy. The buildings were furnished like grand private houses, with thick carpets, marble fireplaces, rich upholstery, beautiful looking-glasses ('always of one pane – a feature of solid English luxury', as Prince Puckler-Muskau wrote with the envy of an impoverished German), and extremely comfortable chairs. These armchairs were a revelation to the Prince, accustomed to the straight-backed formality of European furniture:

... In the first place, the foreigner must admire the refinement of comfort which the Englishman brings to the art of sitting; I must confess that anyone who does not fully understand that work of genius, the English chair, designed for every grade of fatigue, illness and peculiarity of constitution, has truly missed a great part of earthly life. It is indeed a real pleasure just to see an Englishman sit, or rather lie, in one of those bedlike chairs by the fireplace, an arrangement like a writing desk placed on the chair arm and furnished with a light, so that with the slightest pressure he can push it nearer or further away, right or left, as he wishes. Moreover a curious device, of which several stand around the great fireplace, holds up one or both of his feet, [presumably a padded footstool, an essential accessory in an age of gout] and the hat on his head completes the charming picture.[3]

Certain aspects of club life, however, seemed distinctly odd to the Prince; for example the prevalence of scales and the members' habit of weighing themselves every day, which he referred to as 'a favourite hobby of the English'. Similarly he was much struck by the occasional lapse of principles, notably in the case of umbrellas: 'These last attract great care in England since umbrellas, which are so necessary, are stolen in a quite shameless fashion if one does not watch very closely after their safety.' Finally, his comments on the club servants provide an interesting light on the relative economies of Germany and England. He was obviously surprised to see that they all wore proper shoes: 'You never see the numerous domestic staff without shoes, but clad in plain clothes or livery as clean as can be . . .'[4]

White's, Brooks's and Boodle's were the three great clubs of the Regency. Of the three, White's was arguably the smartest and most exclusive: Walpole declared that when an heir was born to a great house, the butler was sent to White's to put his name down in the candidates' book before he went on to record the child's birth at the registry office. White's was basically a social club which prided itself on holding aloof from party politics; Boodle's belonged to the country squires and the fox-hunting set, while Brooks's was the most openly political of the triumvirate. These three clubs, despite their professed individuality, were, in fact, remarkably similar in character and often shared the same clientele. For example, those two great political rivals, Pitt and Fox, were members of both White's and Brooks's at the same time. If White's was considered the most aristocratic of the clubs, Brooks's was the most interesting.

Brooks's was founded in 1778 by one of the ex-managers of Almack's, a man named William Brooks. The original twenty-seven members of Brooks's were all Macaronis, young dandies who specialized in outrageous dressing and enormous wigs. The average age of the founder members was twenty-five; they were all of them rich, smart and extravagant, so it is hardly surprising that the club acquired a reputation for wild behaviour and sensational gambling. Astronomical sums changed hands: according to the club records, one of the founder members, a Mr Thynne, 'Having won only £12,000 during the last two months . . . retired in disgust.'[5] At the same time, these young men were, for the most part, scions of the great Whig families, and as such had been indoctrinated with politics and the concept of liberalism from the earliest age. Thus, in tandem with its reputation as a gambling hell, Brooks's soon became known as a breeding ground for Whig politicians and, within a few years, as the ex-officio headquarters of the party. It was the stamping ground of Charles James Fox, who was elected at the age of sixteen, and other like-minded advocates of reform. Trevelyan described Brooks's as 'the most famous political club that will ever have existed in England.'[6] Gambling and politics were yet to be condemned as mutually exclusive occupations. Membership of Brooks's, however, was by no means confined to politicians: other celebrities included Burke, Reynolds, Garrick, Horace Walpole, Gibbon, Sheridan, Wilberforce and the Prince of Wales, who joined so that he could talk to Fox in comfort and privacy (and enlist Fox's support in parliament over his debts and other complaints against his father and the government). Sheridan, incidentally, was proposed three times for membership of Brooks's and blackballed on each occasion by George Selwyn. Selwyn's objection to the playwright was not, as might have been justified, on account of Sheridan's wild and drunken behaviour, but because his father had been on the stage. Selwyn was a terrible snob. In the end, however, Sheridan did get in: he and his friends tricked Selwyn into leaving the premises during the election meeting by sending a fake message that the Prince of Wales wanted to see him.

The great common denominator between all these clubs was gambling, the passion which dominated high society in London from the reign of Queen Anne to that of Queen Victoria. The clubs of St James's were descended from the chocolate and coffee houses of the seventeenth and early eighteenth century: White's club, for example, was the offspring of a chocolate house of that name which flourished at the end of the seventeenth century. The Cocoa-Tree Club, of which Byron was a member during the Regency, was originally a Tory chocolate house, famous for having once been the headquarters of the Jacobite Party. As gambling increased in popularity, however, it became clear that such houses were unsuitable meeting places, because they were open to the public at large and it was therefore impossible to vet the customers. They were an obvious magnet to cheats and card-sharpers who specialized in making the acquaintance of young men newly arrived in town and other credulous gamblers. Gambling with strangers could prove embarrassing as well as dangerous: as one critic pointed out, 'even highwaymen of the more presentable type were constantly to be met at the Chocolate House; judges there were liable to meet the man whom they might afterwards have to sentence in the dock; it was no uncommon thing . . . to recognise a body swinging in chains on a heath outside London as a man with whom you had called a main at hazard a few weeks before at White's or at the Cocoa Tree.'[7] The ministers and men of fashion very naturally preferred to lose their fortunes to each other in privacy and decorum, so they formed their own 'private Houses' – or clubs.

During the eighteenth century the passion for gambling reached its zenith. White's was described as 'the bane of half the English nobility',[8] because of the fortunes lost at play, and Lord Lyttelton wrote of his dread that

. . . the rattling of a dice-box at White's may one day or other (if my son should be a member of that noble academy) shake down all our fine oaks. It is dreadful to see, not only there, but almost in every [gambling] house in town, what devastations are made by that destructive fury, the spirit of play.

It was quite true that whole estates could change hands in a single evening. Admiral Harvey, as a young man, lost £100,000 playing at White's, and offered to sell his estate in payment. Fortunately his opponent was an Irish gamester with a conscience, who refused to accept more than £10,000 and suggested they play again for the other ninety. They did so, Harvey won, saved his estate, and went on to serve under Nelson at Trafalgar. Charles James Fox was a legendary gambler, often indulging in marathon sessions which carried on for several days and nights. Walpole wrote that on the occasion of a particular debate in the House,* Fox's usual oratory was notably absent,

nor could it be wondered at. He had sat up playing at hazard at Almack's, from Tuesday evening the 4th, till five in the afternoon of Wednesday, 5th. An hour before he had recovered 12,000*l.* that he had lost, and by dinner, which was at five o'clock, he had ended losing

* 6 February 1772.

11,000*l.* On the Thursday, he spoke in the above debate; went to dinner at past eleven that night; from thence to White's, where he drank till seven the next morning; thence to Almack's, where he won 6,000*l.*; and between three and four in the afternoon he set out for Newmarket. His brother Stephen lost 11,000*l.* two nights after, and Charles 10,000*l.* more on the 13th; so that in three nights, the two brothers, the eldest not twenty-five, lost 32,000*l.*[9]

This sort of gambling had nothing to do with having fun, or an amusing evening: it was a deadly serious addiction, often conducted in silence apart from the croupier's call. Gamblers wore special clothes, partly from superstition, but partly, too, for practical reasons, as the following description shows:

The gamesters began by pulling off their embroidered clothes, and put on frieze greatcoats, or turned their coats inside outwards for luck. They put on pieces of leather (such as are worn by footmen when they clean the knives) to save their laced ruffles; and to guard their eyes from the light and to prevent tumbling their hair, wore high-crowned straw hats with broad brims, and adorned with flowers and ribbons; masks to conceal their emotions when they played . . . Each gamester had a small neat stand by him, to hold his tea; or a wooden bowl with an edge of ormolu, to hold the rouleaus.[10]

At the end of the eighteenth century the most popular games were hazard and faro, which were played against the bank. Hazard was a game of pure chance, in which the players threw dice against a particular number between five and nine, which was chosen by the 'caster'. It could be played by any number of people, who took it in turns to 'call the main'. Since the odds were well known, it was a game of pure chance, similar to the modern American game of craps. Faro was a variation on the theme of roulette, but eventually fell into disrepute because it was so easy for the bank to cheat, and was succeeded by a craze for macao, another game involving several players. At the same time too, of course, there was always plenty of single combat going on in the clubs, members chancing huge sums of money on a hand of piquet or a round of backgammon. Whist was popular as well, but regarded as comparatively harmless, even though it was possible to raise the stakes to dangerously high levels: General Scott, Canning's father-in-law, won £200,000 playing whist at White's, but that was said to have been 'thanks to his notorious sobriety'.[11] Gambling was by no means confined to aristocratic circles and the London clubs: in Assembly Rooms all over the country a quiet room was reserved for players to risk their money at whatever game of chance was in fashion. The Card Room at Bath, added to the new buildings in 1777, was adjacent to the ballroom and of almost equal importance to the company. William Lecky, the nineteenth-century historian, wrote that 'At Bath ... it [gambling] reigned supreme; and the physicians even recommended it to their patients as a form of distraction ... Among fashionable ladies the passion was quite as strong as among men, and the professor of whist ... became a regular attendant at their levées.' It was an established feature of country house-parties – and liable to be one of the hazards for an impoverished guest. At Oatlands, for example, the Duke of York insisted on keeping his guests up most of the night playing whist for stakes which even he could ill afford.

It is generally assumed that serious gambling was a peculiarly eighteenth-century vice or pastime and, in fact, by the beginning of the nineteenth, playing for the kind of outrageous stakes which could, and did, ruin whole families had fallen out of favour. Nevertheless, gambling continued to cause havoc amongst the leaders of the Regency, and 'many a time', as one social commentator mourned, 'after a long night of hard play, the loser found himself at the Israelite establishment of Howard and Gibbs, then the fashionable, and patronised, money-lenders.'[12] But for many, as has already been said, even these resources failed: disgraced and ruined, they fled to the Continent in the wake of such fallen idols as Brummell, Scrope Davies and 'Golden Ball' Hughes.

During the Regency a number of clubs were formed on the basis of a specialist interest, aiming to attract a particular clientele. The Roxburghe Club, for example, was dedicated to bibliophiles and the qualification for membership based on possession of a significant private library: founder members included the Duke of Devonshire, the Earl of Carlisle and Sir Walter Scott. The club was formed as a result of the sale, in 1812, of the Duke of Roxburghe's magnificent library. The sale lasted for forty-one days and caused a sensation, a 'sort of book earthquake', according to Thomas Dibdin, the accepted bibliographical authority at the time. The most important volume of the collection, a copy of *The Decameron*, by Boccaccio, printed by Christopher Valdarfer, at Venice in 1471, was kept to the last day of the sale. The initial bid came from 'a gentleman from Shropshire, who seems almost electrified at his own temerity in offering "100 guineas"'. The bidding developed into a duel between Earl Spencer and the Marquess of Blandford, won by the latter, 'and down drops the hammer before the amazed and excited auditory at the last-named handsome figure, namely £2260':[13] clearly, this was thought too much at the time. The value of rare books was yet to be recognized at the start of the nineteenth century but, largely as the result of the Roxburghe sale, the acquisition of a fine library acquired the cultural status of an art collection.

Members of the Roxburghe, a club which has lasted to the present day, subsidized the preservation and reprinting of rare books and ancient manuscripts. The Society of Dilettanti was founded much earlier but professed a similar aim, practical patron-age of the arts. The membership included Charles James Fox, Garrick, Sir Joshua Reynolds and most of the Whig grandees, as well as the notable connoisseurs of the period. Horace Walpole, however, was thoroughly scathing about the Dilettanti, writing that the nominal qualification 'for membership' was having been to Italy, and the real one being drunk. Nevertheless, the society funded a number of expeditions during the Regency, and has continued to make a significant contribution to the national heritage ever since: the Dilettanti have also carried on meeting to the present day. The Alfred Club, however, which also started off with vaguely intellectual pretensions, seems to have been doomed from the start. It was founded in 1808 with the stated intention of attracting the international literati of the period, but quickly became known as the 'Half-read Club'. During the

Regency, club-addicts were always willing to try out a new venture but their verdicts on the Alfred were scathing. Byron was one of the original members but left fairly smartly, finding it 'a little too sober'. He suggested it was a place to go when all else failed, 'on a rainy day, in a dearth of parties, or Parliament, or in an empty season'. Lord Dudley referred to it as an 'asylum of doting Tories and drivelling quidnuncs', but admitted they were 'civil and quiet'; while Lord Alvanley, when asked whether he was still a member of the Alfred, replied, 'Not exactly. I stood it as long as I could, but when the seventeenth bishop was proposed I gave in. I really could not enter the place without being put in mind of my catechism.' The Traveller's Club, on the other hand, was an instantaneous success when it was launched in 1814 by Lord Castlereagh, the then Foreign Secretary. Prince Talleyrand was one of the founder members and used it as a home from home whenever he was in London, playing whist and weaving schemes in the comfort of the gracious rooms. The Traveller's was adopted by the diplomatic world of the Regency and has flourished ever since, but there was some initial criticism over the procedure of admission. It was said that 'all educated and well-recommended foreigners are admitted, but in a rather humiliating way – they have to ask for re-admission every three months, which is insisted upon with almost impolite strictness and held to the very day.'[14]

The Royal Society was one of the most important and influential clubs of the period. The club was originally named the Royal Philosophers but, towards the end of the eighteenth century, this somewhat daunting title was dropped in favour of the more general name and its members came to be known simply as 'the Royals'. The club became the meeting place for all the most distinguished scientists, engineers, astronomers, explorers and botanists of their day, ranging from Cook to Stephenson. The Royal Society, however, was not solely confined to scientific celebrities: soldiers, sailors, bishops, poets, musicians, writers and artists were all welcome. Gibbon, Sir Joshua Reynolds, Benjamin Franklin, Boswell, Wedgwood, Sir Thomas Lawrence, Turner and Watt were all either regular guests or actual members in their time. It was an age of exciting new ideas, in science, technology and medicine, and many were voiced for the first time to the company of the Royals.

One of the more curious customs inaugurated by the Royal Society was that of allowing presents of game, or other luxury foods, in lieu of the membership fee. The original charter included a resolution to the effect that: 'any nobleman or gentleman complimenting this company with venison, not less than a haunch, shall . . . be deemed an honorary member, and admitted as often as he comes without paying the fee which those members do who are elected by ballot'. The gift of a turtle to the club 'carried the same privileges', and other gastronomic treats presented to the club kitchens by members included carp, *tusks* (rare and delicate fish), water melons from Malaga, Egyptian cos lettuces, pine-apples and 'a mighty chine of beef'.[15]

The eighteenth century was a carnivorous age. The English attitude to meat at the time was like that of the Texans in the twentieth: the size of the steaks on offer was an indication of status, or the generosity of the host, and the amount a man could consume a test of his virility. It was considered manly, rather than greedy, to eat huge quantities of beef, and, in any case, the British male really preferred such basic fare to the complicated French food currently fashionable in private houses. Hence the attraction of dining in the clubs, which traditionally served little else. 'The Sublime Society of Beef-Steaks', as it was christened, appears to have been founded as a protest against the prevalent fashion for French cuisine. An early account reports that the society was 'composed of the most ingenious artists in the King-dom', who met every Saturday in a room at the top of Covent Garden Theatre and never suffered 'any diet except Beef-steaks to appear. These, indeed, are most glorious examples: but what, alas!', complains the food correspondent of the day, 'are the weak endeavours of a few to oppose the daily inroads of fricassées and soupe-maigres?' The drink was equally conservative: no French wines or champagnes, but arrack punch out of pint pots – and a great deal of it. Garrick, who was one of the founder members

NIGHT. MORNING
Caricature by Robert Seymour, *c.* 1828.

of the club, caused a near riot among the customers in the pit and gallery at Drury Lane Theatre because he kept turning up late on stage, thanks to lingering over his steaks and arrack next door. The Prince of Wales, never one to pass up a gastronomic experience, was elected to the club in 1785: other members, over the years, ranged from artists and actors to bankers, politicians and socialites. The list included Hogarth, Kemble, the Dukes of Sussex and Clarence, the radical Wilkes and conservative Lord Eldon, Brougham and Charles James Fox. The most legendary trencherman of all the Steaks was Charles, the eleventh Duke of Norfolk. The Duke was a splendid example of the difference between a gourmand and a gourmet: what the Duke wanted, and what the Duke got, was quantity. In his prime he would start his dinner with a token dish or two of fish at one of the other Covent Garden taverns, and then proceed to the Steaks for the serious business of the evening. The ritual of cooking the steaks was part of the attraction:

As the clock struck five, a curtain drew up discovering the kitchen, in which the cooks were seen at work, through a sort of grating, with this inscription from *Macbeth*: –

'If it were done, when 'tis done, then 'twere well
It were done quickly.'

The steaks themselves were enormous,

. . . and in devouring them no one surpassed His Grace of Norfolk: two or three steaks, fragrant from the gridiron, vanished, and when his labours were thought to be over, he might be seen rubbing a clean plate with a shalot for the reception of another. A pause of ten minutes ensued, and His Grace rested upon his knife and fork: he was tarrying for a steak from the middle of the rump of beef, where lurks a fifth essence, the perfect ideal of tenderness and flavour . . . He would often eat between three and four pounds of beef-steak; and after that take a Spanish onion and beet-root, chop them together with oil and vinegar, and eat them.[16]

Legend has it that the Duke once consumed no less than fifteen of these great steaks at a single sitting. The whole performance, allowing for the preliminary fish session, often lasted from three in the afternoon until well after midnight. Surprisingly, this particular Duke, far from keeling over with a heart attack from a surfeit of cholesterol, lived on into his seventieth year – he died in 1815.

By the beginning of the nineteenth century, however, only the most dedicated carnivores were content with such fare. The Regency was a sophisticated age and, in line with other aspects of fashionable life, taste in food began to favour quality and elegance over simple quantity, even in the clubs. According to Gronow, the Prince of Wales, in the course of entertaining several members of White's and Brooks's, asked them what sort of dinners they got at their clubs and was told that the food was always the same: 'the eternal joints, or beef-steaks, the boiled fowl with oyster sauce, and an apple-tart – this is what we have, sir, at our clubs, and very monotonous fare it is.'[17] Whereupon the Prince sent for his own chef, Jean Baptiste Watier, and asked him to form a club which would put particular emphasis on the cuisine. It was founded in 1807, with one of the French cooks from Carlton House as head chef and Brummell as the permanent president. The food was apparently delicious; Gronow spoke of the dinners as 'exquisite' and insisted that no Parisian chef could better the one at Watier's. Watier, or rather the Prince himself, had clearly discovered a gap in the market. The club, however, overreached itself and came to an end after only a few years, ruined by excessive gambling. The preferred games at Watier's were macao and hazard, but by 1819, it was said, there was no one left to gamble with because, almost without exception, the members of Watier's were ruined. Henceforth gambling in all the London clubs was on a slightly more reasonable level, though still excessive in the eyes of many. Thomas Raikes offered an alternative view, attributing the demise of Watier's to 'the paralysed state of its members', by which, presumably, he meant that they had all over eaten and drunk to such an extent that they had made themselves ill. He wrote a long list in his diary of the members who had recently died, adding a note that 'none of the dead reached the average age of man'.[18] Those who survived Watier's moved on to become members of Crockford's, where they carried on eating and gambling for as long as they were physically and financially able to.

William Crockford began life as a fishmonger in the City, won £100,000 at play and used the money to start his own club in St James's.[19] The building was designed and decorated by Wyatt, in 1827, and was a temple of sumptuous luxury; there was a library with marble columns imported from Sienna, the drawing room was decorated in the style of Louis XIV and filled with the finest French furniture, the walls were covered with paintings *à la Watteau*, the staircase was panelled with scagliola and 'enriched with Corinthian columns' and everything possible was covered in gilt. The glory of the new club-house was described, in the exaggerated style typical of journalism at the time, as:

the New Pandemonium; the drawing-rooms, or real Hell, consisting of four chambers; the first an ante-room, opening to a saloon embellished to a degree which baffles description; thence to a small, curiously formed cabinet, or boudoir, which opens to the supper room. All these rooms are panelled in the most gorgeous manner, spaces being left to be filled up with mirrors, silk or gold enrichments; the ceilings being as superb as the walls.

There was a billiard room on an upper floor, and a number of smaller private rooms 'whose walls will tell no tales'. In Gronow's opinion, Crockford 'won the whole of the ready money of the then existing generation'. He made more than a million pounds over the years, but lost most of it in the end. Crockford knew the importance of feeding his members well; suitably mellowed they would spend more at the gaming tables. His chef, M. Ude, had served his apprenticeship in the kitchens of Letitia Bonaparte, Napoleon's mother, and had later cooked for both the Duke of York and the second Earl of Sefton, who was generally acknowledged to be a most discerning gourmet. Gronow raved about Crockford's in its heyday:

No one can describe the splendour and excitement of the early days of Crockey. A supper of the most exquisite kind, prepared by the famous Ude, and accompanied by the best wines in the world, together with every luxury of the season, was furnished gratis. The members of the club included all the celebrities of England, from the Duke of Wellington to the youngest Ensign of the Guards; and at the gay and festive board, which was constantly replenished from midnight to early dawn, the most brilliant sallies of wit, the most agreeable conversation, the most interesting anecdotes, interspersed with grave political discussions and acute logical reasoning on every conceivable subject, proceeded from the soldiers, scholars, statesmen, poets and men of pleasure, who, when the 'house was up' and balls and parties at an end, delighted to finish their evening with a little supper and a good deal of hazard at old Crockey's. The tone of the club was excellent. A most gentleman-like feeling prevailed, and none of the rudeness, familiarity and ill-breeding which disgrace some of the minor clubs of the present day [i.e. *circa* 1850], would have been tolerated for a moment,[20]

the Captain concluded with evident nostalgia.

*

Gastronomic taste has changed in many ways since the days of the Regency: turtle, for example, has been relegated to the role of a tinned soup today and oysters are a costly luxury. At the beginning of the nineteenth century oysters were so cheap that servants would stipulate that they should not be expected to eat them more than so many times a week: but an invitation to a 'turtle dinner' was a sure indication of a feast. The King's Head tavern in the City was the main London depot for the turtles which formed such a feature of Regency dinners. They were stored in the courtyard and were seen as one of the attractions of the place: '. . . in the quadrangle of the tavern might be seen scores of turtle, large and lively, in huge tanks of water; or laid upward on the stone floor, ready for their destination.' People could go and choose one for a private dinner party, or to be despatched as a present to friends. Turtles, according to a contemporary source, will keep for three months in excellent condition provided they are kept in the same water in which they were brought to this country: changing the water reduces the weight of the turtle and dilutes the flavour. The usual allowance at a turtle dinner was 6 lb live weight per head and the cost could be as high as 3s 6d per lb, even if bought direct from the ship. At one such dinner in 1808, given at the London Tavern, four hundred guests consumed 2500 lbs of turtle.[21] The Shakespeare in Covent Garden, a popular theatrical tavern, was another eating-house famous for the number of turtles kept on the premises. According to a Mr Twigg, who was the cook there in 1815, they always had at least fifty turtles on stand-by, and between ten and fifteen dressed turtles as well as an average of forty quarts of turtle soup were dispatched around the country every week. Orders came in from as far away as Yorkshire and Devon. The largest dinner Twigg ever cooked consisted of 108 'made-dishes', excluding cold meats and vegetables; and on another occasion the menu featured a 40-lb turbot, a Thames salmon, a haunch of venison and a green goose, besides numerous side-dishes. The cost for this feast was 7 guineas a head. (It is a comment on the Regency passion for style in all departments of life that the cooking and presentation of a dish is described as 'dressing'.)

Another surprising delicacy at the time, considering how cheap it is today, was whitebait. A number of riverside taverns used to specialize in serving 'Whitebait Dinners' and the *Morning Post* always reported the annual 'Ministerial Fish Dinner'. The cabinet sailed down the river in a gilded barge to one of the taverns at Greenwich or Blackwall for their feast at which the *pièce de résistance* was fresh fried whitebait. At one of these taverns, twenty-two different fish dishes were served, including four different soups, lampreys in Worcester sauce, fried eels, minced eels and something ominously listed on the menu as 'les casseroles de green fat', which 'feront le tour de la table'. This was probably a gravy made from the fat of a green goose, another regular favourite at Regency dinners.

Some of the taverns concentrated on catering to clients with a particular common interest. The legendary Crown and Anchor in the Strand, for example, was almost an annexe of the House of Commons: it became the rallying point of the Westminster electors and the scene of some of the rowdiest political meetings in London. These were held in the tavern's enormous ballroom – 85 ft by 35 ft 6 ins – which could hold up to 2500 people. Between elections the Crown and Anchor could be hired for parties: Charles James Fox once gave a banquet there for 2000 guests. Offley's tavern in Henrietta Street was another political rendezvous, popular with MPs and a 'right joyously convivial place', according one *habitué*. MPs went to this one for the food as much as the conversation: 'Offley's chop was thick and substantial; the House of Commons chop was small and thin, and honourable Members sometimes ate a dozen at a sitting.' The Albion in Aldersgate was one of the most expensive eating houses, and was said to provide the most munificent food in London. The history of the Albion provides one of the best examples of Regency extravagance: Alderman Sir William Curtis, a famous gourmet, once gave a party there which cost nearly £40 a head: he sent a special messenger to Westphalia to choose the ham. Even an 'ordinary', as the *menu du jour* was called, cost 3 guineas a head at the Albion, which was far more than at most of the London taverns.

The wealth and importance of some of these taverns is obvious from the size of their cellars. The whole basement of the London Tavern in Bishopsgate was

filled with barrels of porter, pipes of port, butts of sherry etc. Then there are a labyrinth of walls of bottle ends, and a region of bins, six bottles deep; catacombs of Johanisberg, Tokay and Burgundy . . . There are twelve hundred of champagne down here; there are between six and seven hundred dozen of claret; corked up in these bins is a capital of from eleven to twelve thousand pounds; these bottles absorb, in simple interest at five per cent, an income amounting to some five or six hundred pounds per annum.[22]

Limmer's was the rendezvous for the sporting world, in particular the boxing fraternity and men of the turf. As one client wrote:

. . . in fact, it was a midnight Tattersall's, where you heard nothing but the language of the turf, and where men with not very clean hands used to make their books. Limmer's was the most dirty hotel in London; but in the gloomy comfortless coffee-room might be seen many members of the rich squirearchy who visited London during the sporting season. This hotel was frequently so crowded, that a bed could not be obtained for any amount of money; but you could always get a very good plain English dinner, an excellent bottle of port, and some famous gin-punch.

One of the popular ditties of the Regency, written by a clergyman who was also a boxing enthusiast, celebrated Limmer's thus:

My name is John Collins, head waiter at Limmer's,
Corner of Conduit Street, Hanover Square.
My chief occupation is filling the brimmers
For spicy young gentlemen frequenting there.

And so it went on for several more, equally silly, verses in the same vein. This sort of song, sung in the streets, by merry young men, was part of the background music of life in London during the Regency.

*

The idea of restaurants, places where men and women could eat together in public with perfect propriety, arose in Paris after the French Revolution. In London, however, the concept was not accepted until much later. A 'lady of quality' could only dine out in one of the smart hotels, and then only if heavily chaperoned, or in the company of her husband. The smartest hotels during the Regency were the Clarendon, Grillon's and the Pulteney. The Clarendon was said to serve the best dinners in London, but it was expensive: £3 or £4 a head in 1814, even without drink, and a bottle of claret or champagne cost a further guinea. Visiting grandees tended to favour the Pulteney, at 105 Piccadilly, which was considered the most modern and luxurious of the three. The Russian royal family took over the whole hotel when they came to London for the Regent's premature peace celebrations in 1814, at a cost of 210 guineas per week. Rooms had been booked initially just for the Tsar's sister, the Grand Duchess of Oldenburg, and her suite as the Emperor himself had been invited to stay with the Regent. But when the Tsar arrived he refused the apartments specially prepared for him at St James's Palace and insisted on joining his sister at the Pulteney instead, thus creating an unfortunate atmosphere from the start of their visit. Grillon's was equally exclusive but more conservative, a family hotel, favoured by ladies up from the country for a few days' shopping in London. Louis XVIII preferred Grillon's to the Pulteney and so did Princess Adelaide and her mother when they came to London for the Princess's wedding to the Duke of Clarence. Evan's, in Covent Garden, established at the end of the eighteenth century, was another family hotel in London and boasted 'stabling for one hundred noblemen and horses'. All these were acceptable places to dine or stay the night: other, less well-known hotels popular at the time included Ibbetson's, which was cheaper and patronized chiefly by academics and clergymen; Fladong's, favoured by the navy; and Steven's in Bond Street, which was rather more raffish, the haunt of guardees and dandies.

9

THE AGE OF
INDULGENCE

Clubs, taverns and hotels, however, are all public places catering
for a variable clientele and therefore settle for a median in matters
of taste, often the most conservative common denominator. In
private households there were no such restraints so the chefs of the
period could give real expression to their skill and imagination.
Marie-Antoine Carême, at one time head chef to the Prince
Regent, was the first and most influential of the great French
chefs who transformed cooking into an art and a science. He was
a phenomenon, a celebrity in his own right courted by royalty
and noblemen throughout Europe. Carême's extraordinary history has been recorded by the French novelist and gastronome,
Alexandre Dumas *père*, who relates that Carême was born shortly
before the Revolution and was the sixteenth child of a stone-
mason.[1] At the age of eleven his father took him to the gates of
Paris, fed him supper at a tavern and abandoned him in the street.
Fortunately for posterity he found employment first in the kitchen
of a tavern and then in an elegant patisserie, where he learnt to
read, write and draw as well as to cook. He became interested in
architecture and spent much of his spare time in the Bibliothèque
Royale, studying prints and engravings of classical buildings –
Grecian, Roman and even Egyptian. Carême's passion for classical
architecture found expression in the elaborate *pièces montées* for
which he became so famous. His tables were always decorated
with beautiful and exact replicas of classical temples, rotundas,

bridges and other follies, created from spun sugar and pastry. These enormous centrepieces were made to be admired, not eaten, particularly as they were held together by wax and poisonous glues. Around 1805 Carème became head chef to the French Foreign Minister Talleyrand, himself a well-known gourmet, and later served both Tsar Alexander and the Prince Regent. Much to the Prince's dismay, however, Carème stayed in his employ for only a few halcyon months and returned to Paris to work for Baron Rothschild.

The principles of *haute cuisine*, as practised by Carème and his peers, originated in Paris at the court of Louis XV in the previous century. According to one of 'the fathers of the table', Grimod de la Reynière, there was a direct link between sex and the new gastronomic culture: the ladies of the court who wanted to win the King's favour went to immense trouble creating new dishes with which to tempt his failing appetite. These rich and elaborate *plats*, the antithesis of medieval fare with its accent on solid meats, became the basis of *haute cuisine*. Grimod gives another reason for the success of extravagant food, mocking the greed of the *nouveaux riches* in a way which is equally applicable to their English contemporaries:

The upheaval that has taken place in the distribution of wealth as a natural result of the Revolution has transferred old riches into new hands. As the mentality of these overnight millionaires revolves around purely animal pleasures, it is believed that a service might be rendered them by offering a reliable guide to that most solid part of their affections. The hearts of the greatest number of rich Parisians have suddenly transformed into gullets, their sentiments are no more than sensations, their desires, appetites . . .[2]

These 'fathers of the table' discussed every aspect of gastronomy with the fervour of serious connoisseurs. Brillat-Savarin, for example, was always inventing new words: *truffivorous* for a truffle eater; *obsegenous* for fattening foods; and it was he who suggested the verb to *indigest*. And when Brillat-Savarin coined the aphorism *On devient cuisinier, mais on naît rôtisseur*, one of the others took issue in print, insisting that the *saucier* was the true genius. 'After all, what is a *rôtisseur?*' he asked scornfully,

. . . a man who manipulates, who lives by routine observation, who has no contact with precise science except one or two superficial notions of physics needed to calculate the heat required for each joint . . . one does not treat a spit holding a joint of beef weighing twenty pounds like one carrying twenty ortolans, or better still, robins, fig-eaters or larks . . . What is a *saucier?* An enlightened chemist, a creative genius, the cornerstone of the monument to transcendental cuisine . . . No sauce, no redemption, no cookery.[3]

The cult of gastronomy and *haute cuisine* was just as strong in London as in Paris. Furthermore, the English writers were just as loquacious on the subject as the French, though rather more likely to concentrate on the evils of over-eating and argue about the relative merits or demerits of various foods. It would appear that medical opinion, or fashion, was just as indecisive 200 years ago as it is today. The writer of one of the most popular manuals of the Regency wrote that:

There is perhaps no article of our usual Diet, however Insignificant or however Important, which has not been at one time highly extolled, and at another extremely abused, by those who have published *Books on Diet*, who, wedded to their own whimsies, and estimating the Strength of other Men's Stomachs by the Weakness of their Own, have, as the fit took 'em, attributed 'all the Evils flesh is heir to,' to eating either too much or too little – Salt – Sugar – Spice – Bread – Butter – Pastry – Poultry – Pork – Veal – Beef – Lamb, and indeed all Meats, excepting Mutton, have alternately been prescribed and proscribed.[4]

The difference between then and now was that nobody took much notice. Occasionally they attempted to diet, for reasons of health or vanity. The new Empire dresses made no allowance for corsets: large ladies wearing them looked like nothing so much as 'a sack of potatoes tied with a piece of string' as one fictional matron declared in despair. Byron, whose tendency to corpulence did nothing for his image as a romantic hero, was always pretending to diet. On one occasion he made a great parade at a dinner party of refusing everything offered and asking for 'nothing but hard biscuits and soda-water'. As neither was available 'he dined upon potatoes bruised down upon his plate and drenched in vinegar'. But his behaviour was straight affectation: on quitting the party he went on to a club in St James's and ate 'a hearty meat-supper'. Harriet Cavendish and her sister made rather more serious attempts to lose weight and invented a peculiarly unappetizing diet of scraps: 'had a dinner after our own hearts, a little in the style of Cumberland's Jew, Egg shells and potatoe skins, but quite enough for people upon régimes as strict as ours.' There were others, too, who objected to gluttony on the grand scale as a matter of principle. The *Quarterly Review* thought it worthy of indignant comment that one of the members of Crockford's ate a *covey* of partridges for breakfast every day during the season. But such carping was rare. By the time of the Regency the whole paraphernalia of eating, as far as those who could afford it were concerned, bore little relation to a need for nourishment. Society took its lead from the Prince Regent, whose indulgence at the table knew no restraint.

Some of the banquets given by the Prince have passed into culinary legend: for example, the magnificent dinner prepared by Carème at the Brighton Pavilion on 15 January 1817. The menu on this occasion included more than a hundred hot dishes:

TABLE DE S.A.R. LE PRINCE REGENT
Servie au pavillon de Brighton, Angleterre
15 Janvier 1817
Menu de 36 entrées

QUATRE POTAGES

| Le potage à la Monglas | Le potage d'orge perlée à la Crécy |
| La garbure aux choux | Le potage de poissons à la Russe |

QUATRE RELEVÉS DE POISSONS
La matelote au vin de Bordeaux
Les truites au bleu à la Provençale
Le turbot à l'Anglaise, sauce aux homards
La grosse anguille à la régence

QUATRE GROSSES PIÈCES POUR LES CONTRE-FLANCS
Le jambon à la broche, au Madère
L'oie braisée aux racines glacées
Les poulardes à la Périgueux
Le rond de veau à la royale

TRENTE-SIX ENTRÉES, DONT QUATRE SERVENT DE
CONTRE-FLANCS
Les filets de volaille à la maréchale
Le sauté de merlans aux fines herbes
La timbale de macaroni à la Napolitaine
La noix de veau à la jardinière
Les filets de volaille à l'Orléans

Le Jambon à la Broche
La darne de saumon au beurre de Montpellier
Le sauté de faisans aux truffes
La fricassée de poulets à l'Italienne
Le turban de filets de lapereaux

Les Truites au Bleu
Les boudin de volaille à la Béchamel
Le sauté de ris de veau à la Provençale
Les ailes de poulardes glacées à la chicorée
Les galantines de perdreaux à la gelée

L'Oie Braisée aux Racines Glacées
Les petites canetons de volaille en haricots vierges
Les poulets à la reine, à la Chevry
Les petites croustades de mauviettes au gratin
Les côtelettes de mouton à l'Irlandaise
Les filets de bécasses à la royale
Les filets de sarcelles à la Bourguignotte
Les petits poulets à l'Indienne
Les petites pâtés de mouton à l'Anglaise
L'épigramme de poulardes, purée de céleri
Le faisan à la Minime, bordure de racines

Les Poulardes à la Périgueux
L'aspic de blanc de volaille à la ravigote
Les filets de perdreaux à la Pompadour
L'émincé de poulardes au gratin
La côte de boeuf aux oignons glacés

Le Turbot à l'Anglaise
Le sauté de poulardes à la Provençale
Le salmis de cailles au vin de Madère
Les escalopes de volaille aux truffes
La salade de filets de brochets aux huîtres

Le Rond de Veau à la Royale
Le pain de carpes au beurre d'anchois
Les côtelettes d'agneau glacées à la Toulouse
Le vol-au-vent de quenelles à l'Allemande
Les ailerons de poulardes aux champignons
Les pigeons à la Mirepoix financière

POUR EXTRA, DIX ASSIETTES VOLANTES DE FRITURE
5 De filets de soles   5 De filets de gelinottes à l'Allemande

HUIT GROSSES PIÈCES DE PÂTISSERIE

La brioche au fromage	Le croque-en-bouche aux pistaches
Le nougat à la Française	Le biscuit à l'Orange
La ruine d'Antioche	L'hermitage chinois
L'hermitage Syrien	La ruine de la mosquée turque

QUATRE PLATS DE ROTS

Les coqs de Bruyères	Les poulets gras bardés
Les canards sauvages	Les gelinottes

TRENTE-DEUX ENTREMETS

Les truffes à la cendre	*L'Hermitage Chinois*
La gelée d'oranges moulée	Les petits paniers aux
Les épinards à l'essence	confitures
La Brioche au Fromage	*Les Poulets Gras Bardés*
Les homards a gratin	Les génoises glacées au café
Les petits pains à la	La charlotte à l'Américaine
duchesse	Les choux-fleurs au Parmesan

Les sckals au beurre

Le pouding de pommes au muscat

Les mirlitons aux citrons

Les Canards Sauvages

Les bouchées perlées aux groseilles

Les oeufs brouillés aux truffes

Le Nougat à la Française

Les pommes de terre à la Hollandaise

La gelée de punch renversée

Les champignons à la provençale

Les navets glacés à la Chartre

Les coqs de Bruyères

Les gâteaux glacés aux abricots

Le fromage bavarois aux avelines

La purée de haricots

L'Hermitage Syrien

Le céleri en cardes à l'Espagnole

La crême Française à l'ananas

Les petits soufflés d'abricots

Les Gelinottes

Les gâteaux de feuilletage pralinés

Les huîtres au gratin

Les Croques-en-Bouche

Les petites carottes à la Flamande

La gelée de citrons moulée

Les laitues farcies à l'essence

La gelée de liqueurs des îles

Les concombres à la Béchamel

Les Biscuits de Fécule à l'Orange

Les truffes à l'Italienne

POUR EXTRA, DIX ASSIETTES VOLANTÉS

5 De Petites soufflés de pommes

5 De petites soufflés au chocolat

This fantastic menu sounds delicious but it must have been a nightmare to serve: and how many of the guests who read it managed to get the dishes they wanted? At the Pavilion, and in other grand households, dinner was still served *à la française*, which meant that the majority of the dishes were arranged in the middle of the table: the people were supposed to help themselves from the nearest dish and then offer it to their neighbours. If, however, someone fancied one of the other dishes, which might well have been placed at the opposite end of the table, he had to ask a fellow guest within range, or one of the servants, to pass it. It was therefore impossible to sustain a conversation because someone was always interrupting and the servants were always on the move. As one dissatisfied diner complained: 'Meaning to be very polite [they, the servants] dodge about to offer each *entrée* to the ladies in the first instance; confusion arises, and whilst the same dishes are offered two or three times over to some guests, the same unhappy wights have no option of others.'[5] At Carême's banquet the guests cannot have been able to sample more than a random selection of the dishes on the menu, and it was clearly a matter of luck which ones came their way. In smaller households hostesses were beginning to adopt the new method of serving *à la russe*, whereby all the dishes were handed round in turn to the guests by servants. With this method there was clearly a limit to the number of dishes which could be included on a menu, because otherwise the operation would take much too long, but at least dinners were more harmonious. Reay Tannahill quotes a charming story which illustrates a further hazard of *service à la française*. A shy young divinity student, invited to dine with an archbishop who was due to examine him in the scriptures, found a dish of ruffs and reeves in front of his place; unfortunately the young man had no idea that these wild birds were the main delicacy of the dinner:

Out of sheer modesty the clerical tyro confined himself exclusively to the dish before him, and persevered in his indiscriminating attentions to it till one of the resident dignitaries (all of whom were waiting only the proper moment to participate) observed him, and called the attention of the company by a loud exclamation of alarm. But the warning came too late: the ruffs and reeves had vanished to a bird, and with them . . . all the candidate's chances of preferment.[6]

There are no simple dishes in Carême's menu, no plain cooking, so that even the finest ingredients could not be appreciated in their natural state. The turbot is served in a lobster sauce and the lobsters in a cheese sauce; the trout with garlic and tomatoes, the pike with oysters and the eel with quenelles, truffles and cocks' combs; the woodcock is cooked in red wine, the quails in

Madeira, the partridge à la Pompadour and the roast larks encased in pastry lined with chicken livers. Everything is smothered in sauce, or disguised, to create a complication of tastes which seems not only much too rich to digest but a terrible waste of expensive ingredients. The most humble dish on the menu is cauliflower cheese; even the scrambled eggs are no more than a vehicle for truffles. Truffles are featured at least seven times on the menu and cost at the time between eight and sixteen shillings a pound, according to quality. It is surprising, too, that there is no concession to the English taste for plain meat; no roast joints, (even the côte de boeuf is garnished with glazed onions), no steaks and no grills.

The Prince Regent must have sanctioned this menu because he wanted to impress his guests, for his own tastes were far more carnivorous. In one month, between 6 May and 5 June 1816,[7] the Carlton House records show that the household used 5264 lbs of meat, excluding sausages, pork and poultry. This works out at an average consumption of more than 40 lbs a head, well over a pound a day, as the records indicate that the Carlton Household averaged around 120 resident members. And that was during the summer; the amounts could have been even higher during the winter months. As far as the quantity of dishes on the menu was concerned, however, it would be wrong to discount Carème's feasts as unique, served only on special occasions. The account books and ledgers in the Royal Archives show that gargantuan meals were prepared every single day and spectacular amounts of food consumed on a regular basis. The menus ordered for the Prince's own consumption certainly contained more meat, with never less than a choice of three or four roasts, but they also featured an endless succession of entrées, entremets and side dishes.

The menus for one day, Wednesday 22 July 1812,[8] illustrate the scale of the Prince's dinners on occasion. The number of guests is not specified but most of his banquets have been well documented and there is no reference to one on that date, so it must have been a relatively small party. The menu for the Prince's table starts reasonably enough with a choice of two soups, turtle or jardinière, which were removed with turbot, lobsters and trout à la genevoise. Hereafter it is a matter of multiple choice between fourteen entrées, including a large capon, dressed 'à la financière' as well as 'fillets of capon aux consommé', several more dishes of fowl, loin of veal in a béchamel sauce, lamb cutlets with French beans (relatively pure), lamb sweetbreads with stewed lettuce, croquettes of sweetbreads 'au salpicon', quenelles of whiting in a cream sauce, escalopes of turbot aux fines herbes and a sauté of mutton, 'au naturel' for once. The second course lists a further 22 dishes, including 6 roast quails, 2 roast chickens, a roast peafowl and a roast hare, truffles with wine, a pudding made of 50 crayfish, lobster salad, pineapple jelly and cherry tarts. There are four different joints of roast meat, four more sweet dishes and a side table which bears a hot haunch of venison, a saddle of mutton, 4 pullets, a casserole of beans and bacon, and a pheasant pie as well as all the usual cold meats, ham, tongue, beef, veal, etc. And for supper – still on the same day – the menu lists 14 more dishes, including roast quails again, prawns, asparagus and yet more truffles.

This vast quantity of food was for the Prince's table alone: the provender for the rest of the household was listed separately, in descending order of importance. 'The Family', which also included the aristocratic members of the Prince's entourage, were fed almost as lavishly as the Prince himself. On this particular day their menu must have accounted for the better part of a couple of sheep: the list mentions '2 quarters of G ... [gross] lamb', a leg of mutton and 'shldr. G lamb', plus a shoulder of veal, boiled beef, knuckle of veal, ham and hashed beef. That Wednesday the kitchen used 200 eggs, 17 pints of double cream, 4 bottles of port, 3 of Madeira and 1 each of champagne, sherry and claret: most of the French dishes were heavily laced with alcohol. The chef responsible for all these elaborate dishes, the great Mr Watier, was far more abstemious in his tastes: all he had for his own dinner that day was a simple leg of lamb, roast and served with potatoes and French beans.

The left-over meat was obviously used to make stock but the quantities involved are staggering: one brew, which cannot have lasted for more than two or three days because stock goes bad so quickly, was made from 102 lbs of beef and 30 lbs of veal.[9] Earlier references show that the servants' hall ate the 'stock meat', but they also had freshly boiled beef, roast mutton, hash and vegetables. The stewards' room fare was almost as sumptuous as the guests': at one dinner they were offered a choice of 2 dishes of fish; roast and boiled beef; chine and leg of mutton; roast hare; 2 necks of venison; loin of pork; 2 roast chickens; tongue, ham, pudding and such exotic vegetables as broccoli and celeriac. Both the housemaids and the porters had their own separate menus, with their own enormous joints of meat, the only visible concession to economy being that the servants were usually given mutton rather than lamb. Another entry, under the heading 'Surgeon Phillips' Dinner', shows that even the doctor, dining alone, had a 7 lb joint of roast mutton as well as a whole chicken to his own cheek.[10]

The kitchen Mensils* give further proof of gastronomic culture during the Regency. The Royal Gardens at Kensington supplied the kitchens with all their vegetables and most of their delicacies. In one month the Carlton House kitchens received: 428 bunches of radishes; 153 dozen broccoli; 118 dozen savoy cabbages (usually served in a cream sauce); 10½ bunches of asparagus, each made up of a hundred head; 75 'cucumber braces'; 63 dozen sea-kales and 7 dozen cos lettuce, most of which would have had to be grown under glass.[11] Strawberries arrived at the royal palaces from the beginning of April right through the summer: between 5 June and 6 July 1816,[12] the gardens at Kensington produced 117 large baskets of strawberries, and those of Hampton Court and Kew a further 160 between them. There were huge amounts of all the other luxury fruits: peaches, nectarines, grapes, cherries, figs, raspberries, melons, and pineapples as well as the usual orchard and kitchen garden produce.

All the most expensive foods available at the time are featured again and again in the menus, interspersed with imported

* Monthly accounts.

delicacies: the first grouse, the first green peas, partridges, snipe and pheasant, quails and larks from France, crayfish from Ireland, salmon from Scotland and lobsters from Cornwall, the rarest *cèpes* and the largest truffles. The only mundane item on one of the menus was grilled cabbage but even that was 'aux amandes'. As neither caviare nor foie gras are mentioned it is reasonable to assume that they were as yet unknown, or at least unappreciated, in English* gastronomic circles. The expense would certainly not have been a barrier. 'Rice soup' indicates an attempt on the part of the Prince to diet, and so does the menu which includes plain boiled sliced salmon, poulet au gros sel, and a fricassée of chicken. Nevertheless sweetbreads creep in as well, along with other equally fattening dishes like lobster au gratin, while his passion for spicy food was appeased that day by a sauté of mutton with gherkins. At one time he appears to have thought that abstaining from fish might be a good idea. Two days running there is a laconic entry saying, 'No fish', but such feeble measures were doomed from the outset. Between the spices and the sauces the Prince floundered in gluttony. By the time he was fifty he weighed over seventeen stone and by the time of his death twenty-two and his stomach 'reached his knees'. The jokes and cartoons on the Prince's size and greed amused the public for most of his life: Charles Lamb's poem, for example, published anonymously, was considered hilarious:

THE PRINCE OF WHALES
Not a fatter fish than he
Flounders round the polar sea.
See his blubbers – at his gills
What a world of drink he swills . . .
Every fish of generous kind
Scuds aside or shrinks behind;
But about his presence keep
All the monsters of the deep . . .

* Foie gras was already considered a delicacy in France, and is featured on the menu of a banquet given in Paris in 1808, according to Grimod de la Reynière, in the 'Manuel des Amphitryons'.

Name of title what has he? . . .
Is he Regent of the sea?
By his bulk and by his size,
By his oily qualities,
This (or else my eyesight fails),
This should be the Prince of Whales.

Jean Baptiste Watier had succeeded Carême as head chef in command of the royal kitchens. The Prince could never bear to be parted from his personal chefs, wherever he went and whoever they were, so Watier and his team of minions travelled around in the royal wake. Watier's career illustrates the nuances of service amongst the rich, though it must be said that very few people indeed could afford to live on such a scale. Having started off as a lowly assistant confectioner, Watier worked his way up the confectionary branch of the kitchen hierarchy, via the posts of assistant pastry cook and 'Yeoman of the Confectionery', until he was rewarded with the most important job of all, which carried with it the grandiose title of 'Superintendent of the Household and First Yeoman, Confectionery'. It was his responsibility to compose all the menus and oversee the staff and supplies. The new kitchens at the Brighton Pavilion were described at the time as

admirable – such contrivances for roasting, boiling, baking, stewing, frying, steaming and heating; hot plates, hot closets, hot air and hot hearths, with all manner of cocks for hot water and cold water, and warm water and steam, and twenty saucepans all ticketed and labelled, placed up to their necks in a vapour bath.[13]

The Prince was tremendously proud of the new technology installed at the Pavilion and used to take his friends on a conducted tour, showing off the latest gadgets. In December 1817, he decided it would be fun to dine in the kitchen with a party of friends. Despite this example of egalitarian principles, protocol was not forgotten and the staff laid a red carpet on the kitchen floor. The Prince put on an apron and set about carving, while the giggling ladies scurried about carrying the dishes, which had

A BRIGHTON BREAKFAST OR MORNING COMFORTS
Caricature by Charles Williams, published by Fores, 1802.
Lady Lade (left), a friend of the Prince Regent, with Mrs Fitzherbert (right).

all, of course, been cooked in advance by the resident staff. The *Sussex Advertiser* reported the event under the heading of 'Princely Affability', adding that they were all in a 'merry mood'. The newspaper said that the servants were delighted with this mark of condescension, but this sycophantic conclusion seems a little suspect, considering the temperament of the chef. At that time it was M. Louis Weltje, who was a brilliant cook but known to be difficult at the best of times. Nevertheless, he managed to produce a 'Splendid Repast' and the Prince's party stayed for a 'joyous hour': the public at large, however, were not amused at yet another example of blatant vulgarity, and the 'Royal Kitchen Party' became the subject of several famous cartoons.[14]

The distribution of mince pies was a long-standing tradition of Christmas, a cross between a tip for services rendered and the modern exchange of Christmas cards. There is a long list in the

Royal Archives, under the heading of 'Minced Pyes Distributed to His Royal Highness the Prince Regent's Servants on Christmas Day 1812 and New Year's Day 1813', which gives a good idea of the size and complexity of the royal household.[15] This list applies to his staff at Carlton House alone; the same principles would have been repeated at his other residences.

In all, 124 servants are mentioned, ranging from the Lord Steward of the Household and Colonel McMahon, the Prince's secretary, down to scullery maids and coal porters. Once again status is explicit, this time expressed by the number of mince pies allotted to the various recipients. Thus, Mr Watier and Surgeon Phillips were sent a dozen each, the two master cooks and the head pastry cook four each and the three under cooks and the 'Roasting Cook' three each; the kitchen boys and scullery maids are limited to two each and the six messengers only one. The list includes some wonderfully evocative titles: there was a 'Gentleman of the Silver Scullery', who had his own staff of four assistants, and a 'Gentleman of the Cellar', who had three. The 'Confectioner' was, of course, Mr Watier himself, the head chef and King of the Kitchen. His department employed four assistants, two male and two female. The Prince, who set a particularly high premium on confectionery, considered them worthy of two mince pies each whereas the housemaids and footmen (ten of each) only got one. The list includes a 'Table Decker' and a 'Coffee Room Maid', both of whom also had their own assistant. There were 6 'Pages of the Backstairs' and 4 'Pages of the Presence' and a 'Musical Page', again with his own assistant, 3 coal porters, 3 lamplighters, 4 'Porters at the Gate', 4 watchmen, 2 carpenters, 2 bricklayers and a resident 'Tapissier' looked after the soft furnishings and upholstery. But the list also mentions an 'Inspector of Household Deliveries', a job description which indicates an effort to curtail extravagance. All these people, if not in residence, were on the payroll.

The final entry, under a separate heading, read 'Minced Pyes Sent to Her Majesty at Windsor'. These mince pies, incidentally, were more like Cornish pasties than the sweet variety eaten today. The *Gentleman's Magazine* reported a foreigner's surprise at the ingredients: 'In private families, the English make large pies of beeve's tongues, cut very small, and mixed with eggs, sugar, currants, lemon-peel, &, seasoned with all kind of spices'. The same source, quoting a French commentator, the Abbé Delaporte, says that 'They also serve up on the same day a mixture of dried raisins and boiled prunes, of which they make a detestable pottage.' The magazine asks, 'Is not this what used to be called plumb pottage?', presumably the origin of the modern Christmas pudding.

That Christmas Day the Prince for once refused to go to Windsor and stayed at Carlton House instead. Each department of the household had its own turkey, with all the trimmings, and Watier prepared the Prince his usual feast. He had his own turkey, dressed with livers and sausages and augmented by two soups, two fish dishes, a roast of veal, 4 pigeons 'en Compote', 'Petit Patties à la Béchamel', 4 partridges 'en Cotelette' and his favourite sweetbreads 'à la Dauphine'. The second course consisted of 2 roast chickens, 6 roast snipe, removed with a soufflé au citron, asparagus – obviously out of season at Christmas time – eggs in anchovies, an orange cream and apricot cakes. The side table offered a 26 lb sirloin of beef, a 20 lb chine of pork (one of the very few occasions when pork featured on the Prince's own menu; pork was usually dismissed by the rich as working-class fare), 2 partridges, a pheasant, 2 poulets and a 'plumb broth'.[16]

It is otiose to judge the extravagance of Regency dinners by twentieth-century standards, and to view them simply as examples of vulgar ostentation, because culinary mores were completely different at the time. Lavish dinners, of a size and variety comparable with those at Carlton House, were expected of the nobility. It seems to have been part of the contemporary creed that a hostess should provide and display far more food than the company could possibly eat. It would be thought mean or lazy today to serve less than three courses at a formal dinner party: during the Regency the same criticism would have applied to any wealthy host or hostess who offered less than at least fifteen dishes and often a great many more. Even amongst the middle classes a decent dinner was expected to include a number of choices. It was customary to serve several entrées and side dishes as well as a choice of roasts for the first course, followed by savouries and sweets for the second. As the second course often included several dishes of game, fish and vegetables it could be just as substantial as the first. All this effort and expense, however, was not always appreciated. Captain Gronow, for one, found the entrées thoroughly overrated: after describing a typical dinner and lauding the basic main dishes, roasts, salmon, turbot, etc., he wrote that:

whilst these never-ending *pièces de résistance* occupied the table, what were called French Dishes were, for custom's sake, added to the solid abundance. The French, or side dishes, consisted of very mild, but very abortive, attempts at Continental cooking, and I have always observed that they met with the neglect and contempt they merited.

Furthermore, the dessert for a grand dinner, according to Gronow, was usually ordered from a confectioner's, and 'if for a dozen people, would cost, at least as many pounds'.[17]

Eliza Acton's cookery book *Modern Cookery for Private Families* is based on the principles of 'Elegance and Economy', and aimed at the frugal housewife. Yet she advocates serving such expensive delicacies as truffles on their own as part of the second course. Other suggestions for *entremets* include swans' eggs and syllabubs, Jerusalem artichokes, pheasant breasts and cucumbers, potted mushrooms, or peas, amongst the separate side dishes: and in 1814 early green peas cost 4 guineas a pint in Covent Garden market, according to a contemporary account. It is indicative, too, that Mrs Acton's book is full of recipes for using up leftovers, the natural consequence of such dinners. Although the prospect of a kitchen full of lobsters and oysters rejected by the dining-room may seem unreal today, it was a fact of life during the Regency. Although some of the residue from the dining-room would, of course, be eaten in the servants' hall, the staff in any reasonable upper-middle-class household expected to be given their own, freshly cooked, joint of meat every day. Superfluous food was much more likely to be sold, or given away, by the servants than used up in 'made-dishes' unless the lady of the house kept a careful watch. Hence the demand for imaginative ideas to avoid waste. She suggests oyster or lobster sausages, made by mincing the fish with breadcrumbs and suet, spices and seasoning, which are then disguised in a rich cream sauce. Another way of using up the lobsters was to pound and sieve the flesh to a smooth paste, shape it into cutlets, garnish with the coral and a few shrimps, bake in a gentle oven and again serve with a cream sauce; or they could be made into 'boudinettes', cooked in individual cups. Tremendously rich sweets were always popular: one of the Prince Regent's favourites, for example, was the dish created in his honour by Carême known as 'Nesselrode Pudding', which was basically an ultra-sweet iced purée of chestnuts, mixed with beaten eggs, and a mountain of whipped cream, laced with maraschino and decorated with cherries or dried fruits. Such complicated sweets, and ices, could be bought from patisseries such as Gunter's and it is clear from Mrs Acton's book that the take-away principle was already widespread at the beginning of the nineteenth century. She is all in favour of ready-made meals: 'I would remind [people],' she wrote in her preface, 'that the fashionable dishes of the day may at all times be procured from an able confectioner'[18] (i.e. the delicatessen).

On a more mundane level Mrs Acton points out that calf's head is cheap but even she admits that 'An entire calf's head, served in its natural form, recalls too forcibly the appearance of the living animal . . . not to be very uninviting', and recommends that it should be boned and rolled. But she was not too squeamish to recommend the eye, writing that it was a 'favourite morsel', and should be carefully gouged out of the head 'by passing the point of the carving knife deeply round the eye-hole'. Continuing in her economical vein, Mrs Acton was a great advocate of potatoes, in all forms. Her cookery book includes a recipe for potato salad, invented by one of her friends, which is in fact a glorified mashed potato dish.

THE POET'S RECEIPT FOR SALAD

Two large potatoes, passed through kitchen sieve
Unwonted softness to the salad give;
Of mordant mustard add, a single spoon,
Distrust the condiment which bites so soon;
But deem it not, thou man of herbs, a fault,
To add a double quantity of salt;
Three times the spoon with oil of Lucca crown,
And once with vinegar, procured from town;
True flavour needs it, and your poet begs
The pounded yellow of two well-boiled eggs;
Let onions lurk within the bowl,
And, scarce suspected, animate the whole;
And lastly, in the flavoured compound toss
A magic teaspoon of anchovy sauce:
Then, though green turtle fail, though venison's tough,
And ham and turkey are not boiled enough,
Serenely full, the epicure may say –
Fate cannot harm me, – I have dined to-day.[19]

Potatoes, rather than bread, were the staple fare of the working classes. Twenty pounds of potatoes cost less than a shilling during the post-war years, which was about the price of a single loaf. A large proportion of the working classes lived on or below the poverty line and many families subsisted on potatoes, occasionally enlivened by a small piece of bacon or cheese. A semi-skilled worker earning 15 shillings a week was able to afford a few more 'luxuries': meat, porter, tea and a little sugar, for example. Such facts and figures put the menus of the rich into perspective in relation to the general economic situation and the diet of most of the population: Carême's famous banquet took place in the middle of the Corn Law riots and shortly before the massacre of Peterloo. During the same period, according to the Kitchen Mensils for Carlton House, the royal household bought 67 loaves of bread costing 11d each and 90 at 1s ½d in one month alone.[20] The same accounts show that the Prince spent £258 12s and 3 farthings on meat, including 1854 pounds of beef at

9d per lb., 1625 of mutton at the same price and 1785 pounds of veal at 11d per lb. The poultry bill that month came to £323 5s 6d, with 385 pullets at 8s 6d each; 232 chickens at 5s 6d each; 88 quails at 4s; 31 large capons at 16s 6d; 12 geese at 9s 6d each and 10 rabbits. Fish must have been much less popular, since the bill from the fishmonger's came to no more than £118 and a few shillings that month, but the Prince must have had lobsters virtually every day since 61 were ordered, costing 4s each, as well as plenty of expensive turbot and sole. The 'Oylery' accounted for £51 11s 6d worth of groceries and spices and condiments; 262 lbs of 'new hams' and 118 lbs of 'old ham', costing £13 2s 6d and £7 18s respectively.

At the beginning of the nineteenth century adulteration of various foods was widespread and there was little or no legal control over the merchants. Some of the additives, or methods employed to cut the costs of a product were extremely dangerous, if not lethal. Tea, for example, which could cost anything from 2/6 to 20s a pound, with an average of around five shillings for the genuine variety, was frequently faked. Imitation China tea could be made from thorn leaves, dried and painted with verdigris, which was in itself poisonous, but Indian was difficult to reproduce, so unscrupulous merchants bought up used leaves from taverns and kitchen staff instead. These were then stiffened with a solution of gum, coloured with black lead, which was, of course, equally poisonous, and sold as genuine Indian tea. As for the gin, the ingredients of one eighteenth-century recipe included sulphuric acid and oil of turpentine.[21] Beer was often adulterated with all sorts of 'preservatives' which in fact turned out to contain poisonous substances masquerading under the guise of spices, while tobacco, treacle and liquorice were all added to colour it.[22] In 1820 a German-born scientist, Frederick Accum, published *A Treatise on Adulterations of Food, and Culinary Poisons*. Amongst other iniquities in common practice it revealed:

that 'crusted old port' was new port crusted with supertartrate of potash; that pickles owed their appetising green colour to copper; that many table wines gained their 'nutty' flavour from bitter almonds, which contain prussic acid; that the rainbow hues of London's boiled sweets were produced by the highly poisonous salts of copper and lead; that most commercial bread was loaded with alum and that the rich orange rind of Gloucester cheese came from ordinary red lead.[23]

The book caused such a furore amongst the manufacturers and merchants that the wretched author had to leave the country: but he had proved his point with the public. Copper pans were another serious health hazard during the Regency. The educated classes were already aware of the potential danger inherent in cooking with copper utensils, but most people cherished their shining *batterie de cuisine* and went on using them anyway; the Prince Regent even had his initials engraved on the new set ordered for the Pavilion. Food poisoning was inevitable, even in the strictest households: the Duke of York was reported ill with food poisoning, known to have been caused by a pâté cooked in a dirty copper pan in the Prince's own kitchen.[24]

It was around this time, too, that the idea of preserving food in tin cans was first suggested. By the end of the eighteenth century a basic form of bottling was already in common usage, along with the traditional methods of salting, curing and drying various foods. Another comparatively recent form of preserving food was to cover it with a layer of thick fat, thus excluding air, but this was known to be no more than a temporary measure and was, in any case, far from foolproof. In 1795 a Frenchman, Nicolas Appert, had invented the predecessor of the Kilner jar, in which the food was hermetically sealed, and from there it was a natural progression to canning. A few years later an Englishman, Brian Donkin, who had an interest in an iron works, adopted the same principle and began enclosing meat, fruit and vegetables in tinned iron containers.[25] By 1810 Donkin had his own canning factory, selling tins of cured beef, boiled beef, carrots, stews and soups. They were taken up by the luxury market and by the end of the Regency those who could afford it were able to enjoy imported delicacies from around the world, either canned or bottled.

*

Gluttony was a rich man's vice, by definition confined to those who could afford to indulge: drunkenness was a much more democratic curse, as prevalent amongst the working classes as the nobility. At a time when many people were unable to afford to buy bread they could afford gin: 'drunk for a penny, dead drunk for twopence' was a sad comment on the state of society, but no exaggeration. Drink, drunkenness and drink-related illness coloured daily life at all levels during the Regency. At the beginning of the nineteenth century, according to one estimate, there were 50,000 pubs to cater for a population of 9 million, and they were open all day. In London the 'Gin Parlours' were everywhere, serving the poor as temporary sanctuary, and gin was their favourite opiate. It was the subject of many a street song, such as the following, which was sung to the tune of 'Home, Sweet Home'.

GIN, GIN, SWEET, SWEET GIN!
Walk through London Town, in Alley, Lane or Street,
Eight to ten of all the folks you overtake, or meet,
List to what they talk about, you'll find amid the gin,
The end of every conversation is a drop of Gin.
Gin, Gin, sweet, sweet Gin
There's no drops like Gin.

When the world was young, as we read in classic page,
The shepherds drank the purling stream, and passed the golden age;
For purling streams or golden age folks don't care a pin,
So that they can raise the brass to keep this age of Gin.
Gin, Gin, Hodge's Gin & . . .[26]

There were plenty of impromptu variations, and if the words are intended to be satirical the sentiment is true enough and the message is clear.

Drinking to excess or getting drunk on a regular basis were a fact of life during the Regency, not a matter of concern. One of the dandies, recalling the habits of his dissolute youth, wrote that, at a dinner party, a perpetual thirst seemed to come over people, both men and women, as soon as they had tasted their soup; as from that moment everybody was taking wine with everybody else, till the close of the dinner; and such wine as produced that class of Cordiality which frequently wanders into stupefaction. How all this sort of eating and drinking ended was obvious, from the prevalence of gout, and the necessity of every one making the pill-box their constant bedroom companion.[27]

Lord Byron voiced the sentiments of the leisured classes in an ode from *Don Juan*:

> Few things surpass old wine; and they may preach
> 　Who please – the more because they preach in vain.
> Let us have wine and woman, mirth and laughter,
> 　Sermons and soda water the day after.
>
> Man being reasonable must get drunk;
> 　The best of life is but intoxication . . .[28]

It was even considered rather dashing to spend the better part of life in a state of semi-intoxication, a proof of masculinity. 'Drinking was the fashion of the day,' Gronow remembered, adding that, 'The Prince, Mr Pitt, Dundas, the Lord Chancellor Eldon, and many others, who gave the tone to society, would, if they now [thirty years later] appeared at an evening party . . . be pronounced fit for nothing but bed. A three-bottle man was not an unusual guest at a fashionable table; and the night was invariably spent in drinking bad port-wine to an enormous extent.' On another occasion he refers to 'four, or even five bottle men', and says that 'the only thing that saved them was drinking very slowly, and out of very small glasses.' The modern historian Christopher Hibbert has found evidence that, in fact, the quantities were often even greater: 'According to Gilbert Eliot, men of all ages [drank] abominably. Fox a "great deal", Sheridan "excessively", Pitt "as much as either" and Grey "more than any of them", but none was a match for Dr John Campbell, who – while Pitt and Sheridan were content to drink six bottles a day – was said to get through thirteen, and they were of port.'[29] These references to the number of bottles drunk in an evening, however, need explanation: at the time port was a much lighter drink than it is today. It is only since 1878, when the Douro vines were decimated by phylloxera, and replanted with a stronger strain, that port has been fortified. Furthermore the bottles themselves were much smaller, holding about half a litre, or less than two-thirds of an ordinary bottle today.

Nevertheless, the quantity of alcohol consumed on a daily basis by the majority of men was almost incredible and, furthermore, they carried on drinking round the clock. It began with ale or claret for breakfast, possibly even a nip of brandy to get going in the morning, or a glass of hock and soda to cure the hangover; mid-morning the fashion was for Madeira or sherry and biscuits, and a glass of ratafia for the ladies; those who went hunting or shooting took their silver flask of brandy to sustain them throughout the day; at dinner champagne and wines were followed by port, brandy and yet more champagne at supper. And the pattern was repeated day after day until gout, alcoholic poisoning or death called a halt.

Then, as now, there was a good deal of snobbery about wine and connoisseurs were prepared to pay comparatively high prices for a good vintage. At the sale of the Duke of Queensberry's effects in 1811, a particularly fine Tokay was sold for £84 per dozen quarts, or £7 a bottle. The figures quoted from the sale of the Duke of Cumberland's cellar are more representative of contemporary prices, but, taken in relation to other costs, and in view of the quantities drunk, prove the point that good wine was a major expense: . . . champagne fetched 11 to 12 guineas a dozen; hock about 11 guineas; Hermitage 14, Madeira and claret 7 per dozen; and port between £4 10s and £5 5s.[30] The most popular drinks amongst the Regency bucks were port, sherry, Madeira, rum punch and 'Brown Brandy', which was the Prince's favourite tipple and he always called it '*diabolino*'. Whisky was almost unknown but punch was enormously popular: the basic ingredients were rum, brandy, lemons and sugar, but variations included green tea and milk. As far as the serious drinkers (or drunkards) were concerned, claret and even burgundy were dismissed as 'poor, thin, washy stuff'. (To be fair, light French wines were harder to come by during the war, although, as has already been said, a certain amount was smuggled.) After the ladies had left the dining-room the men settled down to drinking port, often for hours on end: 'female society amongst the upper classes was most notoriously neglected; except by romantic foreigners, who were the heroes of many a fashionable adventure that fed the clubs with ever-acceptable scandal.'

Gronow's description of Twistleton Fiennes, Lord Saye and Sele, makes a suitable epitaph on the subject of Regency greed:

Twistelton Fiennes was a very eccentric man, and the greatest epicure of his day. His dinners were worthy of the days of Vitellius or Helio-gabalus. Every country, every sea, was searched and ransacked to find some new delicacy for our British Sybarite. I remember, at one of his breakfasts, an omelette being served which was composed entirely of golden pheasants' eggs. He had a very strong constitution, and would drink absinthe and curaçoa [sic] in quantities which were perfectly awful to behold. These stimulants produced no effect upon his brain; but his health gradually gave way under the excesses of all kinds in which he indulged ... I shall never forget the astonishment of a servant I had recommended to him. On entering his service, John made his appearance as Fiennes was going out to dinner, and asked his new master if he had any orders. He received the following answer, – 'Place two bottles of sherry by my bedside, and call me the day after tomorrow'.[31]

10

THE PURSUIT OF
PLEASURE

The Regency was an intensely social age, an era which revelled in parties of every kind and saw entertaining as a creative art. Furthermore, the social life of the period was unique, differing from its forbears and successors both in composition and performance. During the eighteenth century high society was limited almost entirely to those who had been born and bred amongst the upper classes, to an aristocratic and highly privileged elite who conducted their lives according to their own standards, mores and morals. Society was also much more fastidious: the *grandes dames* of an earlier generation would have condemned the extravaganzas of the Regency as flashy and vulgar. As for the subsequent generation, the Victorians, they were in a state of outraged reaction to the behaviour of their parents and grandparents about almost everything. From a distance, at least, there is something much more attractive in the attitude of the society which came in the middle, that of the Regency period: something glorious about that very extravagance, that dedication to glamour and gaiety, colour and fun, in spite of the subtext, which was an awesome indifference to reality. It seems almost unbelievable in the context of the political and economic situation at the time that one small section of the population, including the Prince Regent himself, should have devoted so much of its energy to a series of dazzling parties. The leader of society, however, was a man who had no interest in economy, only a qualified interest in politics, but every interest in parties.

The Prince started as he meant to go on, celebrating his coming-of-age in 1783 with a fête 'of the most expensive, magnificent and varied description, prolonged in defiance of usage, and almost of human nature, from the noon of one day to the following morning'. The Prince waited on the ladies himself, and according to one observer, was a perfect host: 'on these occasions, for which he seemed particularly formed, he appeared to great advantage. Louis XIV himself could hardly have eclipsed the son of George III in a ballroom, or when doing the honours of his palace surrounded by the pomp and attributes of luxury and royal state.'[1] (At another party around the same time he fell over drunk in the middle of dancing a quadrille and was then sick in front of the guests.) For the rest of his life the Prince gloried in showing off his flair as a host, with a succession of increasingly splendid breakfasts, balls and fêtes, given, for the most part, at Carlton House. Therein lay the problem, for Carlton House, however much he changed it and however much he spent, would never be large enough to satisfy his social ambition. The solution was to treat the property as ephemeral, to add and modify, to decorate and redecorate, to gild and embellish again and again. At the same time, the Prince, who was a master of illusion, forced the house to expand via corridors into the garden, where he built a series of temporary structures, follies and elaborate tents. The epicentre of social life was really a palatial gypsy encampment. In the end the Prince demolished the whole thing and began enlarging Buckingham House* instead. The short history of what must have been one of the loveliest houses in London encapsulates the transient spirit of the Regency, a compound of style and vulgarity, waste and generosity, charm and chaos.

Carlton House was built in 1709, for Lord Carlton, and passed into the royal gift a few years later. In 1783, when the Prince of Wales, as he then was, came of age, George III reluctantly agreed

---

* The building, by then renamed Buckingham Palace, was still incomplete when George IV died.

that his heir needed his own residence in London, and gave him Carlton House. For the first time in his life the Prince was able to express his aesthetic ideas and indulge his passion for grandeur. At once he began to transform the house, a process which continued intermittently for the next thirty years. The Prince was a compulsive spendthrift and the debts he incurred over Carlton House became a running sore for the rest of his life. Over the years the Prince employed five different architects to work on Carlton House, including Henry Holland, James Wyatt and John Nash. The Prince was never satisfied: each new architect was allowed to scrap much of his predecessor's work and start all over again, but always under his employer's personal supervision. The Prince was obsessed with Carlton House and determined to create the showiest palace in Europe, a setting which would do justice to his position and personality. He brought in the best (and most expensive) decorators and craftsmen from all over Europe, but chose everything that mattered himself: colour schemes, furnishings, paintings, lighting and even the design of the servants' quarters. He built new kitchens, wine cellars and larders, a separate pastry scullery and another for silver, a coffee-room pantry, a footman's hall, a maid's kitchen and a confectionery. The Prince's new apartments included the famous Bow Room, his personal sitting room where he entertained particular cronies in privacy and at leisure. It was decorated in scarlet and gold, with scarlet flock wallpaper and matching curtains embellished with black velvet. The master bedroom suite featured a large dressing-room, where the chosen few could attend his *toilette,* and a 'hot bathe' room, complete with all the latest plumbing. The Prince, like Brummell, put particular emphasis on personal hygiene. During the eighteenth century no one had bothered too much about cleanliness – partly because powdered wigs and elaborate costumes made it virtually impossible to sustain – but during the Regency it was at last recognized as the first priority of fashion, for both men and women.

The initial alterations to Carlton House, under the direction of Henry Holland, were extensive but they were also necessary and efficient, and the interior decoration of the house was relatively simple. At this stage the Prince was still young, good-looking and popular; and so was his house with the general public. In 1785 Horace Walpole wrote that

There is an august simplicity [about it] that astonished me. You can not call it magnificent; it is the taste and propriety that strike ... In all the fairy tales you have been, you never was in so pretty a scene ... How sick one shall be after this chaste palace, of Mr Adam's gingerbread and sippets of embroidery.[2]

He added, prophetically, that he could not imagine how the Prince was ever going to be able to meet the bills: 'All the tin mines in Cornwall would not pay a quarter.'

Holland's taste, however, was much too austere for the Prince and after a series of clashes between them, he withdrew, to be succeeded by Wyatt, the most flamboyant architect and decorator of the period. From then on all the apartments all over the house were in a constant state of flux; barely five years after the Prince had moved in, Lady Mary Coke wrote in her journal, 'the fine apartment which you saw at Carlton House is in part destroy'd in order to make some alteration ...' And by 1806 Farington was writing in his Diary that 'Although Carlton House as finished by *Holland* was in a complete and *new* state He [i.e. the Prince] has ordered the whole to be done again under the direction of Walsh Porter who has destroyed all that Holland has done & is substituting a finishing in a most expensive & motley taste.'[3] A couple of years later a contemporary magazine reported that 'almost the whole of Carlton House is undergoing alterations and improvements':[4] and by 1810 all Walsh Porter's innovations had been scrapped and yet another decorator employed. Even the enormous marble chimney pieces, which most people would regard as permanent fixtures, were moved about all over the house, up and down stairs, and installed in different rooms only to be moved on again a year or two later.

In spite of all this, certain themes predominated throughout the decoration of Carlton House, notably Chinese, Gothic and classical. Furthermore, the emphasis was always on magnificence, brilliance, colour, gold, cut glass and reflected light. In 1819 the

Prince commissioned, at a cost of thousands, an illustrated history of the royal residences which gives the best contemporary description of Carlton House. The author, William Pyne, points out that the Ante Room 'prepares the visitor for the increasing splendour of the superior apartments [to come]. The walls are of a bright blue, coloured in distemper, and surrounded by mouldings in burnished gold; the carpet is also of a bright blue ground, powdered with gold fleurs de lys': and this was only a waiting room. The Golden Drawing Room was 'entirely gilt in burnished and matted gold ... and the frieze, in imitation of rose-wood, is ornamented with Grecian honeysuckle, relieved by burnished gilding.'[5] The folding doors of this room were made of a single vast looking-glass panel, framed in carved and gilded rosewood; the walls covered with more elaborate mirrors and the windows festooned in scarlet silk, 'with sub-curtains of figured muslin, and, between them, the piers are filled with large looking-glasses.' In another of the drawing rooms the walls were covered with rose-coloured satin damask, with gold mouldings, matching curtains with heavy gold fringes and 'embellishments ... of furniture in the Chinese style', while the Crimson Drawing Room was even more theatrical in design, combining great swathes of crimson silk with gilt stucco-work and a light blue velvet carpet. Pyne, at least, saw nothing wrong with this particular colour scheme and wrote enthusiastically of the Crimson Drawing Room that

On entering this spacious apartment, the eye is agreeably struck with the happy combination of splendid materials tastefully arranged; consisting of a profusion of rich draperies, large pier glasses, grand chandeliers of brilliant cut glass, massive furniture richly gilt, candelabra, tripods, bronzes, elegant vases and other corresponding decorations.

The Circular Room was a prime example of the Regent's passion for designing rooms to look like tents. This time the accent was on silver, light blue and red marble, with a smattering of lavender and bronze. Pyne described the Circular Room as

a rotunda of the Ionic order, the parts selected from the purest specimens of ancient Greece ... red porphyry columns with statuary plinths and silvered capitals: the principal ornaments of the cornice and architraves are also silvered, relieved by a ground of lavender tint; and the ornaments of the frieze, consisting of boys supporting festoons of foliage and fruit, are judiciously painted in imitation of bronze . . . The intercolumniations form four recesses . . . [and] from the soffit of each recess is suspended a Roman tent drapery of light blue silk, ornamented with silver, with which silk the walls are in part covered, creating a sort of tent-like character; and these are relieved by sub-curtains of white taffeta.[6]

Ambassadors and ministers of state were usually received in the Blue Velvet Room, one of the suite of state apartments on the first floor. In here, the walls were covered with panels of dark blue velvet with

surrounding margins of light peach blossom, and bordered by a burnished gold moulding . . . The draperies to the windows are arranged in festoons, supported by a staff ornamented by foliage, swans . . . and gilt in burnished gold, and are of blue satin embellished with fleurs de lys of gold coloured satin, and gold fringes, cords and tassels, and lined with white taffeta.

There was a blue velvet 'closet' to match. (The word 'closet' was normally used at the time to indicate a lavatory, not a cupboard; but it could also mean a larger cloakroom, or dressing-room, with a washbasin.)

As for the famous Conservatory, even Pyne must have realized that it might not be to everyone's taste: he refers to it with some ambivalence as 'this unique edifice' and describes the design as 'florid Gothic'. The Prince's Conservatory was built to resemble a small cathedral, with a nave and two aisles, a fanned glass roof, supported on elaborately carved pillars and stained-glass windows, upon which were painted the arms of all the 'sovereigns of England from William the First to the present reign; the Electoral Princes of the House of Brunswick; and those of all the Princes of Wales, in chronological order.'[7] The artist had to include the Prince of Wales or otherwise the man responsible for all this deification of his ancestors and, thereby, himself, would have been left out: in 1819 George III was still alive and the Prince was still only heir apparent. Nevertheless, he created a Throne Room at Carlton House, in happy anticipation of his future role, which was even more splendid than the rest of the house, using real gold rather than gilt for the decorations. According to another description, the walls of the Throne Room were hung with crimson velvet,

with embroidered ornaments in pure gold, and most massive gold fringes and laces. The Canopy, superbly carved and gilt, was surmounted by four helmets of real gold, having plumes of the finest white ostrich feathers, many of them 17 inches high. On each side the Canopy [there] were magnificent antique draperies; decorated to correspond with it, and forming backgrounds to two superb candelabra, after the antique, executed in the finest manner, with *lions couchant*, and other appropriate ornaments. Under the Canopy stood a grand state chair and foot-stool. The compartments of the room were decorated with the richest gold ornaments on a crimson velvet ground, with draperies enriched with gold fringes, *en suite*. There were two superb glasses about twelve feet high, with oriental alabaster tables, on frames, carved and gilt, in the most magnificent style . . .

And so on and so forth, one might have thought *ad nauseam*.

The magnificence of the décor at Carlton House was a subject for comment and criticism throughout the Regency, particularly as the Prince kept changing it. According to taste it was either garish to the point of vulgarity, or an enchanting example of fantasy, but at least it was never dull. Miss Mitford mocked the décor of Carlton House in *Our Village*: 'Every room is in masquerade,' she wrote, 'the saloon Chinese, full of jars and mandarins and pagodas; the library Egyptian, all covered with hieroglyphics . . . They sleep in Turkish tents, and dine in a Gothic chapel';[8] and Canova dismissed the house as an 'ugly barn', adding that there were at least a thousand buildings in Rome which were more beautiful and better suited as a princely residence. Opinions differed: another guest at one of the levées wrote of the 'Great crowds, splendid liveries, and hussars of all colours', adding that 'Carlton House [is] finer than anything in

England and not inferior to Versailles or Saint Cloud'.[9] And the Hanoverian minister thought that even the palace at St Petersburg, despite its great size, 'was not equal to this in elegance and richness'. The surreal element of fantasy created by the décor of Carlton House was described by Lady Elizabeth Fielding, who seems to have fallen in love with the whole performance. Having been to a party there in 1813, she wrote to her sister as follows:

I am afraid all my powers of description would fail to give you an idea of the oriental air of everything in that Mahomet's Paradise, Carlton House. I do not know whether *we* all looked like *Houris,* but I for one was certainly in the seventy-seventh heaven ... Imagine yourself ascending a flight of steps into an immense saloon lighted up to the ceiling with a profusion of candles and a display of gold plate on either hand that dazzled the eye, with a *sonorous* band of turbaned slaves playing 'God save the King'.

The sight and sound were both animating, the kettledrums and cymbals, the glitter of spangles and finery, of dress and furniture that burst upon you were quite *éblouissant . . .*[10]

The Prince Regent was a legendary host, at his best and happiest when entertaining on the grand scale. Moreover, he was able to forget how unpopular he had become as he watched society scramble for an invitation to Carlton House. However much they disapproved of their host, no one would have dreamt of refusing: puritans could always justify themselves on the grounds of *lèse-majesté.* These royal parties were always glittering occasions, but they were never really intended to be social gatherings: the point of the proceedings was to admire, not to talk or meet friends. The Prince was a regal impresario who used Carlton House as a stage and entertaining as a means to show off his aesthetic taste, talent and imagination. He spent weeks planning the setting for the next ball or fête, supervising every detail from the lighting to the silver and plate. As Prince of Wales, parliament had exercised a degree of control over his expenditure, but as soon as he became Regent, and sovereign in all but name, he had a much freer hand: and, naturally, decided to celebrate in suitable style.

On 19 June 1811, the Prince gave a fête at Carlton House to inaugurate the Regency which was the ultimate, to date, in grandeur and extravagance. It was said that

Upon no previous occasion, and at no Court in Europe was ever the experiment made to sit down 2000 of the principal nobility and gentry of a kingdom to a regular supper, as was the case at the Prince Regent's fête. The largest entertainment, at the most brilliant period of the French Monarchy, was that given by the Prince of Condé at Chantilly, to the King of Sweden, when 400 covers were laid. Here covers were laid for 1600 under canvas, and 400 in the house.[11]

The guests were asked for nine o'clock, but an hour before that the queue of carriages formed a solid block stretching all the way back from Carlton House to the top of St James's Street, and eventually to Bond Street. The Prince made his entrance at 9.15, wearing the Field Marshal's uniform which he had designed himself, a suitably splendid garment of which even the seams of his coat were heavily embroidered. The party was nominally in honour of the Bourbon family and the principal guests included the Comte de Provence, later Louis XVIII, the Comte d'Artois, the Duc de Berri, the Duc d'Angoulême, the Duchesse d'Angoulême, Louis XVI's only surviving child, the Prince de Condé and the Duc de Bourbon; in other words nearly all the exiled French royal family. The list did not, however, include the Prince Regent's wife, Princess Caroline, or his mother Queen Charlotte, or his sisters, the royal princesses: the former was not allowed to attend and the latter refused. The 'First Gentleman of Europe' was wonderfully indifferent to protocol or convention, even in the context of a *soi-disant* royal occasion.

The main supper table ran the whole length of the Gothic conservatory and dining room, 200 feet in all. The guests were stunned to find that the table decorations included a real stream flowing along above the middle of the table:

a fountain of real water . . . springing from a silver fountain at the head of the table [i.e. in front of the Prince]. It ran in an irregular stream, about six inches above the surface, between banks covered with real moss and artificial flowers, and in its current a number of goldfish sported up and down . . . Three or four fantastic bridges were thrown over it, one of them with a small tower upon it, which gave the little stream a picturesque appearance . . . The excellence of design, and exquisiteness of workmanship could not be exceeded; it exhibited a grandeur beyond description; while the many and various purposes for which gold and silver materials were used were equally beautiful and superb in all their minute details . . .

The superlatives continued in most of the subsequent accounts.

The rest of the party was seated at tables in specially constructed tents, decorated with fleurs-de-lis in compliment to the Bourbons, dotted about in the gardens but all linked by canvas corridors to the main building. Everyone dressed up in their finest clothes and jewellery (the pawnbrokers lent out diamonds for the night, at 11 per cent interest); there was masses of iced champagne and the food was sumptuous, even if it did have so far to travel from the kitchens that it arrived cold. *The Times*'s account of the fête mentions 'thousands of lights' and flowers, and concluded that the whole effect 'was inexpressibly delightful and even magically impressive'.

Princely optimism in the planning stages of the fête, however, had prevailed over common sense and the festivities ended in farce and tragedy. The day after the fête, the Prince opened Carlton House to the public, so that they might see the decorations. The result was pandemonium and many people were injured in the crush: *The Times* reported that, amongst the casualties,

One young lady, elegantly attired, or, rather, who had been so, presented a shocking spectacle; she had been trodden on, until her face was quite black from strangulation, and every part of her body bruised to such a degree, as to leave little hope of recovery . . . The situation of almost all the ladies who were involved in this terrible rush was truly deplorable; very few of them could leave Carlton House until furnished with a fresh supply of clothes; they were to be seen all round the gardens, most of them without shoes or gowns; and many almost completely undressed, and their hair hanging about their shoulders.

And the *Morning Chronicle* confirmed a few days later that

The number of stray shoes in the courtyard of Carlton House . . . was so great that they filled a large tub, from which the shoeless ladies were invited to select their lost property. Many ladies, however, and also gentlemen, might be seen walking away in their stockinged feet. About a dozen females were so completely disrobed in the squeeze, they were obliged to send home for clothes, before they could venture out into the streets, and one lady was so completely disencumbered of all dress, a female domestic, in kind compassion, wrapped her up in an apron.[12]

During the autumn of 1813 Wellington crossed the Pyrenees and by 31 March of the following year the Allies were in Paris. A few days later Napoleon abdicated and left for Elba; Louis XVIII was restored to the throne of France. In May the French king came to London on a state visit and was followed in June by the Tsar of Russia, the King of Prussia and a covey of lesser foreign princes, statesmen and generals. All that summer the celebrations continued all over England and in London the Prince Regent surpassed himself. There were public fêtes and private dinners; ridottos and banquets; masquerades at Vauxhall and receptions at Carlton House; parties on the river and parties in the park. The Prince showed great imagination in planning these spectacular entertainments, whether for the privileged few or the public at large. As one of his friends, Lady Vernon, said, 'Our Prince Regent is never so happy as in show and state, and there he shines incomparably.' Possibly; but his efforts were not always appreciated. The success of a public fête depends less on the magnificence of the show than the mood of the people and the Prince's audience at the time were distinctly hostile: he had recently tried to divorce his wife, Princess Caroline, whom he had loathed from the start of the marriage, but whom the public decided to champion. During the festivities that year the Prince's carriage was frequently booed and on one occasion, when he ventured into the City, it was surrounded by a hissing mob, shouting insults and asking, 'Where's your wife?' Such was the Prince's unpopularity during this period, according to Creevey, that 'All agree that he will die or go mad. He is worn out with fuss, fatigue and *rage*.'[13]

He did neither, to the chagrin of his detractors, but carried on with the celebrations, showing rare grace and courage in view of such wounding hostility. The first of the state visits to London, in April 1814, was that of Louis XVIII, who had just been restored to the throne of France. A royal state carriage was sent ahead to meet the King at Dover and a procession arranged which included an escort of a hundred gentlemen on horseback and two detachments of Horse Guards. The royal carriages were accompanied by a phalanx of outriders and decorated with white cockades in honour of the Bourbons; last of all came the state carriage, drawn by eight cream-coloured horses, bearing the King and the Prince, waving away at the populace – who were less than impressed. The visit, in fact, fell sadly flat and the crowds remained largely indifferent. Byron, for one, refused to turn out for the grand procession, even though it passed right by his chambers in Albany. In a letter to Tom Moore he wrote, 'At this present writing, Louis the Gouty is wheeling in triumph into Piccadilly . . . the Most Christian King "hath no attractions for me".' The Bourbons were not particularly popular with the general British public either, many of whom still venerated Napoleon as a potential champion of the working classes. Furthermore the King of France was old and lame by this time, and in no fit state to enjoy the festivities: on arriving at his hotel, Grillon's, he could barely walk and had to be assisted, physically, by the Prince. Once inside he collapsed into a large armchair, specially decorated with golden fleurs-de-lis, which had been placed in the main room of the hotel, and held court from there. As usual, it was left to Peter Pindar to express the general feeling about the royal visit in satirical verse:

And France's hope and Britain's heir
Were, truth, a most congenial pair;
Two round tun-bellied, thriving rakes,
Like oxen fed on Linseed cakes.

The visit of the Allied sovereigns a few weeks later, however, was a great success, at least from the point of view of the public. The chief guests were the Tsar of Russia and the King of Prussia, with their respective retinues, but the party also included Prince Metternich, representing the Emperor of Austria, and General Blücher, who became a national idol, welcomed with cheers wherever he went. Unable to vent their enthusiasm for Wellington, who had not yet returned from the Continent, they adopted the Prussian victor of Paris instead. Lady Frances Shelley wrote in her diary that

Blücher came to the door to please the mob, who had been drawing him about the streets all morning. Lord Burghersh had accompanied him; and it was all they could do to get Blücher safe into the house as he was nearly crushed to death. He told Lord Burghersh that he had never been so frightened.[14]

London went mad with royalty fever and chased all over town to get a glimpse of the visitors. Windows along the route of the Grand Procession were let for 50 guineas, a fortune at the time (the equivalent, today, of about £2500.) Mary Frampton's Journal shows that even the most *blasé* members of society were thoroughly over-excited by what one correspondent referred to as 'the present fortunate and distinguishing hugging of the Kings and Emperors of Europe'.[15] Mr Wollaston wrote to Mary Frampton that he had been 'Emperor-hunting' for two mornings running without success, and therefore intended 'to sit in my carriage opposite his house, and by that means they say it may be done, as he comes to the window when the mob call for him to appear.' Another of her friends was delighted to report that she had had a splendid view of the whole party: 'I do not in general like a crowd,' she wrote,

but I ventured into a pretty great one in order to get a good sight of all the Royal strangers . . . ; and I saw the King of Prussia, the Regent, the Duchess of Oldenburg, the Queen, the Princess Augusta, the Emperor of Russia, all standing side by side as I have named them. I was retiring much gratified and well satisfied, when a cry was raised that Marshal Blücher was coming. The air resounded with the cheers the populace gave him, and . . . a few minutes after arrived General Platoff, the latter being the only person in regimentals.

She added that the royals were all dressed so plainly that it was impossible to tell which was which, and the point was emphasized by another royal-watcher who wrote, 'I wish they would all go about *ticketed* – it would save a great deal of trouble in finding out their names.'[16] Celebrity-watching was carried to ludicrous lengths: people even gave parties in their kitchens and basements just to get a glimpse of the royals through the area grating. Mary Frampton's brother received a note saying that 'if I would come to Mrs Fielding's *kitchen* at St James's Palace, I should see a fine sight; so off I set and saw the Emperor, Duchess of Oldenburg, Prince of Oldenburg, &, and the Lord Mayor go to present the Address – old Blücher being in sight the greatest part of the time. In this kitchen were Mrs Arnold and Lady Harriet Frampton'.[17] Others were delighted to be offered a place to sit on the stairs or the landing when the royals were going to a private dinner, presumably so that they could hang over the banisters and gawp at the guests as they passed into the dining-room. Lady Harriet Frampton wrote that she 'had a delicious treat of famous people one evening at Lansdowne House'. The plum of her evening was a German general who was able to tell her all about Napoleon, as he had travelled with the Emperor to Elba, and stayed on with him for several days. (Napoleon remained an object of hero-worship amongst society ladies long after his defeat.) Lady Harriet's next outing was to a dinner at Lord Stafford's, where she was able to report there were twenty-two princes of the blood-royal. Tickets for the magnificent ball to be held at White's club were sold on the black market for 80 or 100 guineas. 'Such is the temporary insanity,' she comments, clearly loving every minute of it.

Ordinary London life became virtually impossible during the royal visit, thanks to the public hysteria. 'It is quite ridiculous how wild London is,' James Frampton wrote to his mother towards the end of the visit, 'the bankers say that they had never so many mistakes on their books, Bills forgot to be accepted . . . No tradesman can get anything done.' There was no milk because the cows were all frightened out of the Green Park by the guns and the noise of cheering, no fresh bread because the bakers delivered it first to the royals at the Pulteney Hotel, and then stayed there all day watching the comings and goings. People could not even get their clothes washed because all the washer-women had deserted their regular customers for the same reason, and 'the confusion beggars all description'.

The royal visitors themselves, however, were irritated by all the fuss, and the Tsar and his sister were actively rude to their host. The Prince had prepared special apartments at Carlton House for the Tsar, but he refused to stay there, joining the Grand Duchess and the rest of the Russian contingent at the Pulteney Hotel instead. According to Creevey the royals all became fed up with the constant ceremony, and were 'sick to death of the way they are followed about'; the King of Prussia was as 'sulky as a bear'; the Tsar grumbled about the long dinners at Carlton House and annoyed the Regent by flirting with his mistress, Lady Jersey; and General Platoff became 'so cursedly provoked at the fuss' that he refused to go out at all. As for the wretched Prince who had spent so much time and energy, let alone public money, on all this entertainment, he had a miserable time, dreaded appearing in public and 'lives only by the protection of his visitors. If he is caught alone, nothing can equal the execration of the people who recognise him.'[18]

At least the Prince was left in peace at his private parties. When the Duke of Wellington finally returned from the Continent the Prince held a fête at Carlton House in his honour which was even more extravagant than the one he had given to inaugurate the Regency: Nash was commissioned to build a series of reception rooms in the gardens dominated by a huge polygon-shaped hall, 136 feet in diameter. Although it was never intended to be a permanent building, the polygon room was made of brick and had a lead roof. Inside, the walls were completely covered in white muslin drapery, broken only by mirrors, and even the umbrella-shaped roof was painted to resemble muslin, making the whole room wonderfully light. In the middle of the room there was a temple made of masses of artificial flowers, which concealed the orchestra. Covered walks, similarly draped in white muslin, led to various supper tents, decorated with regimental colours in silk. In the largest tent, which was designed as a Corinthian temple, a huge mirror hung on the wall facing the entrance, with a brilliant star suspended above it and the letter W engraved on the cut class, in tribute to the guest of honour. On this occasion the Queen and the rest of the royal family did attend the party, which was voted a great success and went on until 6.00 in the morning. (Wellington himself was less than polite about his host: soon after the fête he was reported to have said of the Regent: 'By God! you never saw such a figure in your life as he is. Then he speaks and swears so like old Falstaff, that damn me if I was not ashamed to walk into a room with him.')

Some idea of the cost of a great ball during the Regency may be gathered from the accounts, still extant, of the one given around the same time by White's Club.[19] The Duke of Devonshire lent Burlington House for the occasion and tickets were by subscription. More than 2000 people attended, ranging from the Prince Regent, and assorted visiting royalty, via most of *Debrett's*, to the likes of Harriette Wilson and her sisters, for whom their aristocratic lovers bought tickets. This particular ball cost just under £10,000 and a breakdown of the bill shows the relative values of various items at the time – and how very different the accounts would be for a similar function today. For example, the cost of lighting, at £473, comes to more than half the cost of the drink (which was only £900); and, presumably, that only refers to the candles themselves, rather than the hire of chandeliers and lamps since another entry, for £800, is listed as 'Handcock & Co, for lustres'. The food, listed as 'supper, etc.' at £2575, cost nearly three times as much as the wine: but the band – one of the most expensive items today – less than £70. But it is the charges for service which really highlight the difference in emphasis of expenditure: £20 for the waiters and £12 10s to the porters and White's servants for their extra trouble. The accounts do not specify how many servants were needed, but for such a large company there must have been hundreds.

The summer of 1814 ended with 'The Grand Jubilee', a vast fête for the public held in the London parks. It was the Prince's final attempt to placate his subjects and even the preparations, which went on for weeks, were watched with tremendous excitement by the crowds. The Prince was going through his Oriental phase, so he commissioned Nash to transform St James's Park with a Chinese bridge across the lake, various vaguely Eastern temples, pagodas and other ornamental follies. As usual, however, the press started carping as soon as the programme was announced: 'The public will first gape at the mummery,' wrote *The Times*, 'then laugh at the authors of it and lastly grumble at the expense. We are chiefly sorry on account of the contemptible light in which it will exhibit us as a people to foreign nations. The Pagoda, the Balloons and Girandolles of Rockets, the Chinese bridge ... Alas! Alas! to what are we sinking.'

In the event, the fête was a great success as *The Times* was forced to admit, writing that it was 'an indisputable fact that so immense a number of people at large were never brought together in any previous instance by any description of public rejoicings or any of the great events which have so often gilded the pages of British history.'[20] (More or less what they said about the Prince's Inauguration fête three years earlier: the standard of journalism during the Regency was abysmal.) The Jubilee had originally been planned to synchronize with the State Visit of the Allied Sovereigns, but the building work in the parks took so much longer than expected that it was postponed until 1 August, the ostensible reason then being to celebrate the centenary of the accession to the English throne of the House of Hanover. It was a lovely sunny day and the festivities got off to a suitably flying start with a balloon ascent by Mr Sadler, who scattered favours from the sky on the eager crowds below. At eight in the evening there was a mimic naval battle on the Serpentine, representing the victory of Trafalgar, and at nightfall a continuous display of fireworks, described as 'a contest in brilliancy between the two parks' (St James's Park and Hyde Park). The *pièce de résistance* of the show was a huge Gothic structure, over a hundred feet tall, called the 'Castle of Discord', intended to symbolize all the 'horrors of fire and destruction', i.e. war. For the grand finale of the fête more fireworks were let off from the battlements of the castle, the whole building was obliterated completely by smoke: and lo! and behold!, when the smoke cleared away the Gothic fortress had disappeared to reveal a delightful 'Temple of Concord', all lit up and radiating peace. This complicated construction was designed by Sir William Congreve, the inventor, who happened to be a close personal friend of the Regent's. The only disaster of the day was perceived at the time as part of the fun: the Chinese pagoda on the bridge, which was lit by gas, caught fire and the whole structure burst into flames and collapsed into the lake – to roars of approval from the crowd, who thought it was part of the entertainment. In fact, two men were killed, including one of the carpenters who had been involved in building it, and several more injured. Many of the swans on the lake suffered a similar fate, either suffocated by the smoke or burnt to death.

All day long, and all night long for that matter, and for several days afterwards, the crowds made merry amongst the booths and bars which filled all the parks. A week later Charles Lamb wrote to Wordsworth complaining that Hyde Park was ruined and the party was still going on:

all that was countryfy'd in the Parks is all but obliterated. The very colour green is vanished, the whole surface of Hyde Park is dry crumbling sand (Arabia Arenosa) ... booths and drinking places go all round it for a mile and a half I am confident – I might say two miles in circuit – the stench of liquors, *bad* tobacco, dirty people and provisions, conquers the air and we are stifled and suffocated in Hyde Park.

... Meantime I confess to have smoked one delicious pipe in one of the cleanliest and goodliest of the booths – a tent rather, 'O call it not a booth!' – erected by the public Spirit of Watson, who keeps the Adam and Eve at Pancras (the ale houses have all emigrated with their train of bottles, mugs, corkscrews, waiters, into Hyde Park – whole Ale houses with all their Ale!) in company with some of the guards that had been in France and a fine French girl (habited like a Princess of Banditti) which one of the dogs had transported from the Garonne to the Serpentine. The unusual scene in Hyde Park, by Candlelight in open air, good tobacco, bottled stout, made it look like an interval in a campaign, a repose after battle ... After all, the fireworks were splendid – the Rockets in clusters, in trees and all shapes, spreading about like young stars in the making, floundering about in Space (like unbroken horses) till some of Newton's calculations should fix them, but then they went out. Any one who could see 'em and the still finer showers of gloomy rain fire that fell sulkily and angrily from 'em, and could go to bed without dreaming of the Last Day, must be as hardened an Atheist as *** [name omitted].[21]

A contemporary newspaper's account, describing the same scene, is rather less lyrical: 'Never, within the memory of man, has there been witnessed such scenes of drunkenness and dissipation as these fooleries have given rise to, and the miseries they have brought upon thousands is extreme.' The paper goes on to add the sanctimonious comment that

A report from the pawnbrokers would be an awful lesson to governments how they encourage such riot. Since the delirium, from the example of the highest quarter, began, the pawnbrokers have more than trebled their business; clothes, furniture, and, worst of all, *tools*, have been sacrificed for the sake of momentary enjoyment; industry of every kind has been interrupted, and many hundreds of starving families will long have to remember the *aera* of the Park Fetes.[22]

It is a killjoy attitude, but true. The whole saga of the Regency fêtes is typical of the schizophrenic nature of the period, a constant shifting from one extreme to another, from unnecessary extravagance to unnecessary poverty, from frenetic gaiety to dramatic despair. It was a case of the ends failing to justify the means: for, in the end, neither the aristocracy nor the general public gained more than a temporary pleasure from such an exhausting summer.

There is a similar paradox in the attitude of the educated classes towards the theatre. The Regency was an age when society prided itself on its sophistication and culture, yet its behaviour on occasion belies any such image. In 1788, the time of the first Regency crisis, Sarah Siddons and her brother John Kemble dominated the London stage: one of the Queen's ladies-in-waiting wrote that Mrs Siddons, playing tragedy, 'was making ladies faint and gentlemen weep whenever she performed'. A few years later Edmund Kean appeared and made his name playing Richard III, Shylock and Iago. One critic wrote of his performances in Shakespearean roles that 'he is never out of his part for a moment, entirely absorbed in the character he undertakes, and nothing for an instant draws him from it.' Yet other contemporary accounts make it clear that it was acceptable behaviour on the part of the audience to arrive an hour and a half late and then to talk all the way through the performance. As far as many members of society were concerned, including the intelligentsia, the theatre was simply an arena for social life, for flirting, seeing and being seen: the play, whatever it was, and whoever was acting, came a poor second. Prostitutes and courtesans paraded in the lobby; young men in the pit quizzed the girls in the boxes and called on them in the intervals, while the dowagers scanned the auditorium for potential scandal. One of the Regency wits was reputed to have said that the trouble with the opera was that they sang so loud one couldn't hear oneself talk. And Lady Caroline Lamb clearly sees nothing odd in writing to her mother, Lady Bessborough, after a visit to the theatre, that 'Ld Stair & Mr James agreably enlivened us at the play where Caro* sat flirting with George, & I like Susannah and the elder discoursing with them.'[23] She doesn't bother to say what play they had seen or who was in it, let alone whether it was any good. And yet both mother

* Caroline St Jules, the fifth Duke of Devonshire's illegitimate daughter by Lady Elizabeth Foster. She married George Lamb, William's brother, in 1809.

ACTING MAGISTRATES . . .
Caricature by Isaac and George Cruikshank, 1809.
After the fire at Covent Garden Theatre in 1808, John Kemble attempted to raise the price of tickets, to pay for rebuilding the auditorium. The subsequent 'Old Price Riots' stopped every performance for seventy-one nights.

and daughter were amongst the most highly educated women of their generation and moved in the most cultivated circles of Regency society. Part of the trouble may well have been that the evening went on so long, at least five hours, the performance starting at six or seven and carrying on until midnight, or even later. It was the custom to offer a double bill, following the main drama with a jolly farce, or pantomime, thus giving the audience full value for their money: Edmund Kean playing Macbeth, for example, would be succeeded by *Aladdin*.

On occasion the audience had a genuine grievance against the management, and the public were far more capable of making themselves and their complaints known at the beginning of the nineteenth century than they are today. The 'Old Price Riots' of 1809 stopped the show at Covent Garden every night for nearly three months. In 1808 there had been a fire at Covent Garden

Theatre which virtually demolished the auditorium, and in order to finance the rebuilding, John Kemble, who was manager at the time, proposed to increase the number of private boxes at the expense of the cheaper seats, and at the same time raise the price of the tickets for the pit by sixpence. The public's response was immediate:

. . . for seventy-one nights, between the 18th September and the 16th December, no performance was possible on account of the uproar. The invention of new noises for Covent Garden became a fine art. One gentleman took a watchman's rattle, which he sprung from a private box at propitious moments; another occupied the centre of the pit with a large dustman's bell. Drums, horns, cat-calls and bugles were the arms, so to speak, of the rank and file, while some of the more inventive geniuses of the opposition contrived to introduce live porkers into the theatre, their ears being pinched at proper intervals when a variation in the harmony was required. There was a regular performance called the O.P. Dance, which consisted, apparently, of a simultaneous and measured tramping of the feet all over the house. It was impossible to hear a word a few feet from the stage, and as soon as the curtain rose the audience turned their backs on the performers and devoted themselves to the diversions of the house. Any attempt at the arrest of individuals always led to a free fight, and the magistrates had little to do for three months but to settle disputes arising from the O.P. diversions at Covent Garden.[24]

In the end a compromise was reached but, in any case, the new boxes were a failure. Lady Susan O'Brien wrote to a friend two years after the riots that 'The O.P.'s need not grudge the ladies the private boxes, as they can neither see nor hear in them, two things requisite, or at least used to be so – the only good thing is getting out easily.'

Drury Lane, Covent Garden and the Haymarket Theatre held, between them, a virtual monopoly of the London theatre. Sheridan, when he became manager of Drury Lane, encouraged a certain degree of amateur patronage – Lord Byron, for one, took an active interest. In 1814, however, the management of Drury Lane was taken over by Robert Elliston, who was, above all, a showman. He began with a performance of *King Lear*, with Edmund Kean in the title role, but soon abandoned Shakespeare in favour of more popular productions. He realized that, despite all their protestations to the contrary, the majority of the audience came for the second part of the evening's entertainment, rather than the first, which was the real reason why so many of them were late: musical comedy sold more seats than highbrow drama. Elliston was a manager who based his shows on the principle of the more girls the better, and the more scantily dressed they were the more popular they would be. His greatest success was with 'Vestris',* an Italian girl of eighteen, who made her début in 1815 and was hailed by *The Times* as 'the most faultless and bewitching débutante that we have ever seen.' Vestris became the star of Drury Lane and the darling of London, largely thanks to her legs. She played the Don in a production of *Giovanni in London* and Macheath in *The Beggar's Opera*,[25] wearing breeches in both parts. Vestris was a cross between a music-hall comedienne and an opera singer, with more than a dash of the courtesan thrown in. She was the theatrical forebear of Marlene Dietrich, with her top hat and tails, or the principal boy in pantomime. Whenever possible she dressed in boy's clothing and breeches became her trademark. Her marvellous legs spawned a whole industry – for example, one sculptor had the bright idea of selling plaster casts of *'la jambe de Vestris'*, and made a fortune. When she played the breeches parts, Giovanni or Macheath, theatre managers put the price of the seats up and if she actually showed her legs the receipts went up by £300 per performance. One reviewer wrote that her 'beautiful legs . . . are of such a symmetry, a *moelleux* and a play of muscle, that the mere sight of them is enough for the art lover. Her grace and the inexhaustible wit of her playing are really enchanting, although not infrequently lascivious and too coquettish with the public.' Her hordes of admirers included the Prince Regent, who chose Vestris to star

---

* 'Vestris' was born Lucy Bartolozzi and married, at the age of sixteen, Armand Vestris, a celebrated dancer, rake and playboy. She was what was known as an 'opera-dancer' in Regency parlance.

at the Command Performance to celebrate his daughter's engage-
ment; on another occasion, when he had to miss a performance
he sent round a 'substantial form of apology in gold'.[26]

11

CHARADES AND EPIGRAMS:
THE COUNTRY HOUSE

The Regency satirists, particularly in their prints and cartoons, give the impression that society was solely composed of licentious and spendthrift drunks. But it must be remembered that their target was usually the Prince Regent himself, or his immediate circle, men whose behaviour invited such criticism, and who were by no means representative of the majority of their peer group. Lord Byron dismissed social life at the beginning of the nineteenth century as a round of dissipation and gossip, of 'routs, riots, balls and boxing-matches, cards and crim. cons., parliamentary discussions, political details, Masquerades, mechanics, Argyle Street Institution and aquatic races, love and lotteries, Brooks's and Buonaparte, opera-singers and oratorios, wine, women, wax-work and weathercocks.' Byron's intention was to deride; but in fact it evokes an unusually interesting society. Daily life amongst the upper classes during the Regency may have been spent largely in the pursuit of pleasure but it was often pleasure of the most rarefied and cultivated kind. There were a number of truly formidable intellects on the social circuit at the time, and they both enjoyed and worked at the art of clever conversation. An account of a dinner party shows one of the ways the finer brains of society chose to relax. The host was a Mr Planta, who had been a colleague of Lord Londonderry's, and remained at the Foreign Office as an Under Secretary of State, and the guests included George Canning, the Foreign Secretary; the Russian and American ambassadors, Count Lieven and Richard Rush respectively; Frederick Robinson, the current Chancellor of the Exchequer; Lord Granville; Lord George Bentinck; Lord Howard de Walden; and Charles Ellis, an eminent MP.

'It would not have been easy to assemble a company better fitted to make a dinner party agreeable,' Richard Rush wrote afterwards. 'There was much small talk, some of it very sprightly. Ten o'clock arriving, with little disposition to rise from table, Mr Canning proposed that we should play "Twenty Questions".' It was decided that Canning and Robinson should put the questions and Rush and Granville should give the answers. Nothing too abstract, occult or technical was to be allowed as the thought to be guessed, 'but something well known to the present day, or to general history'. In the event the object in Canning's mind would hardly apply to such qualifications today:

First question (by Mr Canning) – Does what you have thought of belong to the animal or vegetable kingdom?
    Answer – To the vegetable.
    Second question – Is it manufactured, or unmanufactured?
    Manufactured.
    Third – Is it a solid or a liquid?
    A solid.
    (How could it be liquid, said one of the company, slyly, unless vegetable soup!)
    Fourth – Is it a thing entire in itself, or in parts?
    Entire.
    Fifth – Is it for private use or public?
    Public.
    Sixth – Does it exist in England, or out of it?
    In England.
    Seventh – Is it single, or are there others of the same kind?
    Single.
    Eighth – Is it historical, or only existent at present?
    Both.
    Ninth – For ornament or use?

Both.

Tenth – Has it any connexion with the person of the King?

No.

Eleventh – Is it carried, or does it support itself?

The former.

Twelfth – Does it pass by succession?

(Neither Lord Granville nor myself being quite certain on this point, the question was not answered; but, as it was thought that the very hesitation to answer might serve to shed light upon the secret, it was agreed that the question should be counted as one, in the progress of the game.)

Thirteenth – Was it used at the coronation?

Yes.

Fourteenth – In the Hall or Abbey?

Probably in both: certainly in the Hall.

Fifteenth – Does it belong specially to the ceremony of the coronation, or is it used at other times?

It is used at other times.

Sixteenth – Is it exclusively of a vegetable nature, or is it not, in some parts, a compound of a vegetable and a mineral?

Exclusively of a vegetable nature.

Seventeenth – What is its shape?

(This question was objected to as too particular; . . . it was not counted.)

Seventeenth (repeated) – Is it decorated, or simple?

(We made a stand against this question also, as too particular; but . . . I had to answer it and said that it was simple.)

Eighteenth – Is it used in the ordinary ceremonial of the House of Commons, or House of Lords?

No.

Nineteenth – Is it ever used by either House?

No.

Twentieth – Is it generally stationary or movable?

Movable.

The whole number of questions being now exhausted, there was a dead pause. The interest had gone on increasing as the game advanced, until, coming to the last question, it grew to be like neck-and-neck at the close of a race. Mr Canning sat silent for a minute or two; then, rolling his rich eye about, and with a countenance a little anxious, and in an accent by no means over-confident, he exclaimed, 'I think it must be the wand of the Lord High-Steward!' And it was – EVEN SO.

This wand is a long, plain, white staff, not much thicker than your middle finger, and, as such, justifies all the answers given.[1]

Canning's performance on this occasion was obviously a *tour de force*, but what is even more remarkable, by present day standards, is the general assumption that all those present would know about such an esoteric object as the wand of the Lord High Steward. Nor was such intellectual games-playing confined to political and diplomatic circles. At country-house parties, for example, even the younger guests were expected to sing for their supper with wit and charm. After an evening spent gambling at Tixhall, the Granvilles' house in Staffordshire, Charles Greville came down the next morning with an ode to macao which he had written overnight about the various winners and losers; and Henry Luttrell, a fellow guest, produced a whole page of epigrams on the subject at the breakfast table. (Breakfast, in this case, was never before noon and often later; it was a substantial meal in its own right, with plenty of drink to reactivate the mood of the night before.) 'Thus we trifled life away,' Greville wrote, adding that the parties at Tixhall were the epitome of '*le bon goût, les ris, l'aimable liberté.*' After another weekend, his diary records (again, it is worth noting, in French) that '*Nous faisions la bonne chère, ce qui ajoute beaucoup à l'agrément de la société.*'[2]

Lady Granville, the hostess at Tixhall, was one of the cleverest women in society, but in spite of her brains and her wit she seems to have been universally popular, possibly because she was also plain and good-natured, an unusual combination in her particular family. She was born Harriet ('Hary-O') Cavendish, daughter of the fifth Duke of Devonshire and his wife, the beautiful Georgiana. When Harriet married Earl Granville her brother, the sixth Duke, said that the marriage 'spoiled the looks of the two handsomest families in England', the Cavendishes and the Leveson-Gowers:

Granville was considered one of the best-looking men of his generation.[3] In the context of morality, it was a remarkable union, for Granville already had two illegitimate children by his wife's aunt, Lady Bessborough, with whom he had had a running affair for years: the young bride not only accepted the children but went on to bring them up with the same care as her own. As Hary-O herself was prone to take a high moral tone over other people's peccadillos, it can only be assumed that she did not believe in visiting the sins of the father on the child. Or that she was so besotted about Granville – as her aunt had been before her – that he was above criticism. In any case, the marriage prospered and, indeed, seems to have been one of the most successful of their generation. Charles Greville, who knew Lady Granville well, described her as having 'a great deal of genial humour, strong feelings, enthusiasm, delicacy, refinement, good taste, *naiveté* which just misses affectation, and a *bonhomie* which extends to all around her.' Greville was a dedicated country-house visitor, moving between one grand establishment and another, except when it was time to go to Epsom or Newmarket or Brighton, or back to London for the season. He revelled in the way of life of a country-house party and, anyway, fitted into one of the categories of ideal guests – aristocratic bachelor with brains, wit and money, who liked gambling and was good at indoor games as well as sport.

Lady Airlie's book, *In Whig Society*, based on the letters of her great-grandmother, Elizabeth, Lady Melbourne, and the latter's daughter Emily, who married Lord Palmerston, shows the leaders of the Regency at their legendary best and evokes a world of culture and sophistication which has never been surpassed. At Inverary Castle, for example, during the summer of 1802, there was a large and jolly house party, larded with pretty girls and clever young men. They amused themselves by producing their own 'Domestic Newspaper', which they took it in turns to edit: one week the editor was William Lamb, later Lord Melbourne, the Prime Minister. They also played elaborate charades, which, with amateur theatricals, were a regular feature of country-house parties in that particular circle. A letter from 'Monk' Lewis* to Lady Melbourne describes the party:

Inverary is as full as it can hold – & *fuller* too as the Irishman said. Bed-rooms are in great request and William [Lamb] and [Douglas] Kinnaird being the last comers, are moved about from chamber to chamber, never knowing one night where they are to sleep the next. Whoever passes a few hours out of the Castle is certain of finding one of the two new-comers established in his room when he returns; & a formal complaint was lodged yesterday by a great Russian Count, that he only stept out for half an hour, and the first thing which He saw lying on his bed when He came back, were a dozen pair of Kinnaird's leather breeches.[4]

The future Prime Minister was chary of making too much of a fool of himself even then: when dragooned into playing the lead in one of their amateur productions, Monk Lewis complained that 'He obstinately refuses to be dressed as a shepherd with a wreath of roses & a bunch of cherry coloured ribbands ornamenting his hat, which I am clearly of the opinion is the proper dress for the character.'[5]

It was taken for granted amongst the upper classes that a large part of the year would be spent in travelling around the country visiting friends and relations; and that they would be welcome at short notice even though the party often consisted of the whole family and a retinue of servants, lady's maid, valet, nanny, governess, secretary and the ubiquitous family doctor. During the summer of 1807, the Bessboroughs, with all their children, did a social tour of the North, staying in turn at Bolton, Wentworth, Howick, Castle Howard and Alnwick. Another year they travelled all over the country: from wintering in Cornwall, where they rented a house, they went back to London for the season, on to Bognor in the summer, and then, in the autumn, after a visit to Lord Egremont at Petworth, looked in on Chatsworth, Holywell,

---

* 'Monk' Lewis was the author of *The Monk*, a Gothic novel which caused a scandal at the time owing to its strong sexual element.

Hardwick, Wentworth and Woburn, and, by December, they were back in London. This was the usual form of the social year, not an exceptional case. A visit to one of these great country houses was like staying in a luxurious hotel, but free, a factor of importance to some, particularly those who were in danger of being pursued in London by duns. House parties often lasted for weeks on end, with every kind of entertainment on offer and no demands made upon the guests other than that of amusing the company. The circumstances were ideal for prolonged flirtation, and adulterous love was seldom a problem either. Husbands and wives amongst the upper classes always occupied separate rooms and only slept together by mutual arrangement; and in such large houses it was easy to move around in secrecy. As Lady Airlie pointed out, 'Good breeding demanded that outward conventions should not be violated, but asked few questions as to what went on beneath the surface. Scandals were glossed over by the decent acquiescence of the wife or husband.'

The form varied, of course, from house to house. The Priory, for instance, country seat of the Abercorns, was also famous for amateur theatricals, but the atmosphere was rather more subdued than that of Inverary. Caroline Lamb, who was staying there for Christmas one year with her husband William, described the daily routine in a letter to her grandmother:

... for while many go to bed before eleven, few sit up after twelve. We dine exactly at six, & and though I am never down for breakfast there is a regular one which, as Lord Abercorn remarks, lasts generally from daybreak till dinner ... it is extremely pleasant here & a kind of general indulgence prevails so that everybody does what they like best, & even at night some read, others talk, some sing & play, & others go to chess & backgammon.[6]

Supper was served at half past ten, and it would have been another prodigious feast. Caroline goes on to say, with obvious relief, that Lord Abercorn has banished politics from the conversation so that everyone is in a good mood, '& much quieter than any place I ever yet was in, for I do not think it is the fashion of the house to be in a Devonshire bustle.' As usual, at the Priory, the guests were involved in producing their own full-scale production of a contemporary play, in which both the Lambs took leading parts. Mary Berry, another frequent visitor, gives an indication of the type of theatre favoured by the Abercorns: *Who's the Dupe?* and *The Wedding Day* were both performed with an all-star cast of aristocrats, including one of Princess Charlotte's ladies-in-waiting.[7] The plays were followed, as was the custom in the West End theatre itself, by a farce, which was specially written for the occasion by George Lamb. The Abercorns also invited various fashionable professionals to join the party and advise on the productions: Thomas Lawrence was presumably brought in to supervise the stage sets and Mrs John Kemble to direct the actors.

Mary Berry was another amateur playwright. One of her plays, a comedy called *Fashionable Friends*, was first produced privately, at Strawberry Hill, but it was thought so good by her friends, headed by Lord Palmerston, that she was encouraged to try it out on the public. The play was produced anonymously at Drury Lane, with an excellent cast, led by Charles Kemble and Mrs Jordan, the two most popular stars at the time, but was a flop. After only three performances, the play was withdrawn. The main complaint, surprisingly, was its lax morality: presumably Miss Berry had forgotten that the kind of sexual innuendo and loose behaviour which the upper classes took for granted shocked the general public.

One of the most eccentric hostesses of the Regency was the Duchess of York, whose weekend parties at Oatlands, her country house in Surrey, were a well-known endurance test for the guests. The house appears to have been run as a cross between a gambling den and a zoo. At one time the Duchess had more than a hundred dogs roaming around the premises; there was an aviary, with eagles, parrots, macaws and other exotic birds; monkeys played on the lawns and she even kept tame kangaroos. Charles Greville wrote that 'Oatlands is the worst managed establishment in England; there are a great many servants, and nobody waits on you; a vast number of horses, and none to ride or drive.' As usual, however, he seems to have gone there whenever he was asked, and clearly enjoyed himself. Describing a large house party at Oatlands one summer weekend, he wrote that 'We played at whist till four in the morning. On Sunday we amused ourselves with eating fruit in the gardens, and shooting at a mark with pistols, and playing with the monkeys. I bathed in the cold bath in the grotto, which is as clear as crystal and as cold as ice.'[8] The Duchess entertained throughout the summer, but only at the weekends, the guests arriving on Saturday and leaving on Monday. Her parties were popular but she had no intention of allowing her guests to outstay their welcome. The company was almost always 'the same people, sometimes more, sometimes less. We dine at eight and sit at table till eleven. In about a quarter of an hour after we leave the dining-room the Duke sits down to play whist, and never stirs from the table as long as anybody will play with him.' The difference between the Duke and Duchess was that while, as a true Hanoverian spendthrift, the Duke liked playing for enormous stakes, £5 a point plus £25 on the rubber, the Duchess played for fun rather than money, and usually set the stakes at her table at an upper limit of half-a-crown (12½ p in today's money). The Duchess was an eccentric. She was a clever woman, amusing and kind, but really preferred the company of animals in general, and dogs in particular, to that of her guests. She seldom bothered to go to bed but spent most of the night walking around the house and grounds, accompanied by her hordes of dogs. She would drop off occasionally, for an hour or two, on one of the couches encountered during these perambulations, which made life difficult for the servants in the morning. They would arrive to clean the drawing room and have to work their way around Her Grace, still asleep. She would have breakfast by herself at three in the morning and only met her guests at dinner time. Nevertheless, they all loved her. A typical story about the Duchess concerned Monk Lewis, a famous snob, who was invited to Oatlands for the first time. He was found in floods of tears by a fellow guest, and when asked why he was crying, is said to have replied, 'because the Duchess has just been so very, very nice to me.' Whereupon the other man said 'Don't worry. She's so vague, she probably didn't mean it.'

(The Yorks, incidentally, were famous for running out of cash. Much of the time the steward had no money to pay the tradesmen, who retaliated by stopping supplies. The household often ran short of food and even the water was cut off on one occasion because the bills had not been paid: the workmen refused to reconnect the pipes until they were, and in cash, not promises. And this was a royal Duke. The Duchess, unlike her husband, was extremely scrupulous about money. When she died she left £12,000 to her servants – how she had managed to keep even that amount away from the Duke is a mystery – and had arranged all her affairs 'with the greatest exactitude, and left nothing undone'.)

Country-house visiting, in fact, was a way of life: and as it was an age when the literate were hampered by no fears of publication in their copious correspondence, the character of all these various houses and the hospitality they offered has been reported in acid detail. Arundel, for example, the Duke of Norfolk's house in Sussex, was famed for its discomfort, according to Creevey: Henry Brougham complained when he stayed there that he missed such basics as 'a necessary, towels, water, &&'. Princess Lieven was similarly scathing about Stratfield Saye, the house given by the nation to the Duke of Wellington; she said it was nothing but a bore to have to go there, always put her in a bad temper, the house was ugly and freezing, the park barren and the Duchess stupid.[9] Princess Lieven was never one to mince her words. Lady Holland was a rather more gracious guest: after staying with Lord Grey at Howick, his estate in Northumberland, she wrote that 'the House is one of the most comfortable mansions I know, and the grounds are as pretty as they can be . . . I never expected to be so long in a country house, and yet leave it with regret, which was the case in this instance.'[10] Cashiobury, which belonged to Lord Essex, had a most beautiful library '50 feet in length, full of books and every comfort' and a glorious flower garden. At Lambton the hospitality was particularly magnificent, 'with everything in a suitable style of splendour'. Lord Lambton was one of the richest men in the country but he had a frightful temper, exacerbated by insomnia, and was once heard to complain that he thought it 'damned hard that a man with £80,000 a year can't sleep'.[11] He was so pernickety, furthermore, that whenever he condescended to go and stay in someone else's house, he brought his own provisions with him – his own tea, his own sugar, his own bread and even his own butter. Woburn, the Duke of Bedford's country seat, was a Whig establishment, often used as the party's ex-officio headquarters, and, like Howick, renowned for hospitality on the grand scale. Woburn was also said to offer the best shooting in England, a distinction challenged by Holkham, the beautiful house in Norfolk belonging to the Coke family. In the course of one house party at Woburn, lasting five days, the 'bag' included 835 pheasants, 645 hares, 59 rabbits, 10 partridges and 4 woodcocks; while at Holkham 780 head of game were shot by 10 guns in a single drive, a pattern of slaughter which was repeated all over the country throughout the season. Shooting was seen not only as a sport but as a form of exercise, and any form of outdoor activity was encouraged as an antidote to gout. In the country, hunting, shooting and fishing were almost obligatory during the relevant seasons, but all forms of sport were popular, including archery, badminton, cricket and tennis. Spare horses for the guests to ride were always on offer at such houses, as well as spare stabling for those who preferred to bring their own. Guests of a more sedentary nature took their daily 'constitutional', walking or driving round the grounds. On rainy days the younger generation played billiards or chased each other round the house on treasure hunts, or played 'Hunt the Squirrel', a form of 'Sardines', while the dowagers played chess and wrote letters.

Regency ladies wrote an enormous number of letters to each other, their friends and their family. Many wrote to their favourite correspondents virtually every day, about love, politics, marriage, money, health and despair, anything and everything. Lady Spencer, for one, mother of Georgiana and Harriet Cavendish, expected her children to write to her every single day. Complaining to Harriet, she wrote:

On Friday I had not a line from a single creature, which was rather mortifying, because when the post came in, the whole circle seated at breakfast talked impatiently of what news I should have, as that would be authentic, & at length the letters were brought in & distributed in abundance to every creature but me. So you must *griffonner*, if it is but a line every day to save my credit.[12]

Mrs Jordan was equally prolific, sometimes writing as many as twenty letters a day, and expected a commensurate number of answers. Travelling carriages were equipped with special portable writing tables, which could be propped on the passenger's lap. The quantity of correspondence between the women is an indication of the amount of free time at their disposal as well as their interest in current affairs. These wonderful, clever and entertaining letters were a part of everyday life during the Regency; but then this was a generation which put a very high premium on education, at least amongst certain families.

The level of knowledge was astonishing by modern-day standards; it was taken for granted, for example, that children should be fluent in French and familiar with the classics long before they were allowed into the drawing room. As one visitor to London commented at the time, 'there is scarcely a well-educated person in England who does not speak French, whilst thousands among the best educated in France are ignorant of English.'[13] Nor was this emphasis on the importance of education confined to the elite, the families with a long cultural tradition of respect for the arts and learning. The Parker family of Saltram, in Devon, were typical landed gentry of the middle class, rather than aristocrats, but they, too, had their children educated almost entirely in French, taught by a governess who spoke no English. At the age of nine one of the girls was translating stories from *L'Ami des Enfants* into 'very good English, very exactly done, and very well spelt'.[14]

In the context of women's education, however, it must be added that it was a subject which aroused almost as violent and vociferous opposition as the idea that nicely brought-up girls should work for a living, or married ladies control their own money. (The concept of women's suffrage had not, of course,

ADVANTAGES OF MODERN EDUCATION
Caricature by Charles Williams, published by S. Knights, 1825
Regency society was sharply divided on the subject of female education.

even been suggested during the Regency.) The following diatribe in one of the papers may not be in keeping with the popular image of a sophisticated society, but there is no doubt it voiced the sentiments of a large section of the public. The author was reviewing a new book on the education of women in general, and the growing practice of sending girls to boarding school in particular. After a patronizing introduction, in which he admits that women 'compose one half of the species and are destined to constitute the happiness of the other half', he goes on to say that, in any case, educating girls is a waste of time and money:

It is generally allowed, that her [woman's] *intellectual powers* are as different from his, as her physical properties: hence her incapacity for intense application, and her little aptitude for the study of the sciences. She thinks, but can rarely meditate: she improves, but does not create: she feels more profoundly than man, but has not sufficient energy to depict her acute sensations.[15]

As for the new boarding schools, 'the best of them is good for nothing,' while the teachers, he infers, are usually recruited from dubious sources: 'If we enquire, what situations these persons originally occupied, we shall find that many of them were only chamber-maids and common servants ... Some have been kept mistresses, cast off when the bloom of youth and beauty began to fade.' Others, he points out, have no more qualification to teach than that of having been educated at a boarding school themselves, and have only taken the job because there was no other means of earning their living. The author was right, at least, when he went on to say that teaching was a profession which 'few, who are acquainted with its duties, would embrace from choice or inclination; but which is the only one left for a woman, if we except that of a milliner or mantua-maker.' Furthermore, most of the ladies who run these schools, the head-mistresses, according to this highly prejudiced writer, are frustrated spinsters who spend most of their time in bed, or drunk: '... they indulge in the arms of Morpheus till late in the morning; in sacrifices to Bacchus nearly the whole afternoon; and in scribbling wretched poems, and doleful love-stories, in the evening.'[16] This was the sort of attitude with which Hannah More and her fellow campaigners for female education had to contend.

The majority of girls, however, were taught at home, by governesses and tutors. The level of some of their parents' expectations, and the results of their education from the very earliest ages, can be judged by the letters of the Cavendish family, particularly between its female members. The matriarch of the clan at the end of the eighteenth century, and well into the Regency period, was Lady Spencer, mother of Georgiana (later Duchess of Devonshire) and Harriet (later Lady Bessborough). Lady Spencer was a pious and reclusive woman who devoted her life to good works and crusading for the education of women. She was herself a very well-educated woman and a great reader, though not, on the face of it, of the kind of literature likely to amuse her daughters: she was quoted as saying that she considered Paley's *Principles of Morals and Political Philosophy* a 'good book for any sort of people to turn over and dip into',[17] and described a contemporary tome entitled *Annals of Commerce* as 'a most entertaining work'. However, Lady Spencer must have possessed that rare quality of being able to adapt her style to her audience, for she succeeded brilliantly in passing on her intellectual values to her children and grandchildren. (Even if she made an equally spectacular failure of passing on her Puritan principles.) The Cavendish girls were not only extraordinarily well educated, but imbued with a genuine love of literature and learning for its own sake. According to Lady Spencer, her granddaughter, Caroline Ponsonby (later Caroline Lamb) could read at the age of four and could 'do the greatest part of the map of England very perfectly'.[18] By the age of seven, Caro could 'talk French very tolerably' and was learning to play the harpsichord. A year later she could read Italian as well as French and English, even if it was difficult to keep her attention and her mother had to keep correcting her.[19] Caroline wrote a whole letter to her father in French, which was certainly a bit boring – a series of short sentences on the lines of 'I am well', 'Hope you are well', etc. – and had indeed probably been corrected by her mother, but was still a considerable accomplishment for a child of that age. Even dressing a doll was an oblique lesson; Lady Spencer wrote that the girls were making clothes for their dolls and learning the names of the various items in French. The next generation carried on the tradition: Lady Bessborough, who had, of course, been brought up with the same values, read her niece Voltaire's *L'Enfant prodige* as a bedtime story, and larded her letters to her schoolboy sons with Latin quotations. Whether the children always understood everything is another matter, but a letter from one of the boys, William, at the age of seven, shows that at least they were aware of the classics. 'I have been to Virgil's tomb,' he wrote to his brother. 'If you know any such person, he lived about 1800 years ago. We are at Naples. Virgil wrote poems.'[20] Later on the boy complains that his mother wants him to learn to read and write Italian, 'but that is no such easy matter for me.' Lady Bessborough kept up the pressure even when her children were grown-up, constantly suggesting books they should read. It is hard to believe, however, that she was serious when she suggested that her daughter, Caroline Lamb, should take twenty-four volumes of a book called *Ancient History* on her honeymoon. 'I know your happiness cannot be compleat without [it] . . . Could you not contrive a little rolling booke case you might draw after you, containing these precious volumes?'[21] Nevertheless, in later life Caro Lamb amused herself by writing a letter in Greek to her brother-in-law, although it took her a week to get it right.

The Cavendish girls' governess, engaged by their grand-mother, was Miss Selina Trimmer, who came from a family of well-known educationalists: Selina's sister-in-law was Mrs Sarah Trimmer, a celebrated author, founder of charity schools and friend of Dr Johnson. Miss Trimmer was an excellent teacher and much loved by her pupils, who went on writing to her all their lives. She was also their confidante and mentor. There is a long letter from 'Harriett', as she signs herself, to Miss Trimmer which shows the extent of the latter's influence. Harriet was only just sixteen at the time, a débutante in the full excitement of her first season, and yet she takes the trouble to please her old governess by writing at length about serious matters. The tem-porary peace of Amiens was under negotiation and Harriet feels that England has been slighted:

By the bye are not you rather indignant at the *violent honours* bestowed upon Sanintoni and the inscriptions 'Buonaparte saviour of the uni-verse'? Are we not the only nation who have checked his conquests, did we not drive him out of Egypt in the most glorious manner, and I do not see that even by our own countrymen, we have half enough honour for it. I think the peace seems a sad one, however, peace in any shape almost, I think was necessary. I never heard of anything so delightful as Mr Fox's behaviour, with his superior talents and abilities, he is with all the nature and simplicity of a child, in real high spirits at the happiness he sees diffused over his fellow creatures . . . How true it is of Mr Fox 'on his heart we may rely even should his judgement for a moment fail him'.

At least she ends on a less elevated note: 'Exit in a transport of universal philanthropy! . . . Here I am, *cooled* at Feny Bridge. It is a delightful inn and I feel quite well and have been eating a very good dinner.'[22] But the Cavendish girls were not unique: Prince Puckler-Muskau was amazed, and not best pleased, to discover that

English ladies are best reached through politics. Lately one has heard nothing at table, at the opera, even at the ball, but Canning and Wellington from every lovely mouth; indeed Lord Ellenborough complained that his wife plagued him with politics even at night. She had terrified him by crying out suddenly, in her sleep: 'Will the Prime Minister stand or fall?'[23]

There was one curious omission in all this concentrated education: neither spelling nor punctuation seem to have been considered important during the Regency. For example, Harriet Cavendish wrote that she was 'schocked' by someone's 'stupiddity' without any complaint from Miss Trimmer. As for their calligraphy it was so appalling that it is amazing they ever managed to read each other's letters at all. The truth was that sloppy handwriting was sanctioned on the grounds that it was the sign of a gentleman: only people who needed to work for a living, such as clerks, needed to be legible. The point was made by George Eliot, in *Middlemarch*, when Caleb Garth is so shocked by Fred Vincy's handwriting and insists that he learn to write all over again.

To complicate these intellectual – or social – nuances yet further, the Whig grandees specialized in a particular drawl in conversation, and pronounced certain words in a way which was virtually unintelligible to anyone else. It was a private upper-class slang: they said 'chaney' meaning china, 'yaller' for yellow, went to the 'chimist' and invented a string of nicknames for their friends. The fifth Duke of Devonshire was known as 'Canis', his wife, the beautiful Georgiana, as 'Mrs Rat' and his mistress, Lady Elizabeth Foster, as 'The Racoon' or 'Racky'. The Regent, of course, was 'Prinney', the Duke of Wellington 'The Beau' and the Duke of Norfolk 'Jockey'. Lady Darlington was referred to variously as 'The Pop', 'Poplolly' or 'Haradan' and Lord Lambton as 'The Monarch' or 'King Jog', in deference to his remark that 'one can jog along on £40,000 a year' (his own income was double that amount). The Duke of Gloucester was 'Slice', Lord Goderich 'Snip', Lord John Russell 'Pie and Thimble' or 'The Widow's Mite', Lord Sefton 'The Pet', Charles Greville 'Punch', Henry Brougham 'Wickedshifts' and Douglas Kinnaird 'Vesuvius'.[24] This private language was the password to the inner circle of Whig society; the deb who said cucumber instead of 'cowcumber', laundry instead of 'landry', or failed to realize that when the conversation turned to 'Madagascar' they were talking about Lady Holland, not the island, was branded at once as beyond the pale. Jane Austen mocks this kind of snobbery in *Northanger Abbey* in one of the conversations between Catherine and Tilney:

Catherine: 'I cannot speak well enough to be unintelligible.'
   Tilney: 'Bravo! – an excellent satire on modern language.'

The shades of English snobbery have always been a source of annoyance to foreigners, the more so as they are never explained and seem completely illogical. It has already been said that, by the time of the Regency, the hard and fast rules of the eighteenth century had been superseded by more flexible standards and a more liberal attitude in general: but, to an objective outsider, English society was still a class-ridden minefield, full of inexplicable taboos. 'One must be especially careful to avoid as far as possible anything that the English do not do, and at the same time try to imitate them in everything, because no race of men can be more intolerant,' was the verdict of one maddened visitor. 'Besides, most of them look unfavourably on the admission of foreigners into their closed society, and all consider it an outstanding favour and grace conferred upon us.' The writer goes on to warn the unwary about their table manners:

Of all the offences which one can commit . . . and for which, apparently, all further entrance into English society would be barred to one, the three following are the greatest: to put a knife into your mouth like a fork; to take sugar or asparagus with your hand or to spit anywhere in a room . . . the only ridiculous thing is the extraordinary importance which is attached to these things. The last named crime especially is, in England, so pedantically forbidden that one can seek in vain through the whole of London [for] such an article as a spittoon. A Dutchman, who found himself very uncomfortable here for that reason, declared with great annoyance that the Englishman's spittoon is his stomach.[25]

On a more serious level there is no doubt that, despite the new mood of liberality, and despite the odd exceptions, Regency society was not in the least democratic at heart. Class distinctions were a fact of life: aristocratic liberals might, and indeed did, attempt to ameliorate the lives of the working classes, but they never for one moment thought of them as their equals. The campaign for Reform was about injustice, not equality. Sometimes this blatant discrimination was unimportant, at others it caused real distress. At the Gentlemen v. Players match at Lords the Gentlemen wore top hats and the Players wore caps, and nobody took offence or thought it worthy of comment. A more serious example of discrimination was the custom of private pews, bought by the rich and reserved exclusively for their use, which often meant that there was no room for the poor in the church at all. The idea of buying a place in church was taken for granted by most of the population at the beginning of the nineteenth century, but only in England. A book published in 1816, titled *Brief Remarks on English Manners*, whose anonymous author was described simply as 'An Englishman', was one of the first to criticize this iniquitous system. Writing in the form of a letter to a Catholic friend living abroad, he cites the segregation of the classes in church as evidence of the extent of English snobbery:

You will not be prepared, I think, for another proof of the aristocratick spirit which I am about to mention – the pernicious practice of dividing our churches into pews; which is never done in foreign, at least not in Roman Catholick countries . . . the poorer classes are not only separated from their superiours, but in many instances they are shut out of the church for want of means to *purchase* a seat within its walls . . . in London scarce a place is provided in churches for the lower classes, and no accommodation afforded them without the payment of a sum quite beyond their means . . . I do not contend that the system is adopted *for the sake* of shutting the church door against the lower classes. But the effect is precisely the same as if it were so intended . . . Almost all the places are hired by the rich; – scarcely any convenient seats are provided for those who do not pay; and I believe it is well ascertained that taking all the parish churches and chapels of the metropolis together, they will not be found to furnish accommodation *of any kind* for more than one tenth part of the poorer population . . . In ancient times probably the great man of each parish had his family pew, but by degrees, as the influence of money prevailed, his rich neighbours continued to vie with him and with each other, till at last all our churches have become disfigured to the eye by their tasteless divisions, resembling pens for cattle, and many of them *dishonoured* by being made *receptacles for the rich to the exclusion of the poor.* Many fine ladies and gentlemen would shrink from the thought of the seats in a church being open to all classes. But in countries where the practice exists I am not aware that any inconvenience arises from it. The poor people do not think of intruding on the rich; nor would they here, and the objection to seat oneself by a well-dressed tradesman's wife or daughter can only proceed from a feeling of aristocratick superiority unsuited to the sacred place.[26]

12

FASHION, MANNERS
AND MORES:
THE NEW LIBERALISM

The years of the Regency period saw a complete revolution in dress for both men and women. As James Laver, the great authority on English fashions, wrote, 'For a whole century the accepted forms of male and female costume had remained fundamentally the same. Once the tradition was broken, anything might have happened.' What actually happened was the direct result of the French Revolution:

In their hatred of the embroidered garments of the nobility, the men and women of 1789 turned, on the one hand, to English country fashions, and, on the other, to what they imagined was the clothing of the ancient Greeks. The result was that top-boots for men and a single, flimsy, chemise-like garb for women became the accepted wear. Men abandoned knee-breeches, long flapped surcoats and wigs; women gave up loops, brocade and the use of powder on their hair.[1]

However, as Laver explains elsewhere, the change in style which followed the events of 1789 was in itself a paradox:

. . . people only began to adopt the costume of the ancient world when the ideals of Republican virtue had been abandoned for the frank pursuit of pleasure. The frivolity which the Republicans thought they had extinguished for ever with the blood of aristocrats burst forth with renewed intensity once the threat of the guillotine was removed . . . women found themselves suddenly emancipated, and their first reaction was to cut their hair short and to take off most of their clothes.[2]

The dresses of the Directoire period exposed the female form to a degree which would have been unthinkable in the previous century:

Single garments of diaphanous materials replaced the elaborate panniers and stomachers of a former age. Dresses were split up the sides, to the knee and beyond, and revealed inside limbs clothed in flesh-coloured tights, or sometimes not clothed at all ... Dresses were cut very low at the neck, and although a few daring spirits, who went so far as to expose the breasts, were hissed in the street, the costume of the majority of women was not very much more prudish.

The new styles, based on the classic ideal of female beauty, were intended to emulate the simplicity of ancient Greek dress and invoke a spirit of democracy rather than wanton freedom. However, by definition, such light unstructured dresses naturally clung to the body and showed every curve: some daring ladies damped the muslin of their dresses to make the contours of their bodies even more noticeable. Stiff corsets, or stays, would obviously have ruined the silhouette, so the modest solution was to wear a long knitted undergarment of silk, or cotton, moulded to the figure like a modern 'body'. The result may have looked free and easy but, in fact, was the reverse, according to those who had to wear them. One reluctant sufferer, Lady Morgan, remembered that

the most uncomfortable style of dress was when they were so scanty that it was difficult to walk in them, and to make them tighter still, invisible petticoats were worn. They were woven in the stocking loom, and were like strait waist-coats ... but only drawn down over the legs instead of over the arms so that, when walking, you were obliged to take short and mincing steps. I was not long in discarding mine and, of course, shocking my juvenile acquaintances by my boldness in throwing off such a fashionable restraint.

In continuation of the classical theme, the emphasis in fashion was on white, flowing dresses; hair was dressed '*à la Sappho*', '*Brutus*' or '*Titus*'; and there was a vogue for garlands, laurel leaves and antique cameos in place of flashier jewellery, and for sandals instead of high heels.

All this simplicity of dress, however, lasted no more than a few years and, by the time of the political Regency, had been modified out of all recognition. The English have never been entirely happy with foreign influences, even classical ones, and by 1812 they had gone back to their false bosoms and familiar corsets, albeit in a less exaggerated form. Regency ladies prided themselves on their figures but a corset only helps if the waist is in its normal place. Mary Frampton, remembering the ideals of feminine beauty at the end of the eighteenth century, wrote that

The perfection of figure according to the then fashion was the smallness of the circumference into which your unfortunate waist could be compressed, and many a poor girl hurt her health very materially by trying to rival the reigning beauty of that day, the Duchess of Rutland, who was said to squeeze herself to the size of an orange and a half.

Even then, however, some of the fashion magazines had begun to point out the danger of such tight stays and to advocate a return to the natural form. In 1789 the *Lady's Monthly Museum* wrote that

The advantages of a good shape are often injured by the foolish fondness of having them very slender. Were they to consult the form of the superb antique statue of Venus, they would find a good proportion as far removed from a too slender waist, and uniform, as a clumsy one. Besides, it may be justly observed, that when the corsets are too closely laced, it takes away entirely all ease and grace. The motion becomes stiff, and the attitude constrained; without speaking of the accidents which may result from such an outrage against Nature.

By 1795 it appeared that 'corselettes about six inches long, and a slight buffon tucker of two inches high [i.e. a kind of strapless bra], are now the only defensive paraphernalia of our

fashionable belles, between the necklace and the apron string.'[3]
Four years later the fashion correspondent of *The Times* wrote
sarcastically that 'The fashion of false bosoms has at least this
utility, that it compels our fashionable fair to wear something.'
The *Morning Herald* had a different criticism:

The bosom, which Nature planted at the bottom of her chest, is pushed
up by means of wadding and whalebone to a station so near her chin
that in a very full subject that feature is sometimes lost between the
invading mounds. Not only is the shape thrust out of its proper place,
but the blood is thrown forcibly into the face, neck and arms ...
producing an unattractive flush ... Over this strangely manufactured
figure a scanty petticoat and as scanty a gown are put. The latter
resembles a bolster-slip rather than a garment.

Moreover, having lost their waists, the women all looked pregnant, as the satirists were the first to point out. 'The Short Body'd
Gown', of which a few verses will suffice, was published in 1801:

> Ye lads and ye lasses of country and city,
> I pray you give ear to my humorous ditty,
> Concerning the fashion just come from town,
> A whimsical dress call'd the short body'd gown.
>
> This humorous dress that's now call'd the mode,
> Surpasses all fashions that e'er was in vogue,
> There's not a young miss in the country all round,
> But must be stuff'd up in a short body'd gown.
>
> Both maids, wives, and widows, you'd think were all wild
> And all look as if they were got with child;
> Neither baloons (*sic*), nor turbans, or all fashions round,
> Will fit them, unless they've a new body'd gown.[4]

All the same it is notable that many of the Regency menfolk
preferred their women plump. The Prince Regent, for one, liked
his ladies buxom, if not downright chubby, and so did Lord
Byron, the great romantic hero of his generation. Byron's taste
in women had been formed in the Near East, where the ladies of
the seraglio were rounded, sensuous and uncomplicated. He

positively disliked very thin women, saying that when they were young they reminded him of dried butterflies and when they were old, of spiders. (In view of such prejudice it is surprising that he was ever attracted to Lady Caroline Lamb at all: her whole appeal was that of the elfin waif.) In the same context, the popular notion that men wore corsets for reasons of vanity is largely a creation of Regency cartoonists, aided and abetted by the Prince Regent himself. The Prince certainly tried to contain his corpulence with tight stays and elaborate constructions spiked with whalebones; a few of the dandies, too, were prepared to suffer for the sake of a slim waist. But on the whole, if a man wore a corset of any kind, it was as a means of support for his back, particularly when engaged in physical exercise – on the hunting-field, for example. Sometimes such a garment was no more than a wide straight band of strong material, such as jean, duck, leather or webbing, made up as a belt, with three buckles, worn round, or above, the waist.[5] The references in various fashion journals *circa* 1811 to 'elastic' corsets, garters, belts and braces are mislead-ing: the word is being used as an adjective, meaning any knitted silk, cotton or wool material which was particularly pliable. Elastic, as we know it, was not made until the 1840s. (Similarly, Wellington boots, named after the Duke, who wore them during the Peninsular Campaign, were made of leather, not rubber, which had yet to be manufactured in a durable fabric.)

The problem with all underwear at the time was that it had to be made of extremely hard-wearing material in order to survive contemporary laundering. The washerwomen used coarse soap to scrub the clothes in cold water before boiling them, and anything too soft or fine, such as lawn or muslin, would have disintegrated almost at once if subjected to such violent treatment. Chemises, drawers and nightwear, therefore, were always made of plain, good quality linen: colours would run or fade, and embroidery or lace trimmings would have been ruined by the harsh washing. Nightcaps, of similarly washable material, were worn primarily for warmth but also to protect the bed linen, which was often finely embroidered, against dirty hair; during the eighteenth century, when immensely elaborate wigs and hairstyles were in fashion, hair was not washed for weeks, or even months, on end.[6] (A later generation used antimacassars for the same reason — to preserve the fabric on their armchairs from the oil men used on their heads.)

The uncertainty inherent in any period of transition is always reflected in contemporary dress, and fashion, throughout the years of the Regency, was in a constant state of flux. Waists moved in and out, and up and down, with total disregard for the female shape, and at one point disappeared completely; necklines plunged one year and rose the next; frills were *de rigueur* for a season and the next too old-fashioned to be borne; puff sleeves were in and ruffles were out — it was impossible to be sure just which was the latest line. Women must have been in despair at the cost of keeping pace with the ever-changing modes. Crazes came and went every season, but they were also combined with each other, often to disastrous effect: one fashion magazine reported, in all seriousness, that an opera dress they considered the height of chic had a Circassian bodice made of American velvet trimmed with Chinese cord, and was to be worn with an Armenian head-dress and an Eastern mantle. The muddle speaks for itself. Regency hats, too, often verged on the ridiculous, as one fashion writer complained, speaking of the current styles in 1815: 'I do recollect when a lady did not think it necessary to wear a bushel measure on her head . . . when a face was sufficiently pretty without the foil of a coal-scuttle, or when a chimney-pot with a sweep's brush sticking out at the top of it was not thought the most graceful of all models.'[7] Such excesses were a delight to Jane Austen. The vogue for a profusion of trimmings on hats provoked her to write to her sister Cassandra that 'Flowers are very much worn, and fruit is still more the thing. Elizabeth has a bunch of strawberries, and I have seen grapes, cherries, plums, and apricots. There are likewise almonds and raisins, French plums, and tamarinds at the grocers' but I have never seen any of them in hats.' Even during those seasons when the costumes themselves were relatively simple, both men and women were able to ruin the effect by adding a number of accessories which were usually irrelevant and often ridiculous. At one time, for example, there was a craze amongst the beaux for carrying a fur muff or a painted fan. Later, there was a mania for anything vaguely Oriental, which led to a spate of turbans, shawls and exotic jewellery. Few of these innovations lasted more than a few seasons, with the exception of shawls, which served a practical purpose. The best shawls were imported, from India or the East, and made of such luxurious materials as cashmere or silk, but the English manufacturers soon produced cheap copies in serge, wool, cotton and even rabbit fur. Gloves and hats were obligatory for both sexes whenever they went out of doors; ladies carried parasols and a reticule and gentlemen canes, or as the Regency progressed, umbrellas. And, of course, the Regency was the golden age of that ubiquitous accessory, the snuff box.

According to 'Tabaciana', a contemporary treatise on the subject, the practice of taking snuff was originally frowned upon as neither dignified nor respectful: 'To take snuff was formerly considered at least as an act of levity, if not of contempt, when done in the midst of conversation.' Gibbon makes a point of 'having been so much at his ease before the princesses at the court of France as to take snuff.'[8] Towards the end of the eighteenth century, in line with the general change in mores, snuff, and the ritual which went with it, became not merely acceptable but fashionable, and by the time of the Regency the etiquette of snuff-taking had developed into a fine art. It is not easy to look attractive while inhaling snuff, let alone sneezing, but the Regency beaux clearly managed. They spent hours learning how to open a box gracefully, with a flick of the left thumb and a slight wave of the whole hand. The whole performance was designed as much to show off beautifully manicured hands and jewellery as for the pleasure of tobacco. The snuff boxes themselves were some of the most exquisite *objets d'art* of the period, incorporating the skills of the best artists, jewellers, silversmiths, goldsmiths and enamellers of their day. Others were designed to cater for less fastidious tastes: boxes shaped like a lady's leg were popular, and there was always a market for the ones with *risqué* vignettes painted on the inside of the lid. A specially commissioned snuff box could be engraved with a private message or portrait, and others were fitted with a secret compartment. Many of the Regency aesthetes collected snuff boxes, which were displayed in special glass cases or given pride of place on side tables in the drawing room.

Snuff boxes were a traditional royal gift, sometimes carried to excess. The Duke of York, who did not take snuff, received so many that he had them all melted down and had a large salver made from the gold, inscribed with the names of the donors. The Prince Regent, too, admitted to a friend that he never really liked snuff even though he always made a great performance of taking it in public, and spent a fortune on his collection of boxes. Queen Charlotte, on the other hand, was addicted to it and all the ladies of her court followed suit. They had miniatures of their lovers, or children, according to age, painted on the inside lids of their elaborately decorated boxes, many of which were designed to match, or complement, a particular dress. A jewelled and enamelled snuff box became a status symbol as well as an elegant accessory. Even without the cost of the boxes, snuff was an expensive habit, since the best brands cost £3 per lb or more. There were many different sorts of snuff on the market, varying greatly in strength and flavour: some were laced with alcohol, others with scent. 'Spanish Bran' and 'Brazil' were the most popular basic snuffs, both rather powerful in flavour, followed by 'Macouba', a very strongly scented snuff, particularly fancied by the dandy set. Others had even more exotic-sounding names, such as 'Scholten', 'Masulipatam', 'Bureau Demi-Gros' and 'Bolongaro'. Many of the leaders of fashion made a point of mixing their own snuff: the Regent's, for example, was highly scented with attar of roses and the Queen favoured another cloying mixture, scented with violets.

Snuff was the only form of tobacco in evidence at White's as late as 1845. Cigars existed during the Regency, but smoking was considered a disgusting and vulgar habit, banned in the drawing rooms of decent society. The young man, back from the Peninsula, who wanted 'to blow a cloud' had to creep down to the kitchen or out to the stables in order to smoke in peace. In time, however, it was realized that a growing number of men preferred cigars to snuff, and it became the custom to set aside one room in the house as a smoking room.

During the eighteenth century it was customary to use so much rouge, powder and paint that the effect was that of theatrical make-up. It was intended to present an artificial appearance, the direct opposite of the 'natural' look, which came into fashion after the French Revolution. From then on, cosmetics were intended to enhance the complexion rather than to disguise it, and the more discreetly they were used the better. Nothing dated a woman more than covering her face with layers of thick white powder and bright spots of red rouge, or wearing the little black 'patches' which had been considered so alluring in the past. Moreover it had already been proved that many of the eighteenth-century aids to beauty were extremely dangerous to sensitive skins. Both the Gunning sisters, the most famous beauties of their day, lost their looks completely before they were thirty, as a direct result of their addiction to coating their faces with a powder of which the main ingredient was noxious white lead. One of them died of lead poisoning in her twenties and the other became seriously ill from the same cause.

Nevertheless, cosmetics were still big business during the Regency, used as much by men as women. The Prince and many of his fellow dandies all wore make-up, oiled their hair and drenched themselves with scent as a matter of course – it was nothing to do with effeminacy. In fact the Regency men were often more heavily made-up than the ladies because female fashion at the time veered between the rustic, or 'milk-maid' look, and the Grecian, both of which would have been ruined by too much obvious make-up.

Powders, paints, wash-balls, rouges and pomades were made from everything from almonds to violets. Among the more charming names of contemporary cosmetics were 'Royal Tincture of Peach Kernels', 'Carnation of Lilies', 'Liquid Bloom of Roses' (a rouge) and 'Powder of Pearl of India'. Pomatum for the hair included 'Pomade de Nerole' and 'Pomade de Graffa', while

'Olympian Dew' was the favourite eye lotion, guaranteed to produce a seductive sparkle. The best cosmetics then, as now, were made in France but they were expensive, and like all beauty products, highly taxed. Lord Granville Leveson-Gower, sent to Paris on a diplomatic mission, was asked by his mistress, Lady Bessborough, to get her some rouge and in his reply shows a certain reluctance to pay for it: 'you must tell me what cost it is to be, as I am informed here there is a great difference both in cost and deepness of colour'. In any case he may have disapproved of her wanting it at all, as rouge was not only going out of fashion but had already acquired a taint of vulgarity: in 1807 one society lady recommending another to hide her pallor with a little rouge, added that 'husbands never see these things; if Lord O. ever found out he would be furious with me.' Frances, Lady Shelley, describing her first meeting with a famous beauty, wrote that though tears were rolling down her cheeks 'this heightened her beauty, without defacing the rouge, which had been artistically applied'. The lady was apparently dressed 'in the indecent style of the French Republican period', but her make-up, at least, was discreet.

A contemporary book on aids to beauty shows that, in spite of the fashion for imported cosmetics, many of the traditional home-made recipes were still popular: thus, the juice from green pineapples 'takes away wrinkles and gives the complexion an air of youth', and if pineapples were not available, the author says that onion would do just as well; another 'sovereign beautifier of the complexion' was pimpernel water and yet another refresher could be made by mixing 1 lb. of rye breadcrumbs, hot from the oven, with the whites of four eggs and a pint of white vinegar, the whole to be used as a face mask. Powdered parsley seed was believed to prevent baldness and slices of cucumber were recommended for tired eyes. Ripe elderberries could be used to blacken the eyebrows and a mixture of Brazilwood shaving and rock alum, pounded and boiled in red wine, would produce an adequate liquid rouge; grated horseradish immersed in sour milk would get rid of sunburn or freckles 'though we confess to the eccentricity of liking a little dash of sunburn, or a sprinkling of nice, little, delicate freckles on the brow of beauty'.[9] This particular author was ahead of his time: most fashion dictates abhorred such evidence of outdoor activity.

As medical knowledge improved, the link between beauty and health was realized. In an anonymous book, with the grandiose title *The Art of Beauty or the Best Methods of Improving and Preserving the Shape, Carriage and Complexion, Together with the Theory of Beauty*, the reader is told in equally exaggerated prose that 'the colour of the lips, the rich, fresh, ruby tint, so highly praised by poets, painters and lovers' depends chiefly on health. (This style of writing was endemic in such manuals at the time, presumably because it was thought to carry authority.) This was an excellent principle, but the authors had a curious idea of how to achieve their object: the recommended regime for a young lady bans all fruit, vegetables and fish from her diet as well as pastries, cream and cheese. After getting up at 6.00 in the morning and going for a brisk walk of at least three miles she is told to eat steak and ale for breakfast. Though a 'fresh and handsome' girl is advised to leave well alone, it is clear that heavy make-up was still being used by older women: when 'an antique and venerable dowager covers her brown and shrivelled skin with a thick layer of white paint, heightened with a tint of vermilion, we are sincerely thankful to her'.

The practice of wearing hair powder had all but disappeared by the time of the Regency. The Prince Regent himself, for example, gave up wearing powder in later life and favoured, instead, a curly, natural-coloured wig which made him look much younger. (The cartoonists, however, either failed to notice the change or refused to acknowledge it. They continued to portray the Prince to his maximum disadvantage as a fat and ridiculous figure wearing the kind of elaborate powdered wig which went out of fashion decades before.) The decline of powder was partly due to the introduction of an indirect tax in 1795, and partly to the prevailing vogue for simplicity. Nevertheless, it was still worn by ladies who adhered to the fashions of the previous generation, even in the daytime: when Lady Bessborough was prosecuted for evading the tax it was proved that she had even gone to church with a powdered head. As late as 1812, according to the records, 46,000 people still paid the duty, but, of course, the majority of these would have been servants in livery. Powdered hair, or wigs, were always worn by the footmen, coachmen and other senior members of the staff in grand households.

Even though it was no longer fashionable to wear wigs, both men and women made up for any deficiency with false hairpieces, or *toupées*. Lady Stanley, writing to a friend in 1802, asked for help in the matter:

I have a commission or two for you. I enclose a bit of my hair for you to hand over to Marshall as a pattern for a fillet of hair for the front; I have cut off my tail for comfort, and as my hair is always coming out of curl in the damp summer evenings, and as I find everybody sports a false *toupée*, I don't see why I should not have the comfort of one too. I wish it to be as fashionable and as deceiving as possible.[10]

As far as the men's heads were concerned, the nineteenth century saw the demise of the attractive tricorn hat and the arrival of the 'chimney-pot', or 'topper'. These were not the standard top hats which came into general usage later, but came in a variety of sizes and shapes, which could be tailored to suit the taste of the wearer. 'The most wonderful changes in appearance can be effected by a hat', according to a cavalry officer writing in a gentlemen's magazine called *The Whole Art of Dress*. He goes on to cite examples: 'A very high and small crowned hat, with a narrow round brim (as the Tilbury) contrasted with a broad, wide crown and rim (as the Turf), will make a man, if about forty, look about ten or eleven years younger.'

The fashion revolution caused an uproar in Mayfair and the press, with both those in favour of the new styles and those who condemned them on sight equally vociferous in their opinions. The problem throughout the period was that no aspirant to fashion could be certain how far it was safe to deviate. Most of the fashion journalists, along with the dandies and the girls themselves, approved of the new freedom of dress, for men as well as women. They realized that the new simple dresses were not only much more comfortable to wear but much cheaper to make than the elaborate costumes of the previous generation. They were also sexier: 'The female form, after an eclipse of many centuries, has reappeared', was one approving comment. The same authority delighted in the new, natural hairstyles which came into fashion at the same time:

The powder tax first restored [their heads] to their natural colour and curtailed [them] of their dangling encumbrances behind ... The younger branches of large families from economy discarded powder and when taste declared in favour of nature, crop was the word ... [and even] elderly men discarded those immense bushes of cowhair.

'Liberalism', however, could be misinterpreted, even in the guise of fashion, and many of the older generation, backed by the conservative press, were horrified by what they saw as blatant indecency. (Lady Anne Barnard, by then in her eighties, was once heard to ask quite audibly at a dinner party, 'Who is that very handsome naked woman?') The matriarchs of society who continued to sail through the drawing rooms of London in their full dress regalia of silks and satins, wigs and corsets, powder and paint, frowned heavily on the freedom of their granddaughters' scanty shifts. Those who had regulated their lives according to the eighteenth-century code of behaviour were equally censorious of the younger generation's manners. In an article attacking the attitude and behaviour of modern youth, written in 1800, the *Oracle* expressed the views of many contemporary parents: 'To see our young gentlemen cutting a swell, as the fashionable phrase is, and adopting the manners and language of brothel bullies, for that's the go; to behold our amiable young ladies striving to rival in appearance and knowingness the nocturnal trampers of the Strand, is undoubtedly a very edifying prospect.' A few years later the same paper thundered on in the same vein about their appearance as well as their manners: 'What a routine we have had of everything disgusting, in the name of Fashion! Slouched hats, jockey waistcoats, half-boot, leather breeches, cropped heads, unpowdered hair ... the present race of Bucks without blood, Beaux without taste, and Gentlemen without

MONSTROSITIES OF 1822
Caricature by George Cruikshank, published by G. Humphrey, 1822.
The Regency saw a complete revolution in both men's and women's dress. Fashions changed every season and were often carried to outrageous extremes.

manners!' The *Universal Magazine* elaborates the point, writing in 1810, that the manners of the men

have undergone a complete revolution, particularly as they regard the fair sex. From a formal, precise and ceremonious demeanour, constituting good breeding, a mode of conduct almost the reverse is become the distinguishing mark of high life. An indifference to the convenience and accommodation of the softer sex has taken place in our public assemblies ... the extreme of the fashion is little short of brutal rudeness.

As for the ladies, they appear to have forfeited their rights to courtesy by an equal lack of decorum:

from a degree of reserve and strictness of behaviour, [they] have adopted a freedom of manners, a boldness and scantiness of apparel which has often occasioned women of character and condition to be taken for members of a body they affect to look down upon with pity or contempt. Indeed, such has been the revolution in this point that when it was attempted to exclude the Cyprian Corps [i.e. prostitutes] from a theatre . . . the door-keepers were so far misled by appearances that they were very near conveying a *nude* of high rank to the watch-house.

The 'modern young woman' was accused of parading her lack of modesty with her 'impudent leer', 'pert retort' and 'the silly double entendre'. Another newspaper, the *Lewes and Brighthelm stone Journal*, referred to 'the hoity-toity, bold, forward, pert flirts of the present day', and said the girls spent all their time 'gadding' about. The morning, according to this particularly crusty journalist, was 'taken up in preparing dress for the evening where they expose themselves in dancing the Irish wriggle with any fellow in a bit of scarlet and a feather.'[11]

The mores of Regency society may have changed as fast as the fashions, but in one respect, at least, they remained steadfast. The code of honour was as rigid as ever. To the modern mind the idea that a man could be ostracized for life because he once cheated at cards seems unnecessarily harsh: but then so does the concept of fighting a duel over a difference of opinion about politics. In 1809 Castlereagh and Canning disagreed so violently over the management of a military campaign (the Walcheren expedition) that the only resolution seemed to be to fight it out. These two senior cabinet ministers, therefore, went off to Wimbledon Common at dawn, along with their equally distinguished seconds, and shot at each other with pistols. Fortunately neither was killed, though Canning was wounded. Both, understandably, resigned from the government. Even the Duke of Wellington, England's national hero, was involved in a political duel, with Lord Winchilsea, over the question of Catholic Emancipation: the participants met and exchanged shots, but the Duke missed and Lord Winchilsea 'deloped' (fired wide). And that was twenty years later, when the practice of duelling was said to be on the decline. When Lord Charles Lennox felt he had been slighted in the matter of his military promotion he actually challenged his commanding officer, HRH the Duke of York, to a duel. In the event nothing came of it because the Duke was persuaded that his royal status made it impossible for him to accept the challenge and duly refused to fight. For more ordinary men, however, it was impossible to refuse without loss of honour, as in the case of General Thornton, who was forced to resign his commission simply because he declined to fight a duel. There had been a row at a party, between the general and Theodore Hook, the novelist and editor of *John Bull*, in the course of which the latter insulted the former. According to the received notions of honour at the time, the general should have immediately issued a challenge, and when he failed to do so his fellow officers set up a full-scale inquiry into the affair, found him guilty of cowardice, and demanded his resignation.

There were plenty of literary duels as well, usually over libel, or malicious gossip, which had appeared in print. In Scotland, Sir Alexander Boswell, son of the diarist, was challenged to a duel because of a piece he had written anonymously, and killed his opponent. Boswell's initial reaction was to flee the country, expecting to be convicted of murder, but he was persuaded to return, stood his trial and was acquitted, to the general delight of the public. The majority of duels, of course, were fought on the more conventional grounds of love or adultery: Sheridan, for example, fought two with the same man over the same girl.* They fought with swords and Sheridan was nearly killed, but recovered and married her. Gronow, recalling the years of the Regency, wrote later that he could 'scarcely look back to those days of duelling without shuddering. If you looked at a man it was enough; for without having given the slightest offence, cards

---

* She was the beautiful 'nightingale' Elizabeth Linley, the most celebrated singer of her generation. When they married, Sheridan refused to allow her to perform in public ever again, in spite of their financial straits, on the grounds that it would be unsuitable to her position. Dr Johnson concurred: 'He resolved wisely and nobly to be sure. He is a brave man. Would not a gentleman be disgraced by having his wife singing publickly for hire? No, Sir, there can be no doubt here' (L. Kelly, *Sheridan: A Life*, Sinclair-Stevenson, 1997, p. 53).

were exchanged, and the odds were that you stood a good chance of being shot, or run through the body, or maimed for life.'[12]

Towards the end of the Regency a reaction set in against immorality which found expression in a whole new vocabulary of euphemisms. In 1818 a society lady wrote that 'No one can now say "breeding" or "with child" or "lying-in" without being thought indelicate. "Colic" and "bowels" are exploded words. "Stomach" signifies everything.' It was around this time, too, that babies started to be found under gooseberry bushes or dropped by the stork, while trousers, if they had to be spoken of at all, were referred to as 'unmentionables', 'inexpressibles' or 'ineffables'. A few years later Leigh Hunt observed that

so rapid are the changes that take place in people's notions of what is decorous that not only has the word 'smock' been displaced by the word 'shift', but even that harmless expression has been set aside for the French word 'chemise', and at length not even this word, it seems, is to be mentioned, nor the garment itself alluded to, by any decent writer.[13]

The jolly, bawdy speech of the eighteenth century was no longer acceptable in this new, polite, society.

In any period of transition, however, it is a constant battle between the innovative and the traditional, and many of the salons of London society remained eighteenth century in essence to the very end of the Regency. The most famous of the older *grandes dames* was Lady Salisbury, whom Creevey credited, in 1822, with having been 'the head and ornament and patroness of the *beau monde* for the last forty years'.[14] She refused to acknowledge the existence of the revolution in fashion, and maintained the standards and customs of the eighteenth century to the end of her life, often at the expense of her own comfort. For example, she always insisted on being carried around London in a sedan chair, instead of being driven in a carriage, even to the Royal Drawing Rooms when the queue at the gates could take hours. Wherever she went, she was accompanied by an escort of porters and footmen, dressed in the splendid blue and silver livery of the Cecil family. The more Puritan element of society disapproved of Lady Salisbury because she gave regular card parties on Sundays, as had been the custom throughout her youth, but she took no notice of such modern strictures. Lady Salisbury was burnt to death at the age of eighty-five, when the west wing of Hatfield House caught fire. Then there was the elderly and eccentric Lady Cork, who had become an institution on the London scene, rather than a mere hostess, by the beginning of the nineteenth century. Lady Cork devoted her life to entertaining in the grand manner, beginning around 1780, with a salon dominated by Dr Johnson and his circle, and was still collecting celebrities fifty years later. Usually known as 'Corky', she was short and stout but carried on wearing the most flamboyant eighteenth-century fashions, powdered wigs and elaborate make-up. People laughed at her but they liked her and her parties acquired the status of a royal command. In 1834, when Lady Cork was in her eighties, one of her guests described meeting her:

Lady Cork is very old, infirm and diminutive, dressed all in white, with a white bonnet which she wore at table . . . Her features are delicate and her skin fair and notwithstanding her great age she is very animated. She was attended by a boy page in a fantastical green livery with a cap, and a high plume of black feathers. The old lady, who was a lion-hunter in her youth, is as much one now as ever.[15]

Lady Cork's parrot, almost as old as herself, was a notorious hazard at her parties. The parrot pecked the Regent himself at one of them, and took a large bite out of another guest's leg.

Lady Holland, the great Whig hostess, was another matriarch whose drawing room was dominated by a particularly vicious pet: she had a huge cat which scratched the guests whenever it could and had to be kept at arm's length with snuff. Charles Greville, one of the many 'regulars', described the way of life at this famous intellectual salon:

Dined at Holland House . . . The *tableau* of the house is this: – Before dinner, Lady Holland affecting illness and almost dissolution, but with a very respectable appetite, and after dinner in high force and vigour; Lord Holland, with his chalk-stones and unable to walk, lying on his couch in very good spirits and talking away; [Henry] Luttrell and [Samuel] Rogers walking about, ever and anon looking despairingly at the clock and making short excursions from the drawing room; [John] Allen [the librarian] surly and disputatious, poring over the newspapers ... Such is the social despotism of this strange house, which presents an odd mixture of luxury and constraint, of enjoyment physical and intellectual, with an alloy of small *désagréments.* Talleyrand generally comes at ten or eleven o'clock, and stays as long as they will let him. Though everybody who goes there finds something to abuse or to ridicule in the mistress of the house, or its ways, all continue to go; all like it more or less; and whenever, by the death of either, it shall come to an end, a vacuum will be made in society which nothing will supply. It is the house of all Europe; the world will suffer by the loss; and it may with truth be said that it will 'eclipse the gaiety of nations'.[16]

A final, haunting vision of the glamour of high society during the Regency was written by the American ambassador Richard Rush, after his attendance at a Court 'drawing room' (i.e. particularly formal reception). Rush was overwhelmed by the splendour and beauty and grandeur of the whole scene, by the crowds, the carriages, the ladies' dresses and their magnificent family jewels. Describing the reception given by the Queen for her seventy-sixth birthday in 1818, he wrote first of the vast crowds who waited in the streets to see the guests arriving, and of the tangible evidence of England's prestige and prosperity:

Going through Hyde Park, I found the whole way from Tyburn to Piccadilly (about a mile) filled with private carriages, standing still. Persons were in them who had adopted this mode of seeing those who went to court. Tenfold the number went by other approaches, and every approach, I was told, was thronged with double rows of equipages, filled with spectators ... Arrived in its vicinity [the palace], my carriage was stopped by those before it. Here we saw, through the trees and avenues of the Park, other carriages rapidly coming up, in two regular lines from the Horse Guards and St James's. Another line, that had been up, was turning slowly off, towards Birdcage Walk. Foreigners agreed, that the united capitals of Europe could not match the sight. The horses were all in the highest condition; and, under heavily emblazoned harness, seemed, like war-horses, to move proudly. Trumpets were sounding, and the Park and Tower guns firing. There were ranks of cavalry in scarlet, with their bright helmets, and jet black horses; the same, we were told, men and horses that had been at Waterloo . . .

We were not out of time, for, by appointment, my carriage reached the palace with Lord Castlereagh's; but whilst hundreds were still arriving, hundreds were endeavouring to come away. The staircase branched off at the first landing, into two arms. It was wide enough to admit a partition, which was let in. The company ascending, took one channel; those descending, the other; and both were full. The whole group stood motionless. The openings through the carved balusters, brought all under view at once, whilst the paintings on the walls heightened the effect. The hoop dresses of the ladies, sparkling with lamé; their plumes; their lappets; the fanciful attitudes which the hoops occasioned, some getting out of position as when in Addison's time they were adjusted to shoot a door; the various costumes of the gentlemen as they stood pinioning their elbows, and holding their swords; the common hilarity, from the common dilemma; the bland recognitions passing between those above and below, made up, altogether, an exhibition so picturesque, that a painter might give it as illustrative, so far, of the court of that aera . . .

If the scene in the hall was picturesque, the one upstairs transcended it. The doors of the rooms were all open. You saw in them a thousand ladies richly dressed. All the colours of nature were mingling their rays together. It was the first occasion of laying off mourning for the Princess Charlotte, so that it was like a bursting out of spring. No lady was without her plume. The whole was a waving field of feathers. Some were blue, like the sky; some tinged with red; here you saw violet and yellow; there, shades of green. But the most were like tufts of snow. The diamonds encircling them caught the sun through the windows, and threw dazzling beams around. Then the hoops! I cannot describe these. To see one is nothing. But to see a thousand – and their thousand wearers! I afterwards sat in the Ambassador's box at a coronation. That sight faded before this. Each lady seemed to rise out of a gilded little barricade; or one of silvery texture. This, topped by her plume, and the 'face divine' interposing, gave to the whole an effect so unique, so fraught with feminine grace and grandeur, that it seemed as if a curtain had risen to show a pageant in another sphere. It was brilliant and joyous. Those to whom it was not new, stood at gaze as I did. Canning for one. His fine eye took it all in. You saw admiration in the gravest statesmen; Lord Liverpool, Huskisson, the Lord Chancellor, everybody. I had already seen in England signs enough of opulence and power. Now I saw, radiating on all sides, British beauty . . .[17]

It is a fitting epitaph to the world of fashion.

13

ON THE EVE OF
REFORM

By the closing years of the Regency it was no longer possible to ignore the great question of Reform; reform at all levels, of parliament, the Church, the judiciary, penal code, factory conditions, poor laws and child welfare. Even the more enlightened Tories realized that it was not only inevitable but essential. As Charles Greville pointed out, writing in the context of a most distressing murder trial: 'I am afraid there is more vice, more misery and penury in this country than in any other, and at the same time greater wealth . . . The contrasts are too striking, and such an unnatural, artificial, and unjust state of things neither can, nor ought to be, permanent. I am convinced that before many years elapse these things will produce some great convulsion.'[1] Such was Greville's view in 1829, at the height of the agitation for the reform of parliament, the most pressing – and the most controversial – issue of the day.

The need for a more democratic representation is self-evident in the facts. Prior to the Reform Bill, 355 seats in the House of Commons were controlled by 87 peers and a further 213 by 90 of the richest commoners, all by the same means of hereditary rotten boroughs. Except in a very few cases,[2] the tenants on all these great estates automatically voted for whichever candidate their landlord suggested – which was the point of owning a rotten borough. When Lord John Russell first presented the House with his proposals for Reform his figures show just how drastic an approach was needed. The list suggested abolishing sixty whole boroughs, and reducing the number of members returned by a further forty-seven. In the matter of 'safe' seats the Whigs were hopelessly outnumbered, even allowing for the rotten boroughs in their own gift. In 1827, according to statistics compiled by Croker,* out of 276 seats controlled by various patrons, 203 belonged to the Tories. It would, incidentally, be quite wrong to imagine that these 'private' seats were presented free to the chosen candidates. The usual rate for a seat in the House was in the region of £6000, plus an annual fee of between £1500 and £1800.[3] They could, however, cost a great deal more: Castlereagh's first seat in parliament, as the member for County Down, was said to have cost his father, Lord Londonderry, £60,000. (Bribery was particularly necessary in his case: he was an extreme reactionary and one of the most unpopular men of his generation.) When Lord Egremont bought Midhurst from the executors of the seventh Lord Montagu of Cowdray, in 1790, for the benefit of his brothers, he had to pay £40,000. Midhurst was a prime borough for anyone with political ambitions since the patron not only owned all the burgage rights, but was also the only man entitled to a vote. (A few years later, however, Egremont sold it at a loss to a rich banker with social, rather than political, ambitions.)[4]

Seats were bought and sold on the open market, but, of course, tenure was only guaranteed for the life of that particular parliament. Every time parliament was dissolved negotiations had to begin all over again. Even an uncontested seat could cost at least £1000 in 'expenses'. The cost of electioneering was often prohibitive for potential politicians. William Lamb, for example, as a young man pleaded lack of money as his reason for not standing for parliament in the 1812 election. When his mother, the politically ambitious Lady Melbourne, wrote complaining that he had not yet found a seat, Lamb replied angrily:

* John Wilson Croker (1780–1857), Irish MP and satirist.

You say that it is a thousand pities that I have not contrived to make some interest somewhere. You know from my former letter ... my sentiments upon this subject. It is impossible that any Body can feel the being out of Parliament more keenly for me than I feel it for myself. It is actually cutting my throat. It is depriving me of the great object of my life at the moment, that I was near its attainment, & what is more, at a period when I cannot well turn myself to any other course or pursuit. But I have no money ... My income is insufficient ... [and] I receive no assistance.[5]

Charles Wyndham's expenses when he contested East Sussex, in the general election of 1807, standing as an independent candidate against a Tory majority, came to just under £2000. This was a fairly modest amount by the standards of the time, since he was a popular candidate, but, even so, the accounts prove that bribery was taken for granted. They include £408 on beer and dinners, which represents a very large amount of entertaining indeed, considering the cost of food and drink at the time (a reasonable allowance for beer for living-in servants was 1½d per day per head). Then there was £460 on 'transport', i.e. taking people to the polls, always an excellent opportunity for canvassing; 'gratuities to helpers', which is an obvious euphemism, came to £243; and a further £437 for 'disbursements by the Rev. John Austin for favours' is listed without any attempt at explanation. When Lord Egremont gave a great dinner to celebrate his candidate's victory in the general election of 1820 he spent £116 on port alone, the cash equivalent of nearly £6000 in today's money. By 1826, however, Egremont seems to have eliminated effective opposition since his candidate won the seat for the minimal cost to his patron of £249.[6]

Seats in parliament were even offered for sale in the papers. An advertisement in a Cornish newspaper made no attempt to disguise the situation and though the vendor of the seats stops short of actually giving his full name all the locals must have known who he was:

TO GENTLEMEN OF FORTUNE

Any two gentlemen, who would wish to secure seats at the next

Parliament, may be accommodated at the borough of Launceston. There are but 15 votes, majority 3. All letters directed for A.B. to be left at the Exeter post-office, will be duly attended to.

29 January 1819[7]

Advowsons were inherited, bought and sold as freely as rotten boroughs, and very often by the same great landowners. To continue with the example of Lord Egremont, the main landowner in West Sussex, in the course of his lifetime he bought fifteen advowsons, at a collective cost of £45,000. A church living was regarded as a sinecure, a guaranteed income for life: the sale or exchange of one was primarily a financial transaction, to suit the geographical convenience of the parties involved, and had little to do with the politics of the Church. Lord Egremont had to buy in his own home living at Petworth from the previous incumbent, together with two other neighbouring parishes. Others were bought in different parts of the country, as far away as Lincolnshire in one case, and swapped for livings nearer home. A sinecure in the Church was often given as a reward for service, even if the recipient had none of the qualifications one might have thought necessary. Thomas Socket, who had been tutor and general factotum at Petworth for eleven years, had not even contemplated a career in the Church when he was given the main living at Petworth. As he said, 'The offer of a liberal independent establishment is pleasing . . . Having now the idea of going into the church I thought it would be advisable to take a degree, or not, as might suit my convenience.'

The presentation of a living to a younger son was often the means of providing for several generations of the same family: it became a sinecure which could be passed from father to son. For example, several livings in Somerset, in the gift of Lord Portman,* were held by successive members of the Wyndham family for more than a hundred years. In 1775 the Revd John,

* Lord Portman was the titular head of the Wyndham family, with large estates in the West Country.

youngest son of William Wyndham, became rector of Corton Denham and, on his death in 1816, the living passed to his nephew, the son of another Wyndham, who held it until 1852 – the tenures of himself and his uncle thus covering more than three-quarters of a century. Other younger sons of the family were provided for in the same way: the Revd Thomas Wyndham was given the living of Pimperne in 1805 and held it until he died, at the age of ninety-one, in 1862. Yet another Wyndham was appointed rector of Sutton Mandeville, again in the gift of the Portmans. That particular living stayed in the same branch of the family until 1897.[8] All these livings provided a considerable income for the incumbent, out of which he paid a curate to do the actual work of the church, while he himself lived the hunting, shooting and fishing life of a country gentleman with private means. The *Gentleman's Magazine* quoted an advertisement in the *Oxford Journal,* offering for sale by auction one such living, and though it is unclear whether this particular example is intended as a satire on the current situation, or a report of fact, it is a pertinent job description for a Regency cleric:

For Sale . . . The Next Presentation to a most valuable Living, in one of the first sporting Counties: the vicinity affords the best coursing in England, also excellent fishing, an extensive cover for game, and numerous packs of fox-hounds, harriers &; it is half an hour's ride from one of the first cities, and not far distant from several watering-places; the surrounding country is beautiful and healthy, and the society elegant and fashionable.[9]

In defence of the parson who obtained his living by patronage it should be remembered that, by virtue of his status in relation to the landlord, he played an important part in the rural community:

When communication was so difficult and infrequent, he filled a place in the country life of England, that no one else could fill. He was often the patriarch of his parish, its ruler, its doctor, its lawyer, its magistrate, as well as its teacher, before whom vice trembled and rebellion dared not show itself. The idea of the priest was not quite forgotten; but there was much – much even of good and useful – to obscure it.[10]

The principle of multiple benefices, however, was indefensible. According to Cobbett, the revenue of nearly 1500 livings was shared by only 332 parsons: in other words, an average of between four and five per head. Three members of the Pretyman family divided fifteen benefices between themselves; the Duke of Wellington's brother was made, at one time or another, and sometimes simultaneously, Prebendary of Durham, Rector of Chelsea, Rector of Therfield and Rector of Bishopwearmouth, which were all lucrative sinecures in the gift of his family. William Howley, who ended his career as the Archbishop of Canterbury, made a fortune on the way from the system of plurality; in the course of his progress he acquired one rectory, two vicarages and a canonry as well as being made the Regius Professor of Divinity at Oxford and Bishop of London. When Howley died, he left £120,000, all of which had come from the Church.[11] Lord Walsingham was another famous pluralist in this field of easy money. At one time, while receiving a pension of £700 a year from the government, he was also Archdeacon of Surrey, Prebendary of Winchester, Rector of Calbourne, Rector of Fawley, Rector of Merton and perpetual Curate of Exbury. As Trevelyan points out:

The Bishops, the Cathedral clergy and wealthier parish priests were part of the 'enjoying' class; they had obtained preferment not as a reward for work done for the Church, but through aristocratic connection or family favour. The parishes were often perfunctorily served or were left to the ministrations of under-paid curates and threadbare incumbents of poor livings, who were not in the circle visited by the manor house or acknowledged by Lady Catherine de Burgh.[12]

It was a well-known saying at the time that, at the end of the Brighton season, when everyone left the town, 'the coaches go up as full as a vicar's belly, and return as empty as a curate's kitchen.' One of the characters encountered by Doctor Syntax on his journey, when asked about the local dignitaries, expresses the general indignation over the relative finances of the different orders amongst the clergy:

> The land belongs to Squire Bounty.
> One of the best men in the county:
> I wish the Rector were the same,
> Doctor Squeeze'em is his name;
> But we ne'er see him –
>   more's the shame!
> And while in wealth he cuts and carves,
> The worthy Curate prays and starves.

In such parishes, where the nominal incumbent was non-resident, and rarely bothered to visit, the curate who took his place was expected to live on £50 a year or even less. Some of them seem to have managed remarkably well, possibly because they, at least, were men with a genuine vocation for the Church. In 1814 a country paper, reporting the death of the local clergyman after sixty years' service, mentioned that in the early years his benefice had brought in only £12 a year. It was later increased to £18 p.a., which it never exceeded. On this income he married, brought up four children, sent a son to university and 'lived comfortably with his neighbours . . . and left upwards of a thousand pounds behind him.'[13] This was at a time when the Prince Regent and his friends were paying a shilling each for Spanish onions and £1 10s for a dozen Colmar pears. There was a clamour for reform of the whole structure of the Church and an end to sinecures, whether bought or inherited, and the public began to insist that a member of the clergy, however elevated or lowly his status, should carry out the job for which he was paid.

Bribery and corruption in the armed forces had become yet another cause for public concern by the later years of the Regency. The Clarke scandal, in 1809, had shown the extent of illicit trading in army commissions, and though the furore had died down after a few years, there was still an active black market. In any case, in line with the general dissatisfaction with Establishment procedures, liberal thought had begun to question the basic principle that promotion could be bought at all. The official prices of commissions were printed in the Army Lists, but, in fact, they varied according to demand and the number of vacancies; on the black market they cost a great deal more. Commissions in the Guards were by far the most expensive: in 1814 a majority in the Foot Guards was listed at £8300, which was almost twice as much as the cost of a lieutenant-colonelcy in a regiment of the line.[14] After the war vacancies among the higher ranks became even scarcer, and the price of a commission prohibitive to all but the rich. In 1828, for example, the Earl of Lucan had to pay the equivalent of approximately £1,500,000 in modern money for command of the 17th Lancers.

Commissions were not only bought and sold, but exchanged to suit particular requirements. This was usually accomplished by switching regiments. When George Wyndham, an officer in the Grenadiers, wanted to avoid going to the West Indies in 1811, his father, Lord Egremont, simply bought him a majority in the 78th (Highland) Foot. Colonel Torrens, the Duke of York's military secretary, confirmed the exchange in a letter to Egremont which is perfectly open about the price: '. . . the Commander-in-Chief has found the means to recommend your son for the purchase of a majority . . . by which means he will be spared the trip that was contemplated to the West Indies. It will be necessary for your Lordship to lodge £1100 in the hands of the Agents.' Wyndham, incidentally, left the Highlanders after only three months and bought a commission as lieutenant-colonel in the *Régiment de Meuron*, one of the composite European regiments created during the Napoleonic Wars and later transferred to the British army. In the course of nine years, between 1803 and 1812, Wyndham held eight different commissions, from cornet to lieutenant-colonel. In wartime, theoretically, promotion was much faster and could be achieved by merit alone: in fact, such cases were relatively rare, and Wyndham wrote that his commissions were 'all obtained by purchase and by exchange paying a difference'.[15]

One of the greatest attractions of the army to young men of fashion was the glorious uniform, in particular that of the Guards and cavalry regiments. Brummell may have changed civilian fashions for ever in favour of quiet, understated elegance, but even he could not influence the armed forces. The wars of the eighteenth century gave rise to an enormous increase in the forces, and a corresponding variety of gorgeous new uniforms. The coats were beautifully cut, and made of splendid materials in red, gold, blue, green, buff and even pure white, heavily decorated with gold braid, gold epaulettes, gold tassels, gold knots and gold buttons. There were white breeches, enormous fur hats, embossed silver swords and heavy gilt spurs. The soldiers looked extremely glamorous but their uniforms must have been heavy and hot to wear, let alone to fight in. They were also very expensive, another factor which limited the number of men who could afford a commission. The phrase 'to purchase a pair of colours' relates to the uniform of the particular regiment.

Naval officers were equally proud of their uniforms, and, on occasion, even more unrealistic in their design. Prince William, when given the command of his first ship, gloried in the opportunity of choosing new uniforms for his men. The midshipmen were ordered 'white breeches so tight as to appear to be sewn upon the limb – yellow-topped hunting boots pulled close up and strapped with a buckle round the knee ... a pigtail of huge dimensions dangling beneath an immense square gold-laced cocked hat'. These ridiculously impractical outfits provided many a happy giggle amongst the crew since the breeches were liable to burst every time the boys climbed the rigging.

The severity of discipline in both the army and the navy also came under attack during the Regency, together with the whole question of the penal code. The Duke of Kent's brutality to his soldiers has already been mentioned, but even much 'lighter' sentences could mean death, depending on the victim's physique. And there was no reprieve: if a man passed out from pain he was revived by having cold water thrown over him and the punishment continued. When one of the soldiers involved in the riots at St Albans, in 1810, was sentenced to receive 150 lashes, and five others 100, there was a public outcry. William Cobbett was fined £1000 and sent to prison for two years for writing an article in the *Political Register* in which he denounced military flogging. The civilian courts, too, frequently sentenced a petty criminal to a public flogging. An advertisement in a local paper in Cornwall announced the forthcoming attraction of a man sentenced to be flogged through the town, the length of the High Street, on a Saturday, so that everyone would be free to watch. He had been found guilty of stealing oats; another criminal was given a public whipping and a month in prison for stealing 3 lbs of candles from a chandling-house. One of the most appalling punishments was the Tread-Mill, which was introduced by William Cubitt at Brixton Gaol in 1817 and swiftly copied by other prisons. The victim was forced to spend hours and hours treading the steps of a long revolving wheel, christened the 'Everlasting Stairs'. The Tread-Mill was regarded as a new form of preventive punishment and it must be said that it was effective: the prospect of such a sentence so terrified petty criminals that the number of convictions dropped considerably. At the beginning of the nineteenth century 160 types of felony still carried the death penalty. Public executions were still held all over the country, and multiple hangings often took place on the same day, attracting crowds of up to 30,000 spectators. Another familiar sight on a country journey was that of a highwayman hanging in chains at the crossroads, or a rotting corpse on a gibbet.

Many of the most distressing cases involved children: a child of *seven* was held to be legally responsible for its actions and there are cases on record of children even younger than that. A little boy of six was reported to have cried 'pitiably' for his mother on the scaffold. On one day alone, in February 1814, five children were condemned to death at the Old Bailey, one of whom was only eight years old. The sentences were unbelievable in relation to the 'crimes': Matilda Seymour, aged ten, was transported for seven years for the crime of stealing one shawl and one petticoat; and Thomas Bell, aged eleven, received the same sentence for stealing two silk handkerchiefs. Such cases triggered the movement for reform. In 1814, at last, legislation was introduced to prevent the notorious practice of child stealing. The sale of unwanted children and orphans was commonplace: they were sold to chimney sweeps, who used them as 'climbing boys' and lit fires under their feet to force the unwilling up the stack; to professional beggars, as piteous accessories; to thieves as apprentices; and to brothels. The only way it was possible to convict an adult for stealing a child was to link the crime with the theft of the child's clothes: stealing a pair of shoes was an indictable offence, but not stealing the child itself. In the same year a parliamentary inquiry was set up to investigate conditions in Newgate prison, the most infamous gaol in London. One of the witnesses stated that he had an order for the 'removal of fifty-two who are under sentence of transportation, many of whom are seven or eight years old, one nine years old, and others not above twelve or thirteen'.[16] Newgate had been virtually destroyed by fire during the Gordon riots, but was rebuilt in 1782. Felons were still frequently kept in chains and housed fifteen to twenty in a room no more than 23 feet by 15 feet. Gaol fever was endemic.

The conditions under which a prisoner passed his sentence, however, depended entirely on his financial circumstances. When Harriette Wilson went to visit a friend who had been sent to Newgate for debt she was horrified to find that the woman did not even have a bed: the cost of hiring a bed and bedclothes in the debtors' section of the prison was 3/6 a week, in cash. Those who had no money slept on the stone floor, uncovered: but those who could afford to pay passed their sentence in relative comfort. William Cobbett, for example, when sentenced to prison for libel, bought his way out of the common gaol for 12 guineas a week (the maximum fee Newgate gaolers were allowed to charge), and was lodged in the former governor's residence. While he was there, he held what might be described as a political salon, receiving friends and deputations from all over the country. Moreover, he carried on editing the *Political Register*, in which he attacked the government. Similarly, when Leigh Hunt was imprisoned in 1812 for libelling the Prince Regent, he was given luxury quarters and treated like a celebrity. His two rooms were redecorated for his stay, in accordance with his own taste, by the prison staff. He chose a rose trellis wallpaper, a painted ceiling 'coloured with clouds and sky' and Venetian blinds to hide the bars on the windows. Not that there was much point in the bars, since Hunt had his own private garden, with a small lawn, flower beds and fruit trees. His rooms were large enough to house many of his favourite possessions, including books, pictures and a bust of Homer. Charles Lamb wrote that his library was so lovely that 'there was was no other such room except in a fairy tale.' His family moved into 'prison' with him; he had his own servant, special food was provided by friends and he led a perfectly pleasant life, carrying on with his journalism and holding court to all the intelligentsia. 'It became fashionable in progressive circles to be seen in his prison' and his visitors included Brougham, Hazlitt and Byron, who referred to Hunt as 'the wit in the dungeon'.[17] When Hobhouse, too, went to prison for a similar offence he was given the same sort of privileged treatment. Lady Caroline Lamb was one of his regular visitors.[18] There was no disgrace about being sent to gaol during the Regency, provided it was for an acceptable 'crime', i.e. debt or libel.

By the end of the Regency the government had begun the process of reform in the case of nearly all the most controversial issues. The criminal code had been modified and a centralized police force, under the command of Sir Robert Peel, had been organized to tackle metropolitan crime. In 1829 the Catholic Emancipation Bill was finally passed, and three years later the Reform Bill itself became law. At the same time, the economy had at last recovered and England was acknowledged as the richest nation in Europe. In the world of science and technology, too, the English were ahead of their competitors, particularly in the practical application of new ideas. By 1814, for example, the whole of the parish of St Margaret's Westminster was lit by gas instead of oil lamps. In the course of the next few years twenty-six miles of gas mains were installed in central London alone, and more and more towns followed suit. By the 1820s even the lighthouses had been modernized with gas: the Swansea lighthouse was equipped with sixty new gas lamps, arranged in the form of an anchor. Sam Whitbread was one of the first brewers to install gaslight and took great delight in showing dinner guests round the brilliantly illuminated stable, which contained ninety or more great cart horses, each, incidentally, worth 50 or 60 guineas.[19] One enthusiast went so far as to write:

What use of wealth so luxurious and delightful as to light your house with gas? What folly to have a diamond necklace or a Correggio, and not to light your house with gas? ... How pitiful to submit to a farthing-candle existence, when science puts such intense gratification within your reach! ... Better to eat dry bread by the splendour of gas, than to dine on wild beef with wax candles.[20]

But it was the revolution in the speed of transport, and thereby of communications, which caused the greatest sensation. In 1800 Telford was commissioned to create a network of roads over the Scottish highlands. He was given a free hand, even though the new roads often cost as much as £1000 a mile. In the course of eight years he built more than 1000 miles of hard road over bogs, mountains and fells, 20 new ports and bridged 1117 rivers. And in 1815 Macadam began his rival road-building programme, based on a different scientific premise but equally successful. On the inland waterways, the *Comet*, which was launched in 1812, became the first steamship to be run commercially in Europe. In less than fifty years 2600 miles of canal were built throughout Britain, connecting all the major cities to each other, and to London. In 1815 a ship, made in Scotland, and making her way to London, travelled more than 120 miles in just over twelve hours, an amazing phenomenon by contemporary standards. Steam vessels of any kind were still a novelty and attracted great crowds of sightseers wherever they appeared. Pleasure boats came next, powered by steam and built specifically for the tourist trade. A trip on a river launch, up the Thames, or down to the south coast, became a popular outing for those of an adventurous spirit. The fare to Margate on one of the new steamships was 7 shillings, but the voyage was liable to be rowdy, as one of the guidebooks warned: 'A passage in the Margate hoy, which like the grave, levels all distinctions, is frequently so replete with whim, incident and character, that it may be considered as a dramatic entertainment.'[21] Another engineering triumph of the later years was the construction of three new bridges over the River Thames, to ease the chaos of traffic in London itself. Vauxhall Bridge, Southwark Bridge and Waterloo Bridge were all built in the space of only six years, between 1813 and 1819. 'Among the new bridges,' one visitor wrote, 'Waterloo Bridge stands in the first rank, though its promoters must have lost £300,000 in the undertaking. 1200 feet long ... it is almost always comparatively deserted and affords a charming walk with beautiful river views.' A nostalgic thought for the twentieth-century commuter.

Richard Trevithick, a Cornishman, built and tried out his first steam-coach in 1802. Unfortunately, after reaching a speed of 9 mph, it exploded. Other inventors followed and, by the end of the Regency, Goldsworthy Gurney, another Cornishman, was able to run a steam-coach on the Bath road, capable of 15 mph. It carried eighteen passengers, six inside and twelve outside: that particular engine, however, also came to grief. Steam engines became a popular joke:

> Instead of *journeys*, people now
>   May go upon a *Gurney*,
> With steam to do the horses' work
>   By power of attorney;
> Tho' with a load, it may explode
>   And you may all be undone;
> And find you're going up to Heaven,
>   Instead of up to London.[22]

Gurney persevered and by 1831 had a regular service operating between Cheltenham and Gloucester. The coach made three double journeys per day and carried 2066 passengers. Steam-coaches, however, were soon driven out of business by the Turn-pike Trusts, who raised the tolls on the roads to a prohibitive level. The first true train, designed by Trevithick, had made its inaugural run as early as 1804. It carried ten tons of iron and seventy men, at nearly five miles an hour, for nine and a half miles, over the rails used by the horse trams in the mines of Penydarren, South Wales. Four years later Trevithick astonished

THE PLEASURES OF THE RAIL-ROAD — SHOWING THE INCONVENIENCE
OF A BLOW UP
Caricature by Henry Heath published by Gans, 1831.
The first train was dismissed as a dangerous scientific toy. The idea that it might one day become a practical means of transport was as laughable as the thought of a man on the moon.

Londoners with the famous 'Catch-Me-Who-Can', a mini-train which ran round a circular track in North London, specifically built for the purpose. It ran at fifteen miles an hour and Trevithick charged 1s a head for joy-rides: he backed the engine to beat any race horse running at Newmarket over a similar distance. The 'Catch-Me-Who-Can' was a sensation, but the majority of the population were terrified and refused even to consider the steam locomotives as a practical means of transport. The train was dismissed as a scientific toy, its inventor as a crank and the idea that this 'iron horse' could ever replace the real thing was as laughable as the thought of a man on the moon.

The world's first public railway was the Stockton and Darlington, built by Stephenson in 1822 and authorized to carry passengers the following year. In 1829 a competition was organized to test the respective merits of various locomotives powered by steam, with a prize of £500, which was won by Stephenson's *Rocket*. Fanny Kemble, a scion of the great acting family, was one of the very first railway enthusiasts. When she was twenty-one, Stephenson invited her to ride on the new Liverpool–Manchester railway, before it was opened to the public. She was tremendously excited and not in the least frightened. Unfortunately the official opening, in September 1830, ended in yet another disaster: one of the visiting dignitaries* somehow got in the way of one of the engines, was run over and killed.[23] Nevertheless, by the following year, the railway was carrying more than 30,000 passengers a month, 10,000 more than all the coaches running on the same route could have taken even if they were filled to capacity on every journey. Travelling by train was both faster and cheaper than the coaches: there were no hidden extras in the form of tips and meals at the inns *en route*, and it was fun. As Sydney Smith wrote later, when the railways were fully established:

Railroad travelling is a delightful improvement of human life. Man is become a bird; he can fly longer and quicker than a Solan Goose. The mamma rushes sixty miles in two hours to the aching finger of her conjugating and declining grammar boy. The early Scotchman scratches himself in the morning mists of the North and has his porridge in Piccadilly before the setting sun . . . Everything is near, everything is immediate – time, distance and delay are abolished.

All the same most people still preferred to travel by coach, preferably in their own purpose-built carriage. Many of these travelling coaches were so cleverly designed that, on a long journey, the occupant could eat, sleep and work while on the move. One of the trophies of the Napoleonic Wars brought back to England, and put on exhibition in London, was the Emperor's personal travelling coach, which he had had made for the Russian campaign. It had been designed to cater for almost everything the Emperor could either want or need on the long journey, with

---

* William Huskisson, a former President of the Board of Trade and Leader of the House of Commons.

a host of ingenious compartments and appendages. There was a 'Bedstead of Polished Steel', stored in a box under the coachman's seat; a painted Venetian blind covered the front windows (a most practical innovation, since it kept out rain but let in air); a large net hung from the ceiling, filled with various gadgets; and a handsome secretaire had been built into a recess in the side of the coach. The whole equipage was described as being

fitted up with every luxury and convenience that could be imagined, and contained, besides the usual requisites for a Dressing-Box, most of which were of solid Gold; a magnificent Breakfast service, with Plates, Candlesticks, Knives, Forks, Spoons; a spirit Lamp for making breakfast in the Carriage; Gold case for Napoleons; Gold Wash-hand Basin, variety of Essence Bottles, Perfumes and an almost infinite variety of minute articles, down to Pins, Needles, Thread, and Silk . . . at the bottom of this Toilette Box, in divided recesses, were found Two Thousand Gold Napoleons; on the Top, Writing Materials, Looking Glass, Combs &; a Liqueur Case which had Two Bottles, one with Malaga Wine, the other with Rum; a Silver Sandwich Box, containing a Plate, Knives, Spoons, Pepper and Salt Boxes, Mustard Pot, Decanter, Glasses &; a Wardrobe; Writing-Desk, Maps, Telescopes, Arms &,; a large silver Chronometer, by which the watches of the Army were regulated; two Merino Mattresses, a Green Velvet Travelling Cap; also a diamond Headdress, Hat, Sword, Uniform, and an Imperial Mantle &.&.&.[24]

Even the more mundane version of the travelling coach was liable to turn into a pantechnicon on a long journey. It was considered an ordinary precaution to travel with one's own sheets, since in all too many inns those provided would be both dirty and damp. Some form of heating was another essential in draughty carriages, so it was customary to equip the passengers with a pewter, or stone, hot-water bottle, known as a *Califacient*, which they tucked under their feet. Similarly, a writing desk or portable table was needed so that travellers could pass the time writing their innumerable letters or playing games: travelling chess sets, with wooden pegs, were popular, along with backgammon and, of course, dice and cards. Fortunes could change hands as the miles went by. There would be any number of band-boxes, dressing-cases, hampers, flasks and so forth, all regarded as essential 'hand luggage', and therefore carried inside the carriage, or, at least, attached to it somewhere, while the bulk of the trunks and cases followed behind in a separate coach. Rabies was the great dread of nineteenth-century Europe, so travellers were warned to carry at all times a stout stick, or sword-stick, to fend off strange dogs, as well as a 'Brace of Blunderbusses'. The *Gentlemen's Magazine* recommended putting 'the muzzle of one out of each Window, so as to be seen by Robbers!!!' It was, of course, perfectly legal to carry weapons at the time and almost any action could be attributed to self-defence. Thus equipped, travelling could be a positive pleasure: 'I made my preparations for the night straightaway and laid myself comfortably to rest in the carriage,' one tourist wrote in his diary.

One always sleeps even better on the second night than on the first in the carriage, whose movement works, on me at least, like a cradle on children. I felt very well and cheerful the next morning ... I lit the reading lamp in the carriage, and comfortably read through Lady Morgan's latest novel while we rolled at a gallop across the plain.[25]

Improved roads and lighter, faster coaches revolutionized both the comfort and speed of travel for the public sector as much as the private, and the demand grew every year. In 1828 there were twelve coaches a day between Leicester and London alone and the pattern was repeated all over the country. The journey from London to Exeter, 175 miles, took approximately twenty-one hours by stagecoach, including halts for refreshments and changing the teams; and that from Edinburgh to London no more than forty, weather permitting. Passengers booked their seats in advance on the stagecoaches, which usually carried between six and eight passengers on the inside. Those who opted for the cheap seats on the roof ran a very real risk in the winter, particularly on the long night drives. In March, 1812, a Wiltshire newspaper reported that two of the passengers were found to have frozen to death on the roof of a coach and a third was dying: and that was after the relatively short journey from Bath to Chippenham.[26]

Nevertheless, foreign visitors were always amazed by the comfort and ease of travel in Britain. One, a Dr Niemeyer of Leipzig, wrote that the stagecoaches in England were 'so great a novelty to all strangers unacquainted with the mechanical elegance and refinement to which they have arrived in England.' Another German tourist, however, determined to see the dark side of everything, condemned the comfort of the coaches as conducive to immorality. Count Pecchio, travelling post in 1827, was particularly impressed by his reception at the various halts:

At every inn on the road, breakfast, dinner, or supper is always ready, a fire is burning in every room and water always boiling for tea or coffee. Soft-feather beds, with a fire blazing up the chimney, invite repose; and the tables are covered with newspapers for the amusement of the passengers . . . English inns would be real enchanted palaces, if the bill of mine host did not appear to dispel the illusion.

(Even then, however, the economic divide between the North and South was evident. It was said that a better meal was to be had in the North for a shilling than for five in the South.) Visitors were equally surprised by the emphasis on cleanliness to be found in the coaching inns. One delighted tourist wrote:

On your washing table you find – not one miserable water-bottle, with a single earthen or silver jug and basin, and a long strip of towel, such as you are given in all hotels and many private houses in France and Germany; but positive tubs of handsome porcelain, in which you may plunge half your body; cocks which instantly supply you with streams of water at Pleasure; half a dozen wide towels; a multitude of fine glass bottles and glasses, great and small; a large standing looking-glass, foot baths etc., not to mention other anonymous conveniences of the toilet, all of equal elegance.

The arrival of news during the Napoleonic Wars was obviously controlled by the speed of the messenger. Nathan Rothschild heard of Wellington's victory at Waterloo before the cabinet because his courier was better mounted. It had taken him sixty-three hours of hard riding, including the sea-crossing, to reach London. During the war, the Mails became the quickest means of communicating the progress of events to the country people. They were the fastest public coaches on the roads, travelling at an average speed of ten miles per hour, with split-second changing of the teams. The guards shouted out the news of Trafalgar or Waterloo and chalked up headlines on the panels of the coach as they raced through the towns and villages. In any case, whenever there was a victory the splendid decorations on the coaches proclaimed the good news as soon as they came into view: the horses, the men and the carriages would all be dressed up with laurels and flowers, oak leaves and ribbons. By the end of the Regency, too, detailed maps were available to the ordinary traveller. The Post Office commissioned John Cary, at 9d a mile, to compile a new survey of all the roads served by the Mails. On a scale of one inch to a mile, these were not only the first maps to record exact mileages but also acted as a supplementary tourist guide. Information was given about 'Every Gentleman's Seat, situate on or seen from the Road (however distant) with the Name of the Possessor, the Number of Inns on each separate Route and the different Turnpike Gates, shewing the Connection which one Trust has with another.'

It was on 10 March 1812 that Byron awoke and found himself famous, 'the most celebrated young man in the whole of London, the cynosure of admiring and inquisitive glances, the subject of endless talk'. *Childe Harold* had been rejected by two publishers, Longmans and Miller of Albemarle Street, the latter because it contained an attack on Lord Elgin, before being accepted by John Murray. The first edition sold out in three days. Literary tastes then, as now, were unpredictable: Byron sold 10,000 copies of *The Corsair* on the day of publication, but Wordsworth, who was just as valid a Romantic, sold only 500 copies in five years of the 1815 edition of his poems. Sir Walter Scott was by far the most popular novelist of the Regency period, and in two years made £40,000 from his books. But Jane Austen, according to her brother's biographical notice, 'could scarcely believe what she termed her great good fortune when *Sense and Sensibility* produced a clear profit of £150.' Nevertheless she had her admirers, including Scott himself and the Prince Regent, who kept a set of her novels at each of the royal residences. Similarly, the price of contemporary art is always a matter of astonishment to later generations: for example, four paintings by Sir Joshua Reynolds were bought by the third Earl of Egremont for sums ranging from £35 to 200 guineas. One of the paintings was *The Virgin and Child*, which Egremont considered 'one of the finest pictures that ever were painted in any age', and which would today be worth a fortune. On the other hand Egremont was prepared to spend thousands of pounds on sculptures by John Edward Carew, who was popular at the time. One such, *Venus Appeasing the Anger of Vulcan*, was bought for £4200. In the end, Carew became a permanent pensioner of Egremont's with his own apartments at Petworth. Another room in the house was reserved as a private studio for Turner, who first arrived in 1809: no one other than himself and his patron was allowed to enter it. Lord Egremont was one of the great patrons of his generation, a liberal and a scholar, who kept open house to a host of indigent artists.[27]

The greatest patron of all, of course, was the Prince Regent himself. Speaking of his own huge contribution to the national heritage, he explained his dedication to the arts: 'We have lost the magnificent collection of Charles the First; I will do what I can to supply its place.' And, again, 'I have not formed it [the collection] for my pleasure alone, but to gratify the public taste, and lay before the artist the best specimens for his study.' Towards the end of his life the Prince bought the Angerstein collection, of thirty-eight paintings, which formed the nucleus of the new National Gallery. It opened in 1824, with an entrance fee of 1s. The Prince was instrumental, too, in the founding of the Royal Society of Literature, and endowed it with an annuity of 1100 guineas (which was cancelled after his death), and gave the whole of his father's library to the British Museum, 85,000 volumes in all. The British Museum, at the time, was one of the great attractions of London – when the Elgin marbles were brought to England, in 1816, vast crowds went to see them even though at least one society visitor said they gave as much pleasure as 'a

lovely woman with one leg, amputated arms and blinded eyes.'
In spite of such glaring exceptions the Regency was an age which
valued culture.

In 1811 the Prince Regent commissioned John Nash to begin
work on a grand design for the transformation of central London.
The original plans covered an area which stretched from Regent's
Park, via the Regent's Park villas and Regent Street, to Carlton
House. It was a superb piece of town planning by Nash and much
admired: 'The town has . . . greatly gained from the new Regent
Street, Portland Place and the Regent's Park. For the first time
it seems like a royal residence, and no longer simply a boundless
capital for shopkeepers – in Napoleon's immortal words.' The
same source goes on to praise the 'country style lay-out' of the
park, and the design of the new waterways:

You would think that a broad river was flowing far into the distance
between luxuriantly wooded banks and there dividing into several
branches, while in fact all you have before you is a laboriously excavated,
shored up and confined, though clear, piece of water. So charming a
landscape as this, with commanding hills in the distance and surrounded
by a mile-long circus of splendid buildings, is certainly a design worthy
of one of the capitals of the world, and will, when the young trees have
become old giants, scarcely find an equal anywhere.[28]

Unfortunately, Nash's original plans were never executed in
full, but at least 60,000 new houses were built in the Regent's
Park area. The workmanship, however, was notoriously shoddy.
Nash's buildings may have been delightful to look at but their
permanence was considered doubtful even at the time:

> But is not our Nash, too, a very great master;
> He finds us all brick and he leaves us all plaster.

Nevertheless, a combination of the example set by the Prince
Regent and economic prosperity brought about a boom in building during the postwar years. The new middle classes expressed
their wealth in an orgy of self-aggrandizement: 'Gothic' follies,
'Palladian' villas and 'cottages ornés' appeared all over the
country. Some of the loveliest large country houses were built

during the Regency period, small mansions rather than stately homes, family dwellings, surrounded by equally charming farms and cottages for those who worked on the adjacent estate. The first step towards the concept of commuting was initiated with a vogue for country houses within easy driving distance of the cities. The building mania which swept England in the nineteenth century spelt the beginning of the end for the great estates: but it was also the beginning of a far more egalitarian way of life.

On 29 January 1820, George III finally died and the Prince who had waited so impatiently to succeed his father at last became King. The country he inherited had changed at almost every level since 1788, when the throne had first seemed within his reach. Much had been achieved during the years of the Regency but, perhaps, something had been lost as well. The reckless frivolity of the past had been seductive and not wholly offensive: much of the colour faded from life with the advent of the new morality. Lord Melbourne expressed the feelings of many of his contemporaries when he complained to the young Queen Victoria that 'Nobody is gay now: they are so religious.'[29] In the final analysis, however, the Regency was a remarkable era and should not be remembered as a glamorous chimera. In the material sense the tangible achievements of the period had become the wonder of the world. In status, too, Britain was the undisputed leader of Europe. But, by 1820, the might of Britain stemmed from a very different source to that of the late eighteenth century. The ruling class was no longer exclusively aristocratic and a great estate was no longer the only passport to power. The emphases of wealth, and thereby of power, had shifted during the intervening years. In consequence, for the first time in their history, the aristocracy had begun to lose their self-confidence, to doubt the almost divine right to rule they had believed in for so long. It was no longer possible to ignore the new middle class. A different England was emerging based on industry, not land; on the middle class, not the aristocracy; on religion, not irreligion. It was less orientated towards London, less influenced by the French, in either fashions or mores. The new society was richer, better educated, more vocal and therefore more demanding. Power was no longer limited to a tiny minority of the elite but extended to the provinces and the manufacturing towns. At the same time the reaction against eighteenth-century values was almost complete. For example, the code of honour was no longer considered inviolable, or the ultimate arbiter in a dispute: in the past gentlemen settled their differences with swords or pistols, but by the closing years of the Regency they took them to court. Lawyers were among the *nouveaux riches.* The English were developing a strong new identity, based on fundamental values, moral, family-minded and philanthropic. At the end of the Regency, England settled down to a period of peace and prosperity which was to last for nearly a hundred years.

Selected Bibliography

Acton, Eliza, *Modern Cookery for Private Families*, intro. Elizabeth Ray, Southover Press, 1993

Adams, S. and S., *The Complete Servant*, London, 1825

Addison, Sir William, *The Old Roads of England*, Batsford, 1980

Airlie, Mabel, Countess of, *In Whig Society, 1775–1818*, Hodder and Stoughton, 1921

Anon., 'Brief Remarks on English Manners. By an English Gentleman', printed for John Booth, Duke Street, London, 1816

Ashton, J., *Social England under the Regency*, 2 vols, London, 1890s
—*Florizel's Folly*, Chatto and Windus, 1899

Barton, R. M. (ed.), *Life in Cornwall in the Early Nineteenth Century (Extracts from the West Briton Newspaper from 1810 to 1835)*, Bradford Barton, Truro, Cornwall, 1970

Beerbohm, Max, *The Works of Max Beerbohm*, ed. Matthew Arnold, Bodley Head, 1921

Lady Bessborough and Her Family Circle, ed. the Earl of Bessborough in collaboration with A. Aspinall, John Murray, 1940

Blew, W. C. A., *Brighton and Its Coaches*, London, 1894

Boulton, W. B., *The Amusements of Old London*, 2 vols, London, 1901

Buckingham and Chandos, Duke of, *Memoirs of the Court of George IV, 1820–1830*, 2 vols, London, 1859

Burnett, T. A. J., *The Rise and Fall of a Regency Dandy – The Life and Times of Scrope Beardmore Davies*, Oxford University Press, 1983

Calder-Marshall, A., *The Two Duchesses*, Hutchinson, 1878

Carlton House: The Past Glories of George IV's Palace, catalogue published for the exhibition at the Queen's Gallery, Buckingham Palace, London, 1991–2

Cavendish, Lady Harriet, *'Hary-O': The Letters of Lady Harriet Cavendish, 1796–1809*, ed. Sir G. Leveson-Gower, John Murray, 1940

Coleman, V., *The Story of Medicine*, Hale, 1985

Colson, P., *White's, 1693–1950*, Heinemann, 1951

Combe, William, *The Tour of Dr Syntax in Search of the Picturesque*, London, 1809

The Creevey Papers, ed. Sir Herbert Maxwell, John Murray, 1905

The Creevey Papers, ed. John Gore, Batsford, 1963

Devonshire, Duchess of, *The House: A Portrait of Chatsworth*, Macmillan, 1982

Egan, Pierce, *The True History of Tom and Jerry; or the Day and Night Scenes of Life in London*, London, 1820

Ford, J., *Prizefighting: The Age of Regency Boximania*, David and Charles, 1971

Frampton, Mary, *The Journal of Mary Frampton, 1779–1846*, ed. Harriot Georgiana Mundy, London, 1885

Franzero, Carlo, *The Life and Times of Beau Brummell*, Alvin Redman, 1958

Fraser, Flora, *The Unruly Queen*, Macmillan, 1996

Fulford, Roger, *Royal Dukes: The Fathers and Uncles of Queen Victoria*, Duckworth, 1933

—*George the Fourth*, Duckworth, 1935

Fyvie, J., *Wits, Beaux and Beauties of the Georgian Era*, Bodley Head, 1909

Gentleman's Magazine, vol. 1, 1811

George, Dorothy, *English Political Caricature*, Clarendon Press, Oxford, 1959

Girouard, Marc, *Life in the English Country House*, Penguin, 1980

Grant, Elizabeth, of Rothiemurchus, *Memoirs of a Highland Lady*, vol. 2, ed. A. Todd, Canongate Classics, 1988

Gregg, Pauline, *A Social and Economic History of Britain, 1760–1950*, Harrap, 1950

The Greville Memoirs, ed. Henry Reeve, Longmans, 1896

The Greville Memoirs, ed. Christopher Lloyd, Roger Ingram, 1948

Gronow, Captain, *Captain Gronow: His Reminiscences of Regency and Victorian Life, 1810–60*, ed. Christopher Hibbert, Kyle Cathie, 1991

Gronow, Captain, *The Reminiscences and Recollections of Captain Gronow*, Surtees Society, 1984

Harper, Charles G., *Stagecoach and Mail in Days of Yore*, Chapman and Hall, London, 1903

Hibbert, Christopher, *George IV, Prince of Wales*, Longmans, 1972

—*George IV, Regent and King*, Allen Lane, 1973

Johnson, Paul, *The Birth of the Modern*, Orion, 1992

Jolliffe, John, *The Diaries of Benjamin Haydon*, Hutchinson, 1990

Kelly, Linda, *Sheridan: A Life*, Sinclair-Stevenson, 1997

Kitchener, W., *The Traveller's Oracle*, 2 vols, London, 1827

Laver, James, *Taste and Fashion: From the French Revolution until Today*, Harrap, 1945

—*Clothes*, Burke, 1952

—*Handbook of English Costume in the Nineteenth Century*, Faber, 1959

Lees-Milne, J., *The Bachelor Duke: William Spencer Cavendish, Sixth Duke of Devonshire, 1790–1858*, John Murray, 1991

Lewis, Matthew, *Ambrosio, or the Monk*, London, 1796

Lloyd, Christopher, *The Royal Collection*, Sinclair-Stevenson, 1992

Longford, Elizabeth, *Wellington: The Years of the Sword*, Weidenfeld and Nicolson, 1969

Low, Donald, *That Sunny Dome: A Portrait of Regency England*, Book Club Associates, 1977

Lummis, T., and J. Marsh, *The Woman's Domain*, Viking, 1990

MacDonagh, Giles, *Brillat-Savarin: The Judge and His Stomach*, John Murray, 1992

Margetson, Stella, *Journey by Stages*, Cassell, 1967

Masson, M., *Lady Anne Barnard*, Allen and Unwin, 1948

Melville, Lewis, *Beaux of the Regency*, 2 vols, Hutchinson, 1908

—*Some Eccentrics and a Woman*, Martin Secker, 1911

—(ed.), *The Berry Papers, 1763–1852*, London, 1913

—*Regency Ladies*, Hutchinson, 1926

Mitchell, L. G., *Lord Melbourne*, Oxford University Press, Oxford, 1997

Musgrave, Clifford, *Life in Brighton*, Faber, 1970

Oliver, J. W., *The Life of William Beckford*, Oxford University Press, Oxford, 1932

Pinchbeck, Ivy, and M. Hewitt, *Children in English Society*, vol. 2, Routledge and Kegan Paul, 1973

Plumb, J. H., *The First Four Georges*, Little, Brown & Co., 1956

—*The Pursuit of Happiness: A View of Life in Georgian England. Catalogue of the Exhibition*, Yale Center, 1977

—*Royal Heritage*, BBC Publications, 1977

—*Georgian Delights*, Weidenfeld and Nicolson, 1980

Priestley, J. B., *The Prince of Pleasure and His Regency, 1811–20*, Heinemann, 1969

Puckler-Muskau, Prince, *Puckler's Progress: 'The Adventures of Prince Puckler-Muskau in England, Wales and Ireland as Told in Letters to His Former Wife– 1826–9'*, tr. Flora Brennan, Collins, 1987

Pyne, William, *History of the Royal Residences*, 3 vols, London, 1819

Quennell, Marjorie, and C. H. B., *A History of Everyday Things*, revised P. Quennell, Batsford, 1969
Quennell, P., *Byron: The Years of Fame*, John Murray, 1950
—(ed.), *The Private Letters of Princess Lieven to Prince Metternich, 1820–1826*, John Murray, 1948

Radcliffe, Ann, *The Mysteries of Udolpho*, London, 1794
Romilly, S. H., *Letters to 'Ivy' from the First Earl of Dudley*, Longmans, Green, 1905
Rush, Richard, *A Residence at the Court of London*, ed. and intro. Philip Ziegler, Century, 1987
Russell, Lord John, *The Life and Times of Charles James Fox*, Richard Bentley, 1859

Sadleir, Michael, *Blessington D'Orsay: A Masquerade*, Constable, 1933
Smiles, Samuel, *Lives of the Engineers*, John Murray, 1878–9
Smith, Sydney, *Selected Letters of Sydney Smith*, ed. Nowell C. Smith, Oxford University Press, Oxford, 1981

Tannahill, Reay, *Regency England*, Folio Society, 1964
—*Food in History*, Penguin, 1988
Taylor, William, *Diary of William Taylor, Footman: 1837*, ed. Dorothy Wise, St Marylebone Society, 1987
Tillyard, Stella, *Aristocrats*, Chatto and Windus, 1994
Timbs, J., *Club Life of London*, 2 vols, London, 1866
Tomalin, Claire, *Mrs Jordan's Profession*, Viking, 1994
Torr, Cecil, *Small Talk at Wreyland*, Oxford University Press, Oxford, 1979
Trevelyan, G. M., *British History in the Nineteenth Century and After (1782–1919)*, Longmans, 1937
—*English Social History*, Longmans, 1942

Waugh, Norah, *Corsets and Crinolines*, Batsford, 1954
Webster and Parkes, *Encyclopaedia of Domestic Economy*, Longmans, 1844
White, T. H., *The Age of Scandal*, Jonathan Cape, 1950

Williams, Clifford John, *Madame Vestris: A Theatrical Biography*, Sidgwick and Jackson, 1975

Williams, Neville, *Powder and Paint*, Longmans, 1957

Wilson, Anne C., *Food and Drink in Britain*, Constable, 1973

Wilson, Harriette, *Harriette Wilson's Memoirs*, with a Preface by James Laver, Peter Davies, 1929

Wyndham, H. A., *A Family History, 1688–1837: The Wyndhams*, Oxford University Press, Oxford, 1950

Ziegler, Philip, *King William IV*, Collins, 1971

Ziegler, Philip, and Desmond Seward (eds), *Brooks's*, Constable, 1991

Notes

Abbreviations:
RA – Royal Archives, Windsor
CA – Chatsworth Archives

1 An Impolite Society

1 J. W. Oliver, *The Life of William Beckford*, Oxford University Press (Oxford), 1932, p. 108.
2 Flora Fraser, *The Unruly Queen*, Macmillan, 1996, p. 66.
3 Christopher Hibbert, *George IV: Regent and King*, Allen Lane, 1973, p. 32.
4 *Examiner*, March 1812.
5 Clifford Musgrave, *Life in Brighton*, Faber, 1970, p. 108.
6 M. Masson, *Lady Anne Barnard*, Allen and Unwin, 1948, p. 136.
7 *Carlton House: The Past Glories of George IV's Palace*, catalogue published for the exhibition at the Queen's Gallery, Buckingham Palace, 1991–2.
8 Captain Gronow, *The Reminiscences and Recollections of Captain Gronow*, Surtees Society edition, 1984, p. 90.
9 Mary Frampton, *The Journal of Mary Frampton, 1779–1846*, ed. Harriot Georgiana Mundy, London, 1885, p. 198.
10 Mabel, Countess of Airlie, *In Whig Society, 1775–1818*, Hodder and Stoughton, 1921, p. 54.
11 Richard Rush, *A Residence at the Court of London*, ed. and intro. Philip Ziegler, Century, 1987, p. 34.

12 *Lady Bessborough and Her Family Circle*, ed. Earl of Bessborough in collaboration with A. Aspinall, John Murray, 1940, pp. 188−9.

13 Countess of Airlie, *In Whig Society*, p. 172.

14 *Lady Bessborough*, ed. Bessborough, pp. 240−43.

15 T. H. White, *The Age of Scandal*, Jonathan Cape, 1950, pp. 134−5.

16 Gronow, *Gronow*, Surtees edn, p. 241.

17 *The Greville Memoirs*, ed. Christopher Lloyd, Roger Ingram, 1948, pp. 16−17 (24 June 1818).

18 Peter Quennell (ed.), *The Private Letters of Princess Lieven to Prince Metternich, 1820−1826*, John Murray, 1948 (19 March 1820).

19 Countess of Airlie, *In Whig Society*, pp. 169−72.

20 J. Ford, *Prizefighting: The Age of Regency Boximania*, David and Charles (Newton Abbot, Devon), 1971.

21 *Ibid.*

22 *The Creevey Papers*, ed. John Gore, Batsford, 1963, p. 43.

23 Carlo Franzero, *The Life and Times of Beau Brummell*, Alvin Redman, 1958, p. 220.

24 White, *Age of Scandal*, pp. 194−5.

25 Lewis Melville, *Regency Ladies*, Hutchinson, 1926, pp. 121−2.

26 Harriette Wilson, *Harriette Wilson's Memoirs*, with a Preface by James Laver, Peter Davies, 1929, p. 187.

27 Masson, *Lady Anne Barnard*, p. 145.

28 This was Melesina Trench, a beautiful Irish widow who came to London at the end of the eighteenth century. She found London society so degenerate that she left after two weeks and went to live a life of 'tranquillity', 'reflection, and good works in the country'. See J. Fyvie, *Wits, Beaux and Beauties of the Georgian Era*, Bodley Head, 1909, pp. 349−50.

2 Bucks, Beaux and 'Pinks of the Ton'

1 Lewis Melville, *Beaux of the Regency*, 2 vols, Hutchinson, 1908, vol. 1, pp. xxii-xxiii.

2 Prince Puckler-Muskau, *Puckler's Progress: 'The Adventures of Prince Puckler-Muskau in England, Wales and Ireland as Told in Letters to His Former Wife − 1826−9'*, tr. Flora Brennan, Collins, 1987, p. 186.

3 Lewis Melville, *Some Eccentrics and a Woman*, Martin Secker, 1911, pp. 48−9.

4 Carlo Franzero, *The Life and Times of Beau Brummell*, Alvin Redman, 1958, p. 51.

5 *Ibid.*, p. 201.

6 *Ibid.*, p. 48.

7 Matthew Arnold (ed.), *The Works of Max Beerbohm*, Bodley Head, 1921, p. 27.

8 *Ibid.*, p. 20.

9 The admirer in question was Philip Wharton, one of the later dandies. *Ibid.*, p. 5.

10 Franzero, *Life and Times of Beau Brummell*, pp. 49–50.

11 Anon., 'An Exquisite's Diary', from *The Hermit in London*, London, 1819.

12 Captain Gronow, *The Reminiscences and Recollections of Captain Gronow*, Surtees Society edn, 1984, p. 227.

13 *Ibid.*, p. 332.

14 Melville, *Beaux of the Regency*, vol. 1.

15 Gronow, *Gronow*, Surtees edn, p. 285.

16 *Ibid.*, p. 63.

17 Harriette Wilson, *Harriette Wilson's Memoirs*, with a Preface by James Laver, Peter Davies, 1929, pp. 273–6.

18 Melville, *Beaux of the Regency*, vol. 2, pp. 74–7.

3 'The Seventh Heaven of the Fashionable World'

1 Lady Harriet Cavendish, *'Hary-O': The Letters of Lady Harriet Cavendish, 1796–1809*, ed. Sir G. Leveson-Gower, John Murray, 1940. Letter from Lady Harriet Cavendish (later Countess Granville) to Lady Georgiana Morpeth, 14 August 1802.

2 An unnamed captain in the 3rd Guards. Captain Gronow, *Captain Gronow: His Reminiscences of Regency and Victorian Life, 1810–60*, ed. Christopher Hibbert, Kyle Cathie, 1991, p. 177.

3 Prince Puckler-Muskau, *Puckler's Progress: 'The Adventures of Prince Puckler-Muskau in England, Wales and Ireland as Told in Letters to His Former Wife – 1826–9'*, tr. Flora Brennan, Collins, 1987, p. 112.

4 Mabel, Countess of Airlie, *In Whig Society, 1775–1818*, Hodder and Stoughton, 1921, pp. 69–70.

5 *The Greville Memoirs*, ed. Henry Reeve, Longmans, 1896, p. 13 (17 January 1819).

6   *The Creevey Papers*, ed. John Gore, Batsford, 1963, p. 169.

7   Peter Quennell (ed.), *The Private Letters of Princess Lieven to Prince Metternich, 1820–1826*, John Murray, 1948, p. 57 (2 August 1820).

8   *Ibid.*, p. 22 (19 March 1820).

9   *Greville Memoirs*, ed. Lloyd, p. 20 (3 February 1829).

10 Pierce Egan, *The True History of Tom and Jerry; or the Day and Night Scenes of Life in London*, London, 1820, p. 65.

11 *Ibid.*, title page.

12 *Ibid.*, p. 94.

13 Quennell (ed.), *Princess Lieven to Prince Metternich*, p. 114 (10 February 1821).

14 *Lady Bessborough and Her Family Circle*, ed. Earl of Bessborough in collaboration with A. Aspinall, John Murray, 1940, p. 120 (letter dated 5 December 1802).

15 J. Lees-Milne, *The Bachelor Duke: William Spencer Cavendish, Sixth Duke of Devonshire, 1790–1858*, John Murray, 1991, p. 19.

16 Lewis Melville, *Beaux of the Regency*, 2 vols, Hutchinson, 1908, vol. 1, p. 58.

17 W. M. Thackeray, *Vanity Fair*, Odhams Press edn, p. 164.

18 *Ibid.*, p. 354.

4 Relative Values: The Cost of Living

1   Sixth Duke of Devonshire, 'The Sixth (Bachelor) Duke's "Handbook of Chatsworth"', CA, 1844, p. 124.

2   J. Lees-Milne, *The Bachelor Duke: William Spencer Cavendish, Sixth Duke of Devonshire*, 1790–1858, John Murray, 1991, p. 17.

3   'Household Establishments', CA, 1811.

4   Draper, *Chiswick*, Allen, 1923, p. 118 (CA) (diary of Sir Walter Scott, 17 May 1828).

5   Devonshire, 'Handbook of Chatsworth'.

6   J. Ashton, *Social England under the Regency*, 2 vols, London, 1890s, vol. 1, pp. 154–5.

7   Lees-Milne, *Bachelor Duke*, p. 44.

8   *Ibid.*, p. 87.

9   *Ibid.*, p. 68.

10 P. Johnson, *The Birth of the Modern*, Orion, 1992, p. 476.

11 Lord Byron, *Don Juan*, Canto II, Stanza 22.

12 Johnson, *Birth of the Modern*, p. 567.

13 J. Timbs, *Club Life of London*, 2 vols, London, 1866, vol. 1, pp. 198–9.

14 Lewis Melville (ed.), *The Berry Papers, 1763–1852*, London, 1913, p. 288.

15 *Ibid.*, pp. 179–81 (Mary Berry to General O'Hara, *c.* January 1796).

16 W. Kitchener, *The Traveller's Oracle*, 2 vols, London, 1827, vol. 2, p. 18.

17 *Ibid.*, pp. 25–30.

18 Melville (ed.), *The Berry Papers*, p. 340 (Mary Berry to Agnes Berry, Paris, 20 March 1816).

19 *Ibid.*, p. 347 (Mary Berry to Agnes Berry, Paris, 1 April 1816).

20 J. L. Hammond and Barbara Hammond, *The Village Labourer, 1760–1832*, Longmans, 1931, p. 149.

21 H. A. Wyndham, *A Family History, 1688–1837: The Wyndhams*, Oxford University Press (Oxford), 1950, p. 301.

22 Hammond and Hammond, *Village Labourer*, pp. 148–9.

23 Johnson, *Birth of the Modern*, pp. 207–8.

24 Mabel, Countess of Airlie, *In Whig Society, 1775–1818*, Hodder and Stoughton, 1921, p. 175.

5 London: The Most Prosperous City in Europe

1 Reay Tannahill, *Regency England*, Folio Society, 1964, p. 36.

2 W. Kitchener, *The Traveller's Oracle*, 2 vols, London, 1827.

3 Richard Rush, *A Residence at the Court of London*, ed. and intro. Philip Ziegler, Century, 1987, p. 31.

4 Lady Harriet Cavendish, 'Hary-O': The Letters of Lady Harriet Cavendish, 1796–1809*, ed. Sir G. Leveson-Gower, John Murray, 1940, pp. 7–8.

5 Tannahill, *Regency England*, p. 96.

6 *Repository of Arts, Literature, Commerce*, January 1809, p. 54.

7 Donald A. Low, *That Sunny Dome: A Portrait of Regency England*, Book Club Associates, 1977, pp. 190–92.

8 *St James's Chronicle*, 4–7 June 1791.

9 Christopher Hibbert, *George IV, Prince of Wales*, Longmans, 1972, p. 252.

10 RA 29551–638.

11 John Jolliffe (ed.), *The Diaries of Benjamin Haydon*, Hutchinson, 1990, p. 76 (21 July 1821).

12 RA 29284.

13 RA 29237.

14 There are a large number of bills for the Prince's clothes in the Royal Archives: RA 29284–29300.

15 Peter Quennell (ed.), *The Private Letters of Princess Lieven to Prince Metternich, 1820–1826*, John Murray, 1948, p. 110.

16 RA 29398.

17 *The Greville Memoirs*, ed. Henry Reeve, Longmans, 1896, p. 23.

18 Clifford Musgrave, *Life in Brighton*, Faber, 1970, pp. 151–2.

19 RA 29293.

20 RA 29271.

21 RA 26073.

22 RA 25752.

23 *Greville Memoirs*, ed. Reeve, p. 92.

24 Rush, *Residence at the Court of London*, pp. 28–9.

25 Prince Puckler-Muskau, *Puckler's Progress: 'The Adventures of Prince Puckler-Muskau in England, Wales and Ireland as Told in Letters to His Former Wife – 1826–9'*, tr. Flora Brennan, Collins, 1987, p. 27.

26 Cavendish, '*Hary-O*', p. 242 (letter from Lady Harriet Cavendish to Lady Georgiana Morpeth, 12 November 1807).

27 W. B. Boulton, *The Amusements of Old London*, 2 vols, London, 1901, vol. 1, p. 60.

28 Boulton, *Amusements of Old London*, vol. 2, p. 2.

29 *Ibid.*, p. 20.

30 Cavendish, '*Hary-O*', p. 26 (letter dated 15 August 1802).

31 *Gentleman's Magazine*, July 1813.

32 J. Timbs, *Club Life of London*, 2 vols, London, 1866, vol. 2, p. 261.

33 Lewis Melville (ed.), *The Berry Papers, 1763–1852*, London, 1913, p. 360.

34 Captain Gronow, *Captain Gronow: His Reminiscences of Regency and Victorian Life, 1810–60*, ed. Christopher Hibbert, Kyle Cathie, 1991, pp. 74–5.

35 *Gentleman's Magazine*, 1811.

36 Gronow, *Captain Gronow*, ed. Hibbert, p. 31.

6 From the Seaside Resorts to the Northern Meeting

1 Peter Quennell (ed.), *The Private Letters of Princess Lieven to Prince Metternich, 1820–1826*, John Murray, 1948 (25 March 1820).

2 Clifford Musgrave, *Life in Brighton*, Faber, 1970, p. 83.

3 *Ibid.*, p. 53.

4 *Ibid.*, p. 75.

5 *The Creevey Papers*, ed. John Gore, Batsford, 1963, p. 47.

6 *Ibid.*, p. 54.

7 Claire Tomalin, *Mrs Jordan's Profession*, Viking, 1994, pp. 211–16, 234–6 and others.

8 Stella Tillyard, *Aristocrats*, Chatto and Windus, 1994, pp. 35–7.

9 John Gibson Lockhart, *Memoirs of the Life of Sir Walter Scott*, 7 vols, Edinburgh, 1837–8, pp. 118–19.

10 Keats to his brother Tom, 25–7 June 1818. From *Letters of John Keats*, ed. Hyder Edward Rollins, Harvard University Press, 1958, vol. 1, pp. 298–309.

11 *Ibid.*, (1 July 1818).

12 William Combe, *The Tour of Dr Syntax in Search of the Picturesque*, London, 1809, p. 161.

13 *Ibid.*, p. 70.

14 *Ibid.*, p. 108.

15 Elizabeth Grant of Rothiemurchus, *Memoirs of a Highland Lady*, ed. A. Todd, Canongate Classics (Edinburgh), 1992, pp. 329–31.

16 *Ibid.*, pp. 10–14.

17 *Ibid.*, pp. 344–5.

7 'A Mistress Had a Better Deal Than a Wife'

1 Philip Ziegler, *King William IV*, Collins, 1971, p. 78 (*Morning Post*, July 1791).

2 *Ibid.*, p. 81 (*Courier*, 23 August 1806).

3 *Ibid.*, pp. 81–2 (*The Times*, 11 February 1813).

4 Captain Gronow, *Captain Gronow: His Reminiscences of Regency and Victorian Life, 1810–60*, ed. Christopher Hibbert, Kyle Cathie, 1991, p. xi: 'Creevey, in a letter to Miss Orde . . . gives him credit for having negotiated the terms . . .'

5 J. Lees-Milne, *The Bachelor Duke: William Spencer Cavendish, Sixth Duke of Devonshire, 1790–1858*, John Murray, 1991, pp. 87–8 and 117.

6 *Ibid.*, pp. 68–9.

7 Harriette Wilson, *Harriette Wilson's Memoirs*, with a Preface by James Laver, Peter Davies, 1929, Preface.

8 Lewis Melville, *Regency Ladies*, Hutchinson, 1926.

9 *Ibid.*, pp. 195–6.

10 See Michael Sadleir, *Blessington D'Orsay: A Masquerade*, Constable, 1933.

11 *Ibid.*, pp. 30–31.

12 Lady Harriet Cavendish, *'Hary-O': The Letters of Lady Harriet Cavendish, 1796–1809*, ed. Sir G. Leveson-Gower, John Murray, 1940, p. 306.

13 Elizabeth Longford, *Wellington: The Years of the Sword*, Weidenfeld and Nicolson, 1969, p. 235.

14 L. G. Mitchell, *Holland House*, Duckworth, 1980, p. 16 (Byron to J. Murray, 31 August 1820).

15 Mabel, Countess of Airlie, *In Whig Society, 1775–1818*, Hodder and Stoughton, 1921, p. 154 (the Duchess of Bedford to Lady Holland, 13 July 1813).

16 *The Creevey Papers*, ed. John Gore, Batsford, 1963, p. 144 (Lady Holland to Mrs Creevey, 21 May 1816).

17 *Ibid.*

18 Melville, *Regency Ladies*, pp. 239–40.

8 Clubs and Taverns: Gambling and Gluttony

1 J. Timbs, *Club Life of London*, 2 vols, London, 1866, vol. 1, pp. 249–51.

2 Prince Puckler-Muskau, *Puckler's Progress: 'The Adventures of Prince Puckler-Muskau in England, Wales and Ireland as Told in Letters to His Former Wife – 1826–9'*, tr. Flora Brennan, Collins, 1987, p. 44.

3 *Ibid.*

4 *Ibid.*, p. 43.

5 Philip Ziegler and Desmond Seward (eds), *Brooks's*, Constable, 1991, p. 26.

6 *Ibid.*, p. 27.

7 W. B. Boulton, *The Amusements of Old London*, 2 vols, London, 1901, vol. 1, p. 134.

8 Timbs, *Club Life of London*, vol. 1, p. 134.

9 Boulton, *Amusements of Old London*, vol. 1, p. 147.

10 Timbs, *Club Life of London*, vol. 1, p. 85.

11 Captain Gronow, *Captain Gronow: His Reminiscences of Regency and Victorian Life, 1810–60*, ed. Christopher Hibbert, Kyle Cathie, 1991, p. 76.

12 J. Ashton, *Social England under the Regency*, 2 vols, London, 1890s, vol. 2, p. 64.

13 Reay Tannahill, *Regency England*, Folio Society, 1964, p. 7.

14 Puckler-Muskau, *Puckler's Progress*, pp. 42–3.

15 Timbs, *Club Life of London*, vol. 1, pp. 70, 76 and 80.

16 *Ibid.*, pp. 142–3.

17 Gronow, *Gronow*, Surtees edn, pp. 57–8.

18 C. Reay, 'Table Talk', in Ziegler and Seward (eds), *Brooks's*, p. 165.

19 Timbs, *Club Life of London*, vol. 1, pp. 281–6.

20 Gronow, *Captain Gronow*, ed. Hibbert, pp. 80–81.

21 Timbs, *Club Life of London*, vol. 2, p. 278.

22 *Ibid.*, p. 275.

9 The Age of Indulgence

1 *Encyclopaedia Britannica*, vol. 7, p. 941.

2 Giles MacDonagh, *Brillat-Savarin: The Judge and His Stomach*, John Murray, 1992, p. 201.

3 *Ibid.*

4 W. Kitchener, *The Traveller's Oracle*, 2 vols, London, 1827, vol. 1, p. 43.

5 Reay Tannahill, *Food in History*, Penguin, 1973, p. 302.

6 *Ibid.*, p. 301.

7 RA Kitchen Mensil, 6 May–5 June 1816.

8 RA Ledger, Wednesday 22 July 1812.

9 RA Ledger, Christmas Day 1812.

10 RA Ledger, 9 April 1812.

11 RA Vegetable Mensils, 5 April–6 May 1816.

12 RA Brighton Ledger, Carlton House menus, 1816.

13 Christopher Hibbert, *George IV*, Penguin, 1976, p. 521.

14 Clifford Musgrave, *Life in Brighton*, Faber, 1970, p. 154.

15 RA Ledger, 1812, dated 'Christmas 1812 and New Year's Day 1813'.

16 *Ibid.*

17 Captain Gronow, *The Reminiscences and Recollections of Captain Gronow*, Surtees Society edition, 1984, p. 37.

18 Eliza Acton, *Modern Cookery for Private Families*, intro. Elizabeth Ray, Southover Press, 1993, Preface.

19 *Ibid.*

20 RA Kitchen Mensil, 5 April–6 May 1816.

21 Tannahill, *Food in History*, p. 293.

22 *Ibid.*, p. 346.

23 *Ibid.*, p. 294.

24 *Lady Bessborough and Her Family Circle*, ed. Earl of Bessborough in collaboration with A. Aspinall, John Murray, 1940, p. 46.

25 Tannahill, *Food in History*, p. 310.

26 Pierce Egan, *The True History of Tom and Jerry; or the Day and Night Scenes of Life in London*, London, 1820.

27 Gronow, *Gronow*, Surtees edn, p. 38.

28 Lord Byron, *Don Juan*, Canto II, Stanzas 178–9.

29 Captain Gronow, *Captain Gronow: His Reminiscences of Regency and Victorian Life, 1810–60*, ed. Christopher Hibbert, Kyle Cathie, 1991, pp. 226 and 227n.

30 J. Ashton, *Social England under the Regency*, 2 vols, London, 1890s, vol. 2, p. 329.

31 Gronow, *Gronow*, Surtees edn, p. 275.

10 The Pursuit of Pleasure

1 Christopher Hibbert, *George IV, Prince of Wales*, Longmans, 1972, pp. 37–8.

2 Roger Fulford, *George the Fourth*, Duckworth, 1935, p. 46.

3 *Carlton House: The Past Glories of George IV's Palace*, catalogue published for the exhibition at the Queen's Gallery, Buckingham Palace, 1991–2, copyright Her Majesty Queen Elizabeth II, 1991, p. 15.

4 *Ibid.*

5 William Pyne, *History of the Royal Residences*, 3 vols, London, 1819, vol. 1, p. 58.

6 *Ibid.*, p. 24.

7 *Ibid.*, p. 84.

8 Reay Tannahill, *Regency England*, Folio Society, 1964, p. 17.

9 J. B. Priestley, *The Prince of Pleasure and His Regency, 1811–1820*, Heinemann, 1969, p. 36.

10 Mary Frampton, *The Journal of Mary Frampton, 1779–1846*, ed. Harriot Georgiana Mundy, London, 1885, p. 158 (Lady Elizabeth Fielding to her sister, Sackville Street, 10 February 1813).

11 J. Ashton, *Social England under the Regency*, 2 vols, London, 1890s, vol. 1, p. 52.

12 *Ibid.*, pp. 64–5.
13 *The Creevey Papers*, ed. John Gore, Batsford, 1963 (Creevey to Mrs Creevey, 14 June 1814).
14 Priestley, *Prince of Pleasure*, p. 122.
15 Frampton, *Journal*, pp. 200–202.
16 *Ibid.*, p. 215 (C. B. Wollaston to Mary Frampton, 10 June 1814).
17 *Ibid.*, p. 215 (James Frampton to his mother, 12 June 1814).
18 *Creevey Papers*, ed. Gore, (Creevey to Mrs Creevey, 14 June 1814).
19 P. Colson, *White's, 1693–1950*, Heinemann, 1951, pp. 68–9 (21 June 1814).
20 Fulford, *George the Fourth*, p. 145.
21 Priestley, *Prince of Pleasure*, p. 126.
22 Ashton, *Social England*, vol. 1, p. 358 (and see chapters 17 and 18).
23 *Lady Bessborough and Her Family Circle*, ed. Earl of Bessborough in collaboration with A. Aspinall, John Murray, 1940, p. 156 (Lady Caroline Lamb to Lady Bessborough, 15 January 1807).
24 W. B. Boulton, *The Amusements of Old London*, 2 vols, London, 1901, vol. 1, p. 268.
25 Clifford John Williams, *Madame Vestris: A Theatrical Biography*, Sidgwick and Jackson, 1975.
26 *Ibid.*

11 Charades and Epigrams: The Country House

1 Richard Rush, *A Residence at the Court of London*, ed. and intro. Philip Ziegler, Century, 1987, pp. 207–11.
2 *The Greville Memoirs*, ed. Henry Reeve, Longmans, 1896, pp. 11–12.
3 Lady Harriet Cavendish, *'Hary-O': The Letters of Lady Harriet Cavendish, 1796–1809*, ed. Sir G. Leveson-Gower, John Murray, 1940, p. 2.
4 Mabel, Countess of Airlie, *In Whig Society, 1775–1818*, Hodder and Stoughton, 1921, pp. 64–5 (letter from 'Monk' Lewis to Lady Melbourne, October 1802).
5 *Ibid.*
6 *Lady Bessborough and Her Family Circle*, ed. Earl of Bessborough in collaboration with A. Aspinall, John Murray, 1940, p. 140 (letter from Lady Caroline Lamb to her grandmother, Lady Spencer, 9 December 1805).

7 Lewis Melville (ed.), *The Berry Papers, 1763–1852*, London, 1913, p. 224.

8 *Greville Memoirs*, ed. Reeve, pp. 4–6.

9 Peter Quennell (ed.), *The Private Letters of Princess Lieven to Prince Metternich, 1820–1826*, John Murray, 1948 (6 January and 1 April 1820).

10 *The Creevey Papers*, ed. John Gore, Batsford, 1963, p. 150 (Lady Holland to Mrs Creevey, September 1817).

11 *Creevey Papers*, ed. Gore, pp. 182 and 185 (Creevey to Miss Orde, Cantley, 19 September 1822 and from Croxteth, 26 November 1822).

12 *Lady Bessborough*, ed. Bessborough, p. 149 (Georgiana, Lady Spencer to Lady Bessborough, Midgham, 2 November 1806).

13 Rush, *Residence at the Court of London*, p. 34 (20 January 1818).

14 T. Lummis and J. Marsh, *The Woman's Domain*, Viking, 1990, pp. 79–80.

15 *Gentleman's Magazine*, vol. 1, pp. 250–55.

16 *Ibid.*

17 *Lady Bessborough*, ed. Bessborough, p. 4.

18 *Ibid.* (Lady Spencer to Lady Duncannon, March 1790).

19 *Ibid.*, pp. 70 (Lord Duncannon to Lord Bessborough, Nice, 26 March 1792) and 99 (Lady Bessborough to her sons, Lucca, 18 August 1793).

20 *Ibid.*, p. 103 (William Ponsonby to his brothers, Naples, January or February 1794).

21 *Ibid.*, p. 133 (Lady Bessborough to Lady Caroline Lamb, *c.* 5 June 1805).

22 Cavendish, '*Hary-O*', p. 17 (letter from Lady Harriet Cavendish to Miss Selina Trimmer, 10 October 1801).

23 Prince Puckler-Muskau, *Puckler's Progress: 'The Adventures of Prince Puckler-Muskau in England, Wales and Ireland as Told in Letters to His Former Wife – 1826–9'*, tr. Flora Brennan, Collins, 1987, pp. 116–17.

24 *Creevey Papers*, ed. Gore, pp. 9–10.

25 Puckler-Muskau, *Puckler's Progress*, p. 45.

26 Anon., 'Brief Remarks on English Manners. By an English Gentleman', printed for John Booth, Duke Street, London, 1816, pp. 76–7.

12 Fashion, Manners and Mores: The New Liberalism

1 James Laver, *Handbook of English Costume in the Nineteenth Century*, Faber, 1959, Foreword.

2 James Laver, *Taste and Fashion: From the French Revolution until Today*, Harrap, 1945, p. 18.

3 Norah Waugh, *Corsets and Crinolines*, Batsford, 1954, pp. 71–2.

4 James Laver, *Clothes*, Burke, 1952, p. 70.

5 Information kindly supplied by Susan North of the Victoria and Albert Museum, London.

6 *Ibid.*

7 Reay Tannahill, *Regency England*, Folio Society, 1964, p. 26.

8 'Tabaciana', in Barry Charles, *Letters by Roberts*, London, 1814.

9 Neville Williams, *Powder and Paint*, Longmans, 1957, pp. 77–9.

10 Laver, *Clothes*, p. 185.

11 Laver, *Handbook of English Costume*, pp. 12–14.

12 Captain Gronow, *Captain Gronow: His Reminiscences of Regency and Victorian Life, 1810–60*, ed. Christopher Hibbert, Kyle Cathie, 1991, p. 176.

13 Laver, *Handbook of English Costume*.

14 *The Creevey Papers*, ed. John Gore, Batsford, 1963, p. 75 (Creevey to Miss Orde, 3 May 1822).

15 Michael Sadleir, *Blessington D'Orsay: A Masquerade*, Constable, 1933, pp. 148–9.

16 Lewis Melville, *Regency Ladies*, Hutchinson, 1926, p. 292.

17 Richard Rush, *A Residence at the Court of London*, ed. and intro. Philip Ziegler, Century, 1987, pp. 54–6 (27 February 1818).

13 On the Eve of Reform

1 *The Greville Memoirs*, ed. Christopher Lloyd, Roger Ingram, 1948, p. 43 (13 April 1829).

2 The fifth Duke of Devonshire had a most refreshing attitude towards the many rotten boroughs within his gift. Unlike most of his fellow patrons he made no attempt to foist his own political prejudices on to the chosen candidates; it seems that the only stipulation the Duke made was that they must be in favour of any bill for the suppression of cruelty to animals.

3 Philip Ziegler, *King William IV*, Collins, 1971, pp. 181–2.

4 H. A. Wyndham, *A Family History, 1688–1837: The Wyndhams*, Oxford University Press (Oxford), 1950, p. 24.

5 Mabel, Countess of Airlie, *In Whig Society, 1775–1818*, Hodder and Stoughton, 1921, pp. 109–10 (William Lamb to Lady Melbourne, 1812).

6 Wyndham, *Family History*, p. 334.

7 R. M. Barton (ed.), *Life in Cornwall in the Early Nineteenth Century (Extracts from the West Briton Newspaper from 1810 to 1835)*, Bradford Barton (Truro, Cornwall), 1970.

8 Wyndham, *Family History*, p. 230.

9 *Gentleman's Magazine*, p. 309 (9 April 1811).

10 G. M. Trevelyan, *English Social History*, Longmans, 1942, pp. 511–12.

11 P. Johnson, *The Birth of the Modern*, Orion, 1992, pp. 378–9.

12 Trevelyan, *English Social History*, p. 511.

13 J. Ashton, *Social England under the Regency*, 2 vols, London, 1890s, vol. 1, p. 238.

14 Captain Gronow, *Captain Gronow: His Reminiscences of Regency and Victorian Life, 1810–60*, ed. Christopher Hibbert, Kyle Cathie, 1991, p. xiv.

15 Wyndham, *Family History*, pp. 288–94.

16 Ivy Pinchbeck and M. Hewitt, *Children in English Society*, vol. 2, Routledge and Kegan Paul, 1973, p. 352.

17 Johnson, *Birth of the Modern*, pp. 367–9.

18 Peter Quennell (ed.), *The Private Letters of Princess Lieven to Prince Metternich, 1820–1826*, John Murray, 1948 (11 March 1820).

19 *The Creevey Papers*, ed. John Gore, Batsford, 1963, p. 194 (Creevey to Miss Orde, 6 May 1823).

20 Reay Tannahill, *Regency England*, Folio Society, 1964, p. 16.

21 *Ibid.*, p. 25.

22 Stella Margetson, *Journey by Stages*, Cassell, 1967, pp. 204–5.

23 Samuel Smiles, 'George and Robert Stephenson', in *Lives of the Engineers*, John Murray, 1878–9, pp. 223–4.

24 W. Kitchener, *The Traveller's Oracle*, 2 vols, London, 1827, vol. 2, p. 127.

25 Prince Puckler-Muskau, *Puckler's Progress: 'The Adventures of Prince Puckler-Muskau in England, Wales and Ireland as Told in Letters to His Former Wife – 1826–9'*, tr. Flora Brennan, Collins, 1987, p. 73.

26 W. C. A. Blew, *Brighton and Its Coaches*, London, 1894.

27 Wyndham, *Family History*, pp. 322–3.

28 Puckler-Muskau, *Puckler's Progress*, pp. 21–4.

29 L. G. Mitchell, *Lord Melbourne*, Oxford University Press (Oxford), 1997, p. 31.

Index

FOR THE BEST IN PAPERBACKS, LOOK FOR THE

In every corner of the world, on every subject under the sun, Penguin represents quality and variety—the very best in publishing today.

For complete information about books available from Penguin—including Penguin Classics, Penguin Compass, and Puffins—and how to order them, write to us at the appropriate address below. Please note that for copyright reasons the selection of books varies from country to country.

In the United States: Please write to *Penguin Group (USA), P.O. Box 12289 Dept. B, Newark, New Jersey 07101-5289* or call 1-800-788-6262.

In the United Kingdom: Please write to *Dept. EP, Penguin Books Ltd, Bath Road, Harmondsworth, West Drayton, Middlesex UB7 0DA.*

In Canada: Please write to *Penguin Books Canada Ltd, 10 Alcorn Avenue, Suite 300, Toronto, Ontario M4V 3B2.*

In Australia: Please write to *Penguin Books Australia Ltd, P.O. Box 257, Ringwood, Victoria 3134.*

In New Zealand: Please write to *Penguin Books (NZ) Ltd, Private Bag 102902, North Shore Mail Centre, Auckland 10.*

In India: Please write to *Penguin Books India Pvt Ltd, 11 Panchsheel Shopping Centre, Panchsheel Park, New Delhi 110 017.*

In the Netherlands: Please write to *Penguin Books Netherlands bv, Postbus 3507, NL-1001 AH Amsterdam.*

In Germany: Please write to *Penguin Books Deutschland GmbH, Metzlerstrasse 26, 60594 Frankfurt am Main.*

In Spain: Please write to *Penguin Books S. A., Bravo Murillo 19, 1° B, 28015 Madrid.*

In Italy: Please write to *Penguin Italia s.r.l., Via Benedetto Croce 2, 20094 Corsico, Milano.*

In France: Please write to *Penguin France, Le Carré Wilson, 62 rue Benjamin Baillaud, 31500 Toulouse.*

In Japan: Please write to *Penguin Books Japan Ltd, Kaneko Building, 2-3-25 Koraku, Bunkyo-Ku, Tokyo 112.*

In South Africa: Please write to *Penguin Books South Africa (Pty) Ltd, Private Bag X14, Parkview, 2122 Johannesburg.*